T0361175

Terrorist Diversion

Many of the world's 40,000 International NGOs (INGOs) work in places where terrorist financing, sanctions breaches, and diversion are key risks. Almost all of the top ten recipient countries of humanitarian aid alone in 2015 were high-risk jurisdictions, for example, receiving more than £7bn between them. When they feel safe to speak, sector workers share sobering stories about what might have happened to some of this money.

As INGOs struggle to keep up with worsening humanitarian needs, diversion risks and their complexity remain daunting. The demands of internal stakeholders, donors, banks, and regulators are diverse and even contradictory. Public scrutiny has magnified, but is not always well-informed. Institutional donors transfer ever more risk to implementing partners, while some banks seek to avoid this business altogether, pushing some NGOs outside the global banking system. Looming over all of these converging pressures is a latticework of austere international sanctions and counter-terror regimes.

It is no surprise that INGOs find themselves struggling to reconcile this complex set of expectations with their charitable missions. Yet the consequences of failing to do so can be severe; future funding is contingent on reputation, and serious offences litter the regulatory landscape. The implications of breaches can be existential for organisations and criminal for individuals.

Terrorist Diversion: A Guide to Prevention and Detection for NGOs is an accessible, pragmatic guide for international NGOs of all shapes and sizes. Clearly explaining the nature of the challenge, and setting out a programme to meet it, it explores how it is possible for INGOs to manage these risks more effectively through their missions – not in spite of them.

Oliver May is a Director at Deloitte Australia. Formerly the head of counter-fraud for Oxfam GB and an investigator with Britain's Serious Organised Crime Agency, he has helped aid organisations worldwide to manage the risks of fraud, corruption, terrorist financing, and money laundering.

Paul Curwell is also a Director at Deloitte Australia. He was formerly the global lead for intelligence and due diligence investigations at Australia's largest bank, and has almost 20 years' experience in risk management, specialising in financial crime, security, and due diligence.

Terrorist Diversion

A Guide to Prevention and
Detection for NGOs

Oliver May and Paul Curwell

Routledge
Taylor & Francis Group

LONDON AND NEW YORK

First published 2021
by Routledge
2 Park Square, Milton Park, Abingdon, Oxon OX14 4RN

and by Routledge
52 Vanderbilt Avenue, New York, NY 10017

Routledge is an imprint of the Taylor & Francis Group, an informa business

© 2021 Oliver May and Paul Curwell

The right of Oliver May and Paul Curwell to be identified as authors of this work has been asserted by them in accordance with sections 77 and 78 of the Copyright, Designs and Patents Act 1988.

All rights reserved. No part of this book may be reprinted or reproduced or utilised in any form or by any electronic, mechanical, or other means, now known or hereafter invented, including photocopying and recording, or in any information storage or retrieval system, without permission in writing from the publishers.

Trademark notice: Product or corporate names may be trademarks or registered trademarks, and are used only for identification and explanation without intent to infringe.

British Library Cataloguing-in-Publication Data
A catalogue record for this book is available from the British Library

Library of Congress Cataloging-in-Publication Data

Names: May, Oliver, 1981- author. | Curwell, Paul, 1979- author.

Title: Terrorist diversion: a guide to prevention and detection for NGOs/Oliver May and Paul Curwell.

Description: Abingdon, Oxon; New York, NY: Routledge, 2020. | Includes bibliographical references and index. | Summary: "Many of the world's 40,000 International NGOs (INGOs) work in places where terrorist financing, sanctions breaches and diversion are key risks. Almost all of the top ten recipient countries of humanitarian aid alone in 2015 were high-risk jurisdictions, for example, receiving more than £7bn between them. When they feel safe to speak, sector workers share sobering stories about what might have happened to some of this money. As INGOs struggle to keep up with worsening humanitarian needs, diversion risks and their complexity remain daunting. The demands of internal stakeholders, donors, banks and regulators are diverse and even contradictory. Public scrutiny has magnified, but is not always well-informed. Institutional donors transfer ever more risk to implementing partners, while some banks seek to avoid this business altogether, pushing some NGOs outside the global banking system. Looming over all of these converging pressures is a latticework of austere international sanctions and counter-terror regimes. It is no surprise that INGOs find themselves struggling to reconcile this complex set of expectations with their charitable missions. Yet the consequences of failing to do so can be severe; future funding is contingent on reputation, and serious offences litter the regulatory landscape. The implications of breaches can be existential for organisations, and criminal for individuals. Terrorist Diversion: A guide to prevention and detection for NGOs is an accessible, pragmatic guide for international NGOs of all shapes and sizes. Clearly explaining the nature of the challenge, and setting out a programme to meet it, it explores how it is possible for INGOs to manage these risks more effectively through their missions - not in spite of them"– Provided by publisher.

Identifiers: LCCN 2020007185 (print) | LCCN 2020007186 (ebook) | ISBN 9781138338081 (hardback) | ISBN 9780429441929 (ebook)

Subjects: LCSH: Nonprofit organizations–Finance. | Non-governmental organizations–Finance. | Humanitarian assistance–Corrupt practices. | Terrorism–Finance. | Fraud–Prevention.

Classification: LCC HD62.6 .M38393 2020 (print) | LCC HD62.6 (ebook) | DDC 658.15/5–dc23
LC record available at https://lccn.loc.gov/2020007185
LC ebook record available at https://lccn.loc.gov/2020007186

ISBN: 978-1-138-33808-1 (hbk)
ISBN: 978-0-429-44192-9 (ebk)

Typeset in Bembo
by MPS Limited, Dehradun

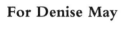

For Denise May

Contents

Figures

Tables

List of acronyms

ACFE	Association of Certified Fraud Examiners
ACNC	Australian Charities and Not-for-profits Commission
ADP	Anti-Diversion Programme
AFA	Asset Freezing Act 2010 (UK)
AML	Anti-Money Laundering
ANCP	Australian NGO Cooperation Program
AUSTRAC	Australian Transaction Reports and Analysis Centre
BOR	Business Obligations Register
CCA	Criminal Code Act 1995 (Australia)
CCEW	Charity Commission for England and Wales
CDD	Customer Due Diligence
CEO	Chief Executive Officer
CFG	Charity Finance Group
CHE project	Counterterrorism and Humanitarian Engagement Project
CIDA	Canadian International Development Agency
CPS	Crown Prosecution Service (UK)
CRA	Country Risk Assessment
CRA	Customer Risk Assessment (Chapter 12)
CSO	Civil Society Organisation
CTBSA	Counter-Terrorism and Border Security Act 2019 (UK)
CTF	Counter-Terrorist Financing
CTP	Cash-Transfer Programming
DFAT	Department of Foreign Affairs and Trade (Australia)
DFID	Department for International Development (UK)
ECSs	External Conduct Standards
EDD	Enhanced Due Diligence
ERM	Enterprise Risk Management
FATF	Financial Action Task Force
FFIEC	Federal Financial Institutions Examinations Council
FinCEN	Financial Crimes Enforcement Network (USA)
FIU	Financial Intelligence Unit
GRC	Governance, Risk and Compliance
HRC	High Risk Customer

IHL	International Humanitarian Law
IMC	International Medical Corps
INGO	International Non-Governmental Organisation
IRIN	Integrated Regional Information Networks (now The New Humanitarian)
IS	Islamic State
ISAF	International Security Assistance Force
ISIL	Islamic State of Iraq and the Levant
ISIS	Islamic State of Iraq and Syria
KYP	Know Your Partner
KYS	Know Your Staff
KYV	Know Your Vendor
LMIC	Low and Middle Income Country
MDB	Multilateral Development Bank
MEL	Monitoring, Evaluation, and Learning
MI	Management Information
MOU	Memorandum of Understanding
MSB	Money Service Business/Bureaux
MSF	Médicins Sans Frontières
NATO	North Atlantic Treaty Organization
NCA	National Crime Agency (UK)
NFI	Non-Food Item
NGO	Non-Governmental Organisation
NGOCB	NGO Co-Ordination Board (Kenya)
NPA	Norwegian People's Aid
NRC	Norwegian Refugee Council
OCHA	UN Office for the Coordination of Humanitarian Affairs
OFAC	Office of Foreign Assets Control (USA)
OFSI	Office of Financial Sanctions Implementation (UK)
OIG	Office of the Inspector General
OPT	Occupied Palestinian Territories
ORA	Organisational Risk Assessment
PEP	Politically Exposed Person
POCAMLA	Proceeds of Crime and Anti-Money Laundering Act 2009 (Kenya)
POTA	Prevention of Terrorism Act 2012 (Kenya)
PRA	Project Risk Assessment
PSEA	Prevention of Sexual Exploitation and Abuse
PSNI	Police Service of Northern Ireland
RfQ	Request for Quotation
RSPCA	Royal Society for the Prevention of Cruelty to Animals (UK)
SCI	Save the Children International
SEA model	Source/Event/Asset model
SLT	Senior Leadership Team
SOCA	Serious Organised Crime Agency (UK)

SPOC	Single Point of Contact
TACT	Terrorism Act 2000 (UK)
TNA	Training Needs Analysis
TPFL	Tigray People's Liberation Front (Ethiopia)
UKFIU	UK Financial Intelligence Unit
UN	United Nations
USAID	US Agency for International Development
WFP	World Food Programme

Acknowledgements

Oliver is deeply grateful to all those who have shared their perspectives, experiences, and stories with him in countless discussions about these issues, all over the world. But in particular, he would like to thank Najwa Al Abdallah, Tim Boyes-Watson of Humentum, Ben Evans of Greenacre Associates, Kay Guinane of the Charity Security Network, Tim Holmes and Mike Parkinson of Oxfam, Anne Miller of the United Nations, Malika Aït-Mohamed Parent (formerly of the International Federation of Red Cross and Red Crescent Societies, IFRC), Martin Polaine, Jeff Rubin of Christian Aid, Yusef Salehi, and Clare Wimshurst of Unicef.

The insights and advice of these professionals were invaluable. Their input into this book does not mean that they necessarily agree with any part of it, and any errors of fact or analysis remain that of the authors alone.

In making this book a reality, Oliver would like to thank Peter Clarke, Sean Barton, and the team at Routledge – especially Rebecca Marsh, Sophie Peoples, Amy Laurens, Alex Atkinson, and Kristina Abbotts, for their support, time, and encouragement. He would also like to thank Paul Curwell, a thoughtful and constructive collaborator, colleague, and friend. And finally, of course, Oliver is unendingly grateful for his family, and in particular his wife and son – both of whom have tolerated this sort of thing for far too long.

Paul would like to thank Nicholas McTaggart (formerly of the Australian Federal Police), Kobus Beukes of South32, and Juliette Ishlove-Morris of Bank of America. He is grateful to his family and friends for their patience.

Foreword

While working at Scotland Yard investigating international terrorist organisations, and later when serving on the board of the Charity Commission, I was never slow either to give, or to welcome with good grace, the well-worn but usually sensible advice to 'follow the money'. Understanding the how, what, why, when, and where of money flows, whether through regulated banks or informal banking systems, was often a key part of investigations. This was so whether the intention was to track missing assets, or to prevent them going missing in the first place.

Over the years, I also came to appreciate the unique vulnerability of international NGOs (Non-Government Organisations) to having their assets diverted towards terrorist organisations, their supporters, or potential supporters. Why are they so vulnerable? Well, there are some striking similarities between the 'business models', for want of a better expression, of many NGOs and terrorist organisations. For instance, in many cases, both will gather donations locally, through a variety of means. Time and again I saw terrorist organisations using 'micro-financing' to gather funds – often accompanied by a liberal dose of fear or fraud. In some ways this is a mirror-image of many NGOs who rely on the philanthropy and generosity of the public at large – minus the fear or fraud. Whether these funds are intended for terrorist or humanitarian purposes, they are then aggregated and moved to their respective theatres of operations. Typically, this will be from a more affluent to a more deprived, less stable, or downright hostile environment. These similarities, and the many potential points of contact, in my experience, created vulnerabilities for NGOs at almost every stage of their operations.

All charities rely upon donors being able to have confidence that their donations will reach the intended recipients and be applied for the intended purpose. At the Charity Commission this was an absolutely fundamental part of our mission to maintain 'public trust and confidence' in charities. I shall never forget how fragile this concept can be. When a global NGO, a household name, had to face the possibility that they had suffered the diversion of assets into a terrorist organisation, the implications were severe not only for that particular NGO, but for the sector as a whole.

In the world of risk management, there is a saying that the threat of a negative outcome occurring can be best assessed if there is a clear understanding of the actual risks (often based on intelligence) measured against the vulnerabilities that might allow the risks to turn into reality. Only when those risks and vulnerabilities are properly understood can effective mitigations or preventive measures be put in place. At the level of neighbourhood crime, this might be as simple as warning the public that there are pickpockets operating at a train station, and to take care of their possessions.

Needless to say, things are rather more complicated for NGOs delivering humanitarian and development operations in some of the most challenging environments on earth. At every stage of their operations there are stakeholders and donors looking for reassurance. There are legal requirements and sanctions to be complied with. Financial and regulatory obligations can crowd in, to the point where the complexities of the risks and vulnerabilities can feel overwhelming. It is also impossible to ignore the ethical, legal, and physical risks that NGOs can face in the field. Looking to divest or minimise some of those risks can actually increase the vulnerabilities still further. The reputational risks for some key stakeholders and donors can become too high, with the potential to undermine or fatally damage the NGO objectives.

The complexities are such that a simple demand that NGOs should be 'compliant' or that there must be a 'zero tolerance' approach to any kind of risk is not helpful. There needs to be a nuanced understanding of the pressures, the risks, and the opportunities to safeguard the mission of NGOs.

Oliver May and Paul Curwell set out with great clarity the risks of diversion, and offer practical, pragmatic responses for NGOs. I have seen for myself that the greatest vulnerabilities for NGOs can arise from a lack of appreciation of the risks of diversion, sometimes bordering on complacency. I commend this book to practitioners, regulators, commentators, policy makers, and anyone who wants to gain an understanding of the tough choices that are often faced by NGOs in delivering their vital work.

Peter Clarke was the UK National Co-ordinator of Terrorist Investigations from 2002–2008, and head of the Anti-Terrorist Branch at New Scotland Yard. He was a non-executive director of the UK Serious Organised Crime Agency from 2009–2014, and served on the board of the Charity Commission for England and Wales from 2013–2016. In 2016 he was appointed as HM Chief Inspector of Prisons.

Introduction

The open secret

In 2004, Ivory Coast descended into a bloody civil war. Thousands of civilians, fleeing the conflict, clustered in makeshift camps near the borders. It was not long before disease began to tear through them – sometimes such outbreaks kill more civilians than the source of the emergency.

Tolu was a co-ordinator for a British International Non-Government Organisation (INGO) in Ghana, tasked with taking lorries of hygiene kits across the border into Ivory Coast. These kits, which contain basics like underwear, soap, and sanitary pads, are critical for preventing the spread of illness and restoring some dignity. The small convoy made it into Ivory Coast without incident, though it took longer than expected and it was getting late. As he sat in the cab of the first lorry, Tolu's heart sank as they rumbled along the dusty, potholed road. Coming into view was a makeshift checkpoint.

"Oh, no," he said, as the smudges in the distance crystallised into a group of armed men, and one signalled for them to stop. The driver did so, and Tolu took a moment to inspect the scene as he stepped down from the cab. There were about a dozen of them, dressed in greens and blacks. They were certainly soldiers – but from whom they took orders was anyone's guess. What was much more certain was that they were drunk and stoned.

A couple of soldiers asked for some kits. Tolu refused, several times despite their insistence – and eventually an older man stepped forward. His bearing left no doubt that he was in charge.

"We are victims, too," he said. "My men have not washed in weeks. We are shitting in holes in the ground. You can help us."

Tolu apologised – the kits could only be given to specific beneficiaries. The man in charge persisted, and Tolu rattled through the usual bribery-avoidance techniques that field humanitarians build up in a mental dossier.

"It's more than my job's worth, I am forbidden by the boss," he smiled, as broadly as he could. "Even if the Queen of England herself asked me for some soap, I wouldn't be able to give it to her!"

Neither this nor any of his other lines worked, and eventually, the man's smile evaporated. Some of the soldiers became angry, shouting at Tolu's team. The man waved them to be quiet, but looked Tolu directly in the eyes. "You will give my men some of these soaps and things," he said. "You will give them now."

Tolu looked at the trucks. The light was fading around them. If they didn't get through this roadblock soon, too much of the journey would have to be completed in darkness. He didn't like their chances at night on these treacherous, bandit-infested roads. He turned back to the man, wondering whether he could hear the sound of rifles being cocked.

This is a true story, albeit with some details changed. These are the situations in which humanitarian emergency staff must make judgements every day. Who were these men, really? Government? A sanctioned or proscribed group? Bandits? All three? Were they requesting kits? Or was it bribery, a polite theft, or diversion? At what point did duress kick in – a legal defence potentially available to Tolu? To what extent did the situation need to escalate before it did? Was it reasonable to expect Tolu to weigh all this up in an instant, with drunk, armed men in front of him? Development staff, though perhaps generally operating in circumstances with less immediate mortality, are also required to make difficult decisions in complicated contexts.

Confused, grey, and chaotic circumstances are normal in humanitarian and global development work. Operating in close proximity to powerful and competing local interests is complex – whether in Low and Middle Income Countries (LMICs), fragile states, or conflict zones. That complexity often defies the carefully agreed positions, policies, and plans of donors, regulators, and INGOs in Washington, London, or Geneva.

Working near sanctioned and proscribed entities has trapped INGOs in a liminal space – an invidious gap between powerful, jostling agendas. On the one hand, they struggle to keep up with worsening humanitarian crises and intensifying global development needs. This is often in places in which the presence of such entities is a key threat, and yet in which donors, governments, and the public expect INGOs to operate. On the other, counter-terrorism legislation, regulatory expectations, and donor requirements create pressures which are not always aligned, and even sometimes contradictory.

Banks, trying to manage their own risks, agitate the situation as do actors who oppose international aid, for whom the issue of diversion is a lever. Underlying all of this is the scrutiny of the public, which is not always well-informed and often open to manipulation.

Against this backdrop, the traditional PR go-to for busy INGO communications staff – that diversion incidents are isolated, and INGOs vet their third parties which shows adequate preventative action – rings hollow in the media. That is rightly so. It is an open secret in the humanitarian and global development sector that diversion to terrorists and other sanctioned entities is more common than many might think. It is under-detected, under-reported, and under-managed – but not well understood.

Despite the complexities they face, INGOs are not alone in dealing with this issue. Private sector organisations and government bodies face it too. But perhaps there is a special repugnance to diversion from INGOs. It is sometimes said that defrauding charitable organisations is the worst kind of theft, but even within depravity, there is hierarchy. Diversion not only robs a person in need, but takes those resources intended for good and uses them for harm – including, perhaps, to that beneficiary. Even though channelling funds and resources to diversionaries can be unintentional – or with the best of intentions – the consequences can be severe.

Anti-Money Laundering (AML) and Counter-Terrorist Financing (CTF) are interrelating disciplines. But there is still limited material to shed light on the nature and extent of money laundering amongst legitimate INGOs. It has happened, certainly, and it is easy to envisage circumstances in which risks exist (see May, 2016a). The focus of this book, however, is diversion, by which we mean the unlawful and dishonest or negligent movement of items of value from INGOs to proscribed or sanctioned entities. Generally, this means assets, funds, or stock, but as we will see there are circumstances in which the provision of other services or benefits might also be covered. When we describe country contexts as 'high' risk, we generally mean in relation to this.

By a 'diversionary', we mean a proscribed or sanctioned individual, group, or other entity that becomes the recipient of goods and services that were intended for the assistance of beneficiaries. By the use of this term, we hope to sidestep two challenges: The political and ideological debate around the word 'terrorist', and the diversity of persons and organisations that might appear on proscription or sanctions lists. Further, when we refer to 'listed' entities, we mean lists in this context.

For us, an INGO is simply an organisation operating in more than one country with charitable aims, for which it obtains funding from institutional donors, private supporters, or both. It is probably registered with one or more national non-profit regulators and would likely recognise itself in the Financial Action Task Force (FATF) definition of a Non-Profit Organisation (NPO) as a "legal person or arrangement or organisation that primarily engages in raising or disbursing funds for purposes such as charitable, religious, cultural, educational, social or fraternal purposes, or the carrying out of other types of 'good works'" (FATF, 2012). For expediency, we will call INGOs and the organisations that work with them 'the aid sector,' though we recognise that this shorthand comes with unhelpful baggage, and inadequately captures the diversity of the humanitarian and global development sector.

This book sets out a simple approach to managing the risk of diversion in two parts. Part I explores the nature of the issue. It looks at the extent of the risk and the complexity of the issue for INGOs, explores some of the common myths and misconceptions, provides an overview of the modern regulatory landscape upon which INGOs must work, and examines what the risks actually look like. In Part II, it sets out how an INGO can manage those risks through an Anti-Diversion Programme (ADP).

Much anti-diversion value can be obtained through traditional good governance and financial management. As we set out the elements of an ADP, we assume that an organisation already has a control framework for the governance of people, assets, and funds. Ideally, it will have a counter-fraud framework too, aligning with that set out in *Fighting Fraud and Corruption in the Humanitarian and Global Development Sector* (May, 2016b) – and to that end, we will avoid going over substantially the same ground where the issues overlap.

Given how few incidents of diversion make it into the public space, this book also draws on examples of which we are aware, but which are not necessarily public. These may variously be cases of which we have had direct experience, or where we rely on the experience of colleagues.

The daunting complexity of this issue does not have a single solution, and we do not pretend that this book presents one. Much can be done to unravel that complexity, however, and this book should be seen as a contributory voice in the spirit of iterative development. The insights here are intended to help INGOs and their partners pick through the issues, understand their risks, and exert greater control over them.

This book does not explore the tension between International Humanitarian Law (IHL) and CTF regimes, nor other key issues like the provision of medicine. These are serious matters at the heart of this subject, without immediate resolution but which could easily consume this book. While sector actors await constructive movement on those matters, this book promotes a pragmatic, risk-based approach to managing diversion within the current dynamic.

The key messages of this book challenge the prevalence of the compliance-based approach, recognise that the term 'zero-tolerance' may have lost some value, and accept that to operate in places of great humanitarian need means that some diversion incidents will not be avoidable. But much more diversion can be prevented than currently is, and this book is about reducing overall risk by successfully managing that which we can do something about, while helping readers to make informed decisions about the incidents that do happen. In Chapter 13, the book sets out how INGOs alone cannot (and should not be expected to) resolve this problem. Instead, institutional donors, governments, lawmakers, peak bodies, the media, and the public must also embrace change. Paul Curwell, with his expertise in financial services, contributes on prevention, due diligence, and bank de-risking.

Some diversion problems might be, at the time of writing, intractable. If an INGO is operating in a place in which a sanctioned entity is in full political control, is there any way to procure goods and services without their vendor paying taxes to the entity, for example? In some places, probably not, and the thought of committing a terrorist financing offence as one orders, eats, and pays for their meal in a local restaurant is enough to make one lose their appetite.

But even those issues, while not within an INGO's sphere of control, are within the INGO community's sphere of influence. In addition to taking more action to reduce diversion through a risk-based approach, INGOs must engage with lawmakers, enforcement bodies, and those that pull their strings to advocate for the INGO context. They must help to ensure that these stakeholders understand the unique and vital role of aid, and its vulnerability to decisions taken elsewhere. And those stakeholders need to listen and respond – after all, today's powerful elite is so often tomorrow's crisis population.

At the time of writing, the media coverage of the #AidToo sexual misconduct crisis is quietening. As the talking heads move on to new scandals, sector professionals speculate about what the next major reputational crisis might be. Suggestions include fundraising, power differentials, the gap between north and south and so on. But if the open secret captured the public imagination, it could rock the sector to its core. Fortunately, this is a crisis that can be avoided, but only if INGOs and other sector actors make investments now.

References

FATF 2012. *International Standards on Combating Money Laundering and the Financing of Terrorism & Proliferation – the FATF Recommendations (Recommendation 8 and Interpretive Note to Recommendation 8)*. Paris: FATF.

May, O. 2016a. The 'Panama Papers': What lessons can NGOs learn? Second Marshmallow. https://secondmarshmallow.org/2016/04/06/panama-papers/

May, O. 2016b. *Fighting fraud and corruption in the humanitarian and global development sector*. Abingdon: Routledge. https://doi.org/10.4324/9781315558301

Part I

1   The challenge

Terrorist diversion and INGOs

Oliver May

This chapter explores the likelihood of diversion for INGOs operating in certain contexts, and the vulnerability of these unique organisations. In broad strokes, it describes some of the key reasons why managing diversion risk is such a complex undertaking for an INGO. These factors, of course, are those of which any Anti-Diversion Programme (ADP) must take account. It also considers the consequences of failing to prevent diversion incidents – whether they are detected or not.

The likelihood of diversion

Determining the likelihood of diversion requires nuance. Other integrity-related risks, such as sexual abuse or fraud, may carry a relatively consistent level of opportunity across most INGOs; they all work with people, they all have funds that can be abused. But diversion is not the same – not all INGOs share exposure to the core risk factors. Determining a general risk level for the sector may fail to appreciate its diversity, nor necessarily be constructive.

That said, there are common factors shared by some organisations within the sector. Indeed, in 2017, three sectoral assessments in the UK (HM Treasury), Australia (AUSTRAC/ACNC), and the Asia region (AUSTRAC) all revised the charity sector's general risk level downwards – but identified a higher risk subset of internationally operating organisations.

INGOs at an elevated likelihood of diversion might be those that can see their situation in three factors identified by FATF (2014): The value of an INGO's resources or activities to a diversionary, the INGO's proximity to that diversionary, and that diversionary's capability and intent to abuse them.

The value of an INGO's resources or activities to a diversionary

In 2016, the top five recipient countries of humanitarian assistance – Syria, Yemen, Iraq, Palestine, and South Sudan – received $7.7bn (£6bn) between them (Development Initiatives, 2018) and were, at the time, all high-risk jurisdictions with active and organised diversionary threats. As significant proportions of these funding streams are delivered through INGOs, their

Figure 1.1 Factors elevating diversionary likelihood.

operations represent a major channel of resources into fragile states and conflict zones. To put it another way, as an INGO security advisor told Benelli et al. (2012), "NGOs are walking dollars."

Funds do not have to be liquid to be of use to diversionaries, either. While both food and Non-Food Items (NFIs) alike can serve diversionaries directly, they can also serve a diversionary's purposes; these items can be liquidated or can be distributed to others to gain legitimacy with local populations. Even non-distributional forms of intervention can be of use to a diversionary, such as the construction of amenities and infrastructure, or training in critical skills.

Indeed, the very nature of humanitarian and development assistance means that, to a diversionary, many of its outputs are likely to be valuable. In fact, Belliveau (2015) found that the perceived value of the service provided by Médicins Sans Frontières (MSF) in Somalia was a critical factor in the agency gaining access in the first place.

Proximity

INGOs do not have to be operating in the base countries of diversionaries to be at risk – merely adjacently. In one matter of which I am aware, Al-Shabaab allegedly levied fees from INGOs in Kenya, across the border from Somalia. And adjacency does not have to be geographic either; risk can rise for INGOs working with particular populations known to be targeted by diversionaries for recruitment purposes.

In fact, of the top ten recipient countries of humanitarian assistance in 2016, nine were either high-risk conflict zones or were adjacent to one (Development Initiatives, 2018). Between them, they received more than

60 per cent of global humanitarian funding that year at over $11bn (£8.6bn). There was known, organised diversionary activity in at least eight.

Diversionary capability and intent

FATF (2014) notes that both capability and intent must be present for a diversionary to pose a threat. A group, for example, may have the capability to divert resources from an INGO but may not wish to do so. Similarly, a group may wish to divert resources, but may not have the ability to do so.

The geographic, social, and political power of diversionaries can be easy to underestimate. Given that many such groups see themselves as governments-in-waiting (in some cases, de-facto governments), it should be expected that they could exact a sophisticated approach to diversion where their value chains and those of INGOs intersect. Al-Shabaab appointed local humanitarian officers to co-ordinate with aid groups and ensure the collection of fees (Jackson and Aynte, 2013), while the Taliban in Afghanistan had a 'minister' for the management of aid agencies (Jackson and Giustozzi, 2012).

The vulnerability of INGOs to diversion

Although every INGO is unique, a number of common enablers of vulnerability may exist for those that work in proximity to diversionaries. Themes INGOs should watch out for include a low risk maturity but a high risk appetite, an over-sensitivity to cost that impedes proportionate investment, the phenomenon of risk transfer, and shared factors with wider fraud and corruption vulnerabilities.

Low risk maturity versus high risk appetite

In East Africa, I once delivered AML/CTF workshops to nearly 50 national and international NGOs. When I asked participants whether any had conducted an AML/CTF risk assessment, none had. Then I asked if anyone had conducted *any* kind of risk assessment at all, and only one hand went up.

In recent years, there has been significant development in the application of risk management across the aid sector. This includes the adoption of Enterprise Risk Management (ERM) (Modirzadeh, 2013), for example, activity by sector collectives and peak bodies, and even the use of compliance software (Harvard Law School, 2014). Even so, the capacity and capability of many INGOs to manage diversion risk remains questionable. The CHE project found that most respondents in a survey of about 500 humanitarian and development workers (mostly from senior or project management, or legal departments) declared only a 'slight' or 'moderate' familiarity with counter-terror laws (Burniske and Modirzadeh, 2017). Debarre (2019) described a lack of understanding amongst humanitarian stakeholders of sanctions regimes.

Meanwhile, many organisations swing between overly simplistic and paralysingly complex approaches to risk. Without meaningful risk assessment, managers cannot be confident that controls are proportionate or effective. The absence of good risk management sits behind not just the absence of controls, but *over*-control in which bureaucratic procedures hinder delivery and do not actually modify the real risks the organisation faces.

And so, a core enabler of vulnerability to diversion is what we might call the 'jaws of trouble' – where low organisational risk maturity meets high risk appetite. Put simply, 'risk maturity' is the extent to which an INGO has implemented effective risk management. The poorest maturity is naivety; no concept of risk nor real management of it. The greatest maturity would see an organisation not just managing hazards well, but managing risk so effectively that it was able to embrace risky opportunities. Meanwhile, 'risk appetite' represents the total volume of residual risk that an organisation is prepared to bear.

There are a range of drivers pushing INGOs towards the jaws of trouble, but four might be particularly common. Firstly, that for INGOs, risk appetite decisions are often powered by a moral imperative. This differentiates them from companies, answerable for their bottom lines and luxuriously selecting operating theatres on the basis of a nuanced analysis of profit, risk, and opportunity. For humanitarian agencies in particular, that 'life and limb' principle – part of the humanitarian imperative – is a heavy weight on the scales and, if it is not treated carefully, can obliterate balanced risk analysis.

The second driver is how the operational ambitions of many INGOs outstrip their resources. This often derives from a fundamental tension: The push to help ever more beneficiaries versus the failure to adequately invest in the business support functions necessary to do so safely. This stretch rapidly becomes untenable, and holes appear.

The third might be the limited extent to which informed self-reflection around risk exists in many INGOs. While the Charity Finance Group's (CFG) 2018 survey of British charities operating overseas found that most respondents thought that they were at a low, or very low, risk of money-laundering or terrorist-financing, this was also the view of that group in Nairobi at the start of my workshop. At the end, the modal response was that they were at a medium risk.

Perhaps this is, in part, a consequence of fourth driver – that diversion often suffers from poor risk visibility. Challenges to incident detection can make it difficult to develop an informed risk picture, while diversion risks can span multiple functions, and change rapidly and unpredictably (Modirzadeh, 2013).

Over-sensitivity to cost

A key enabler for the misalignment of ambition and resource is chronic underinvestment in business support functions. Sensitivity to such costs is hardwired into global development. This is even expressed in the language of some of the key research into diversion. For example, Pantuliano et al. (2011),

Mackintosh and Duplat (2013), Harvard Law School (2014), Metcalfe-Hough et al. (2015), and CFG (2018) all use the term 'burden' – sometimes paired with 'administrative' – to describe aspects of the INGO response to counter-terrorism. This tells us something important about how diversion risk management might be unconsciously seen by many in the sector – as a set of secondary activities, rather than integral to the safe delivery of operations. Certainly, NGOs are known to underinvest in business support (Jones, 2018) and local and national NGOs do not often enjoy substantial funding for 'overheads' in their contracts (Stoddard et al., 2019).

The challenge for us is that the sensitivity to their cost which leads to un-derinvestment is not necessarily driven by a sober risk management equation, but by powerful outside levers. These might include, for example, the unreasonable expectations of uninformed public commentators (such as Gina Miller's 2015 attack on charity cost ratios – see Ricketts, 2015), ideologically-driven political pressures, and sectoral norms at the intersection of fundraising and accounting that create a 'race to the bottom' on 'administrative' cost reporting.

Risk transfer: A systemic flaw

Risk transfer, usually through contractual means, involves shifting a risk onto another party. Generally speaking, this is a sensible way to alleviate the like-lihood or consequences of a risk (particularly its financial liabilities). Perhaps the most commonly-used allegory is home insurance. One pays a small, regular fee so that if one's possessions are stolen or damaged by fire, the insurer will take care of the matter.

Aid operations make extensive use of risk transfer. One of the most common operating modalities in the sector features a long funding chain, in which big government or multilateral donors engage INGOs, who in turn engage local partners, to execute project aims. In a matter I examined in Africa, there were more than a dozen organisations in one such chain.

The rationale for risk transfer seems relatively sound at face value. Other organisations enjoy greater access and local knowledge, and are therefore in a better position to deliver the project's aims and control its risks. While this might sound attractive, there are ways that it might actually elevate vulner-ability to diversion.

Firstly, risk transfer is rarely complete. In the home insurance example, the risk has only been transferred in certain circumstances, and only a particular *consequence* is covered by the transfer. One is still required to reduce the *like-lihood* of theft, for example, by locking doors, or the insurer may not pay out. Donors do not fully transfer the risk of diversion – they are not fully protected from all the consequences, such as reputational damage. Similarly, Metcalfe et al. (2011) also found that INGO staff would still feel a moral responsibility for the partners to whom the risk had apparently been transferred.

Secondly, the concept relies on the ability of the transferee to reduce the likelihood or absorb the consequences. But in this sector, capacity and capability to manage the risks often decline with each step down the funding chain; a phenomenon exacerbated by the increased focus on 'localisation' and the masking of 'partnership' in flowery terms that bely that this is often no more than a subcontracting arrangement. Indeed, Stoddard et al. (2019) found that the use of local partnerships as a cost-effective means to scale up in Nigeria and South Sudan, for example, had the effect of incentivising competition amongst local NGOs to take on more risk. Abild (2009) meanwhile argued that some actually profit from risk transfer and what he called the 'Nairobi field divide'. If that were so, then the opacity inherent in much risk transfer potentially becomes an enabler for payments to diversionaries.

Shared factors with wider fraud and corruption

Diversion shares characteristics with the wider family of fraud and corruption risks, such as insider fraud, vendor fraud, bribery, conflicted interests, and nepotism. Consequently, many of the factors in the sector that enable these wider risks are also relevant to diversion. These include the effect of the sector's reliance on cultures of trust and the presence of hierarchical value structures that may deprioritise anti-diversion (May, 2016), the volatility of funding and its effects on downstream business planning, and decentralised governance (a trend noted by Harvard Law School in 2014, and linked to sanctions breach risk by the US Office of Foreign Assets Control (OFAC) in 2019).

Much has been made of the challenges of implementing meaningful systems to prevent and detect diversion, fraud, and corruption in LMICs, fragile states, and conflict zones. But there is one particular issue for diversion that stands out, and this is that even where countries might have stronger infrastructure, both business planning and due diligence can be impeded by an ongoing 'who's who' question.

This is a well-understood issue for the sector – most respondents in CFG's 2018 survey of British charities operating overseas identified partners and suppliers as the greatest source of ML or TF risk. Put simply, without deep local knowledge, it can be extremely difficult to identify diversionaries amongst local partners, community elders, beneficiaries, vendors, and suppliers. As one NGO worker told Benelli et al. (2012) in Afghanistan, "We can speak to the community elders, but how do we know they are not Taliban?"

Diversionary networks are also complex – while due diligence may help to identify the principals of local entities with links to diversionaries, there are plenty of individuals with those links that will not show a trace.

The complexity of managing diversion risk

For INGOs working in or near LMICs, fragile states, or conflict zones with active diversionary threats, managing the risk is a challenging undertaking. These challenges arise at organisational, programme, and project levels and are exacerbated by a range of complexities. These derive from a number of interlinking issues – the variance between the risk profiles of an INGO's operations, anti-diversion obligations and expectations, and differences of perspectives. Even for INGOs with strong anti-diversion frameworks, there are also risks generated by compliance with CTF regimes in themselves.

Variance in risk profiles

No two INGO operations have identical risk profiles, and there are several layers of variance that make up each. Firstly, the modalities themselves. Modern humanitarian, development, and advocacy programming is diverse. Cash transfers, construction, training and capacity building, technology, distribution of food and NFIs, micro-finance and others all have differing risk profiles. It is also an innovative sector, and so these evolve all the time, while the way in which they are deployed differ too – direct delivery, implementing partners, consortia and other means also bring different risk profiles.

Meanwhile, the array of third parties (and their industries and sectors) with which INGOs work creates further variance, from other INGOs to local Civil Society Organisations (CSOs), educational institutions, municipal authorities, small consultancies and large contractors. Local country and regional contexts themselves offer a fourth layer – offering diversity of environmental risk between and within countries. Compare Syria, Somalia, Afghanistan, and the Democratic Republic of the Congo (DRC), for example, or Belfast and Manchester.

These diverse risk profiles are also affected by several volatility factors. Diversion risk changes throughout the project cycle – different risks move up and down in likelihood depending on where we are from project inception to closure. Because funding is so often contingent on donors, changing donor priorities means that the operational picture pivots rapidly. Finally, of course, local contexts – especially in emergencies and conflicts – can also change quickly.

Variety of obligations and expectations

In Chapter 3, we set out some common features of CTF regimes of which INGOs will need to be aware. But despite those common features, there is huge complexity in delivering compliance with it. INGOs must grapple with the dizzying scale, nature, and variance of obligations, their differing consistency and clarity, and with the ever-present threat of financial exclusion.

Scale, nature, and variance of obligations

INGOs operate within an extensive latticework of anti-diversion obligations and expectations. These arise not just from differing national counter-terror legislation, but also from other legislation, NGO regulations, and donor requirements. Their variance includes definitions, level of preventative prescription, reporting, consequences, and reach. In relation to the latter, they can be local or extraterritorial, project-based or enterprise-wide, present or historical. And they do not always align – in fact, in practice, they can even contradict. An example might be a jurisdiction with local legislation that prohibits discrimination on the basis of political belief. While back-donors may require of an INGO that job applicants are free of 'links' to sanctioned entities, should they defer employment to an individual on the basis of their support for a political group (that happens to be listed) on social media, they may run the risk of legal liability.

How governments enforce these obligations varies too. Banks listed by one government may not be by another, for example. Even within national governments, there may not be internal alignment. Different noises may come from different departments – a situation that has changed little since Pantuliano et al. reported it in 2011. Donor agencies, for example, do not operate in a vacuum and are accountable to other actors. Law enforcement, treasury, and international development departments may approach the issues from very different starting points.

Working in consortia adds another layer of complexity, as different members may be subject to different levels of scrutiny by their national authorities. This can lead to different systems, expectations, and perceptions of risk amongst INGOs themselves.

Variance in consistency and clarity

If the variance in obligations and their enforcement was not problematic enough, INGOs also encounter challenges in how such obligations are interpreted in highly complicated and fluid local contexts. Indeed, many of these obligations were conceived in circumstances different to the operations of INGOs, and perhaps without any consideration of them. Burke (2017) quotes Justin Brady, a United Nations (UN) humanitarian in Somalia: "I'm sure in Washington or London it's clear what [the laws] meant but here it is much more difficult."

In recent years, a common government response to INGOs worried about being caught up in financial integrity legislation has been the intimation that they are not the focus of such legislation, and are unlikely to be pursued. As Burke reported, for example, the "unofficial advice" given to NGOs operating in Al-Shabaab controlled areas of Somalia was that "a blind eye" was being turned to their humanitarian operations. Indeed, the UK government had earlier issued official guidance that described the risk of prosecution for a terrorist offence as a result of involvement in humanitarian efforts as "low" (OFSI, 2016). At face-value, this appears reassuring; a welcome recognition of the complexity of humanitarian work and its vital need. But it is not only unhelpful, but potentially counter-productive.

Firstly, such statements do not carry the comfort of permanence. While prosecution may be unlikely at the time of the pronouncement, that may not always be the case and, in any event, such decisions are taken on the individual circumstances of the matter. This is not a sound basis for developing compliance frameworks and taking governance decisions. In 2014, Burniske et al. quoted Daniel Fried at the US State Department, providing reassurance that the prosecution of humanitarian actors was not an enforcement priority under US counter-terror law. He couldn't "think of cases where the [US] Department of Justice has actually gone after legitimate NGOs," he said. Four years later, of course, the Department of Justice would be settling with Norwegian People's Aid (NPA) in a sector-shaking matter.

Further, as Burke notes, if INGOs are expected to operate 'under the radar' then this can be perceived to preclude large-scale operations, while such a nudge-wink approach may even lead to a dwindling of anti-diversion effort amongst NGOs, ironically increasing the likelihood of incidents and therefore legal action. Encouraging routine non-compliance with the law also risks corrosive effect; how can the INGO ask its own people to follow its own policies while it role-models legal non-compliance? There is also an ethical choice here: Just because one might not be prosecuted for committing an offence, does that make it right to offend? If the public hold a different view, this may sow the seed of a reputational crisis.

But most importantly, responsible INGOs do not want to allow diversion. They are not looking for 'get out of jail free cards,' but for support, guidance, and policy cohesion – including from governments.

Financial exclusion ('de-risking')

Hovering over all of this is the threat of financial exclusion. As CFG (2018) put it, INGO operations in particular jurisdictions represent relatively high risk and low profitability for banks, who have been made liable for customer activities by their own international legislative frameworks. This has led to the practice of bank 'de-risking,' in which NGOs have found that they are unable to access legitimate banking channels. In practice, this means delays to financial transfers, requests for unusual additional documentation, increased fees, or account closures (Kuznia, 2017).

A key consequence of financial exclusion, of course, is that it may worsen the situation. Mission-driven organisations like INGOs do not stop because they do not have bank accounts. As noted by Pantuliano et al. (2011) and CFG (2018), NGOs turn to higher risk mechanisms of financial movement such as cash couriers, staff bank accounts, and Money Service Bureaux (MSBs). Hawala banking has also been used.

Differences of perspective

The relationship of INGOs to diversion is also shaped by how people in the sector may see these issues, which in turn derives from worldviews shaped by culture, context, experience, and an array of factors beyond the scope of this book. 'Human factors,' however, are important to touch on as an awareness of them is required for the design and operation of an ADP.

The impact of local perspectives

Local perspectives on risk, controls, and governance can be significantly at variance to those further up the funding chain, and this can generate tensions and drag on implementation (May, 2016). An example might be due diligence, which Pantuliano et al. (2011) describe as "undermining relations between humanitarian organisations and local communities. USAID partner vetting requirements envisage collecting and reporting personal information about partner and contractor staff to the US government – a requirement that is invariably seen as invasive and accusatory by locals." As we will discuss, there is an alternative perspective on due diligence – but Pantuliano et al. certainly demonstrate how risk and controls can be seen differently between parties.

Meanwhile, the old adage that 'one man's terrorist is another man's freedom fighter' is trite, but holds some truth. The relationships between diversionaries and local communities are complex, and diversionaries themselves can be sprawling collectives occupying political, military, and social spaces.

The humanitarian imperative and principles

In 1994, the Code of Conduct for the International Red Cross and Red Crescent Movement and NGOs in Disaster Relief documented the 'humanitarian imperative' and its primacy. This concept describes that "the right to receive humanitarian assistance, and to offer it, is a fundamental humanitarian principle which should be enjoyed by all citizens of all countries." It goes on to include, amongst other provisions, that access to affected populations should be unimpeded, and that humanitarian aid is not a partisan or political act. It is accompanied by four humanitarian principles: humanity, neutrality, impartiality, and independence.

These are statements of faith for humanitarians, but their relationship with the anti-diversion agenda can be fraught. Some humanitarians see elements of organisational anti-diversion activity as impediments to access, and counter-terror compliance itself as a partisan or political act in which the regulations require INGOs to take sides. This speaks to a core truth at the heart of the sector's relationship with diversion: That humanitarians approach the issue with a completely different mental model to legislators, law enforcers, and compliance professionals. For INGOs to properly manage the risk, any ADP will need to accept this difference of viewpoint and work with it. All sides can learn from each other.

Compliance with the global CTF regime as a risk in itself

For many risks, arriving at a point where they are satisfactorily controlled and humanitarian opportunities can be safely pursued is the objective. But with diversion, arriving at that point can open up a whole new set of risks, and an ADP needs to take account of these. This is because counter-terrorism has been a tool of challenge to civil society, compliance with CTF regimes can create local challenges, and even transparency can be a double-edged sword.

Counter-terrorism as a tool of challenge to civil society

While much commonality exists between the values of many INGOs and the intent of counter-terror regulation, the relationship must be seen against the backdrop of shrinking civil society space and the historic use of counter-terrorism as a tool of persecution and marginalisation. The balance between legitimate accountability and nefariously-motivated scrutiny can be, at best, uneasy. This spectre means that, even where the aims of regulators are legitimate, a climate of mistrust exists. This can affect the readiness of an INGO's internal stakeholders to comply with the counter-terror regime, to practise transparency with regulators, and to participate in open dialogue.

For example, Kenya's NGO Co-Ordination Board (NGOCB) announced the de-registration of 500 NGOs in December 2014, ostensibly as part of a counter-terror initiative (Honan, 2014), and then of a further 959 in October 2015 on the basis of alleged financial non-transparency (IRIN, 2015). Whatever the intent, the moves were characterised in the sector as a civil society 'crackdown.'

Civil society is not just in the crosshairs of certain government actors, either. Private organisations like Shurat HaDin in Israel investigate and scrutinise the operations of civil society for any links to terrorist organisations (Ho, 2014).

More recently, we have seen the rise of what we might call 'bounty activism.' Here, whatever the motivations of a civil actor in bringing an anti-diversion case, they may also be able to pocket a slice of any resulting fine through whistleblower reward provisions. A possible example was the case initiated by US lawyer David Abrams against NPA, which settled at £2m for allegedly breaching the US False Claims Act when it claimed that it had not dealt with sanctioned entities, allegedly erroneously. Abrams told IRIN that he received more than $300,000 (about $240,000) for bringing that case, and that there were further cases to come (Parker, 2018). Recent years have also seen the growth of private prosecutions in the UK (Gibb, 2015), potentially giving private individuals and organisations a further tool by which to hold INGOs to account for real or perceived transgressions.

Counter-terrorism compliance as a source of local risk to INGOs

Mindful of attacks and the inhuman cruelty of Islamic State (IS), for example, some readers may wonder why INGOs might even consider it appropriate to try to 'opt-out' of counter-terror obligations. Yet the ability of an INGO to deliver its mission safely in a conflict zone can be dependent on signalling neutrality, and compliance with the global counter-terror regime may be seen by belligerents as alignment with their enemies.

A vivid example of which I am aware might be a case involving a UK NGO operating in a Middle Eastern conflict zone. The NGO was approached by British anti-terror police officers seeking an expert witness for a criminal case in which the typical supply chain of INGO operations had become a fact in issue. This created a dilemma – supporting the British justice system was well within the NGO's values, but to have been identified with the British anti-terror police would have turned the logos on their vehicles in the conflict zone into bullseyes.

There are also more banal forms of compliance carrying similar risks – the provision of beneficiary data to government donor agencies, for example, or even participation in meetings at embassies or military bases. As noted by one commentator, "through complying [with] national legislation, US [funded] organisations are seen by partners on the ground as endorsing the political view of the government […] particularly in its conception of terrorism and who deserves assistance" (Pantuliano et al., 2011).

Falling foul of a diversionary's sensibilities, then, can affect not only an INGO's access to beneficiaries, but the physical security of their operations, staff, partners, and even those beneficiaries. At a time when humanitarianism is a potentially deadly occupation (Humanitarian Outcomes, 2019), these risks are not easily put aside. In fact, Belliveau (2015) describes that operating in Somalia was "at best an uncomfortable balancing act, at worst a brutal dilemma between impossible choices."

Diversionary fear that INGOs might be aligned with their enemies is well documented. In Afghanistan, paranoia that aid agencies might be 'spying' peppered Jackson and Giustozzi's conversations with Taliban commanders (2012). Donini (2009) reported comments by a UN official that the co-ordination of World Food Programme (WFP) deliveries with the International Security Assistance Force (ISAF) and, in some cases, the execution of pre-convoy patrols by ISAF, gave the impression to locals that ISAF and the WFP were aligned. In Somalia, Jackson and Aynte (2013) reported that a former Al-Shabaab official told them that the expulsion of certain UN agencies was because they were seen as 'spy-friendly.' Certainly, Al-Shabaab indicated that their banning of the International Medical Corps (IMC) and CARE was in response to alleged spying (Pantuliano et al., 2011).

The challenge of transparency

Transparency is critical to reducing the risk of diversion. In addition to its deterrent, preventative, and detective effects, it enables agencies to work together to resolve mutual problems. It does, however, come with its own risks. The public discourse is not always informed or fair. The honest disclosure of integrity risk information by INGOs can lead to political attention and reputationally-impactive media coverage, while institutional donors do not always respond proportionately. INGOs may not be in a position to challenge this, given the expense of legal defences and the existential risks of souring relationships with donors.

Consequently, a form of *omertà* hangs over the sector. In Afghanistan, Benelli et al. (2012) found that paranoia made NGOs secretive and prone to silo-working. "Basically, it's everyone for himself," quipped an NGO country director. Things were not much better in Gaza in 2011, found

Pantuliano et al., where minutes were not taken at meetings to avoid recording any engagement with proscribed organisations. Debarre reports the silence as still extant in 2019, and Humanitarian Outcomes (nd) rightly challenges it.

The consequences of diversion

The ripples of diversion can be extensive. These might touch not only the INGO concerned, but the whole aid sector and the wider community. They are not to be taken lightly. In concert, or in extremis, they can be existential.

It is a common misunderstanding that these effects are activated only upon the detection of incidents. This is not always the case. While some will crystallise only if diversion is detected, others will occur whether the event or its effects are detected or not. Others still can materialise if incidents are suspected, even if not detected.

Contributing to harm

Whatever the political disagreement about whether every entity that appears on a list deserves to be there, whether all those who are alleged to be connected to those entities actually are, or even whether such a system is effective or appropriate, it remains the case that many of these entities do execute their strategies in a manner that is at odds to the vision, values, and missions of legitimate INGOs.

In addition to the violence that fills television screens, diversionaries are often integral to, or the originators of, exploitative power structures that create, maintain, and intensify harm to the people that INGOs seek to help. They are rarely liberal democratic, empowering, or altruistic. Instead they are often authoritarian, controlling, and corrupt.

In fact, all benefits extracted from an INGO to a diversionary risk contributing, in some way, to their agenda. Across different agencies and over time, even small payments become significant in aggregate. There is a chain between the dollar paid to a diversionary in a one-off toll at a checkpoint, and the bullet used to silence a local merchant who challenges the injustices inherent in that diversionary's regime.

Effects upon public confidence

In addition to providing fuel to those who seek to challenge or oppress civil society, a failure to prevent diversion can also impede the social licence of both individual organisations, and the sector as a whole. Given the importance of public trust for fundraising, a collapse in it can be a potentially existential matter.

Effects upon programming

The clearest effect of diversion is its damage to beneficiary outcomes, whether the diversion is detected or not. Where diversion is undetected, this effect is hidden (or, at best, shows up in audit and evaluation as inefficiency). And if it is detected, it comes with further impact for resourcing. Managing a detected incident involves significant time and financial costs, as well as potentially drag on programming activities (whether or not funding is suspended by an institutional donor, which is frequently the case). Forensic audits and investigations are potentially disruptive, lengthy, and complex activities for a project to bear.

In addition to the loss of the resources that were diverted, there may be other financial liabilities too that reduce programming bandwidth. American lawyer David Abrams told IRIN that, in the NPA case, the NGO could theoretically have been liable to pay back every dollar obtained from USAID in triplicate (Parker, 2018). More commonly, institutional donors often expect repayment of the lost funds, which – unless insurance applies – can lead to a 'double-dip' loss for the INGO.

Loss of bank and institutional donor confidence

Earlier in this chapter we described the impact of financial exclusion throughout the sector, and the loss of bank confidence here is very real. In the 2018 CFG survey of British charities operating overseas, nearly 80 per cent of respondents reported some kind of problem accessing or using mainstream banking channels.

It is not just the financial freedom to operate that can be affected, but the confidence of institutional donors too. And donors may apply onerous remedial controls – often with the acceptance of the programme impact such controls entail – and extensive investigative activity.

INGOs could also expect debarment from bidding for future contracts. While this can take a range of forms (temporary or permanent, compulsory or voluntary, unilateral or negotiated), the effect on revenue can be significant and perhaps result in the loss of capabilities that can be hard to resurrect. Following the aid sector sexual abuse scandal in 2018, for example, Oxfam and Save the Children International (SCI) agreed temporarily not to bid for DFID funding (Quinn, 2018). An article in *The Times* linked Oxfam's announcement of significant project and staffing cuts with this crisis (Hurst, 2018).

Regulatory impact

Regulatory interest – though a necessary part of the wider governance of INGO activity – can be intense, reputationally damaging, and disruptive. Failing to adequately prevent diversion runs the risk of activating that interest. Meanwhile, the incidents themselves can come with significant penalties. This is not only limited to, for example, deregistration but can extend to fines and even imprisonment.

Human impact

The effects of diversion can include not only career-limiting disciplinary outcomes for negligent staff, but the loss of wider staff confidence (whether the case is detected and reported, or not). Discovering that diversion has occurred – especially in a project upon which the staff concerned have been working – can be tremendously destabilising. Further, the issue is particularly consequential for board members and trustees, who may not have the specialist expertise to recognise and understand diversion risk, but may still incur personal liability in the event of risks materialising.

And where staff suspect diversion, but it has not been detected or reported, this can damage compliance culture through undermining an INGO's policy line on diversion. The credibility of the INGO's entire anti-diversion position evaporates if staff on the ground believe it may be taking place but that the INGO is unaware or inactive. After all, for many staff, diversion entails the loss of the INGO's moral high-ground.

That high-ground is crucial to the moral mission of INGOs. As values-driven organisations, diversion represents a transgression against their missions and purpose, a failure to 'do no harm', and a malfunction in the application of the humanitarian imperative. For legitimate, trustworthy INGOs, diversion must be a risk to be controlled as far as possible.

References

Abild, E. 2009. *Creating humanitarian space: A case study of Somalia.* Oxford: University of Oxford.

AUSTRAC 2017. *Non-profit organisations and terrorism financing regional risk assessment 2017.* Commonwealth of Australia.

AUSTRAC and ACNC 2017. *National risk assessment on money laundering and terrorism financing 2017: Australia's non-profit organisation sector.* Commonwealth of Australia.

Belliveau, J. 2015. *Red lines and Al-Shabaab: Negotiating humanitarian access in Somalia.* Oslo: Norwegian Peacebuilding Resource Centre.

Benelli, P., Donini, A., and Niland, N. 2012. *Afghanistan: Humanitarianism in uncertain times.* Somerville, MA: Feinstein International Center, Tufts University.

Burke, J. 2017. Anti-terrorism laws have 'chilling effect' on vital aid deliveries to Somalia. *The Guardian.*

Burniske, J. and Modirzadeh, N. 2017. *Pilot empirical survey study on the impact of counter-terrorism measures on humanitarian action.* Cambridge, MA: Harvard Law School.

Burniske, J., Modirzadeh, N., and Lewis, D. 2014. *Counter terrorism laws and regulations: What aid agencies need to know.* London: Overseas Development Institute.

Charity Finance Group 2018. *Impact of money laundering and terrorist financing regulations on charities.* London: Charity Finance Group.

Debarre, A. 2019. *Safeguarding humanitarian action in sanctions regimes.* New York, NY: International Peace Institute.

Development Initiatives 2018. *Global Humanitarian Assistance Report 2018.* Bristol: Development Initiatives.

Donini, A. 2009. *Afghanistan: Humanitarianism under threat.* Somerville, MA: Feinstein International Center, Tufts University.

FATF 2014. *Risk of terrorist abuse in non-profit organisations.* Paris: FATF.

Gibb, F. 2015. Cuts lead to 'growth industry' in private prosecutions. *The Times.*

Harvard Law School 2014. *Counterterrorism and Humanitarian Engagement Project: An Analysis of Contemporary Anti-Diversion Policies and Practices of Humanitarian Organizations.* Cambridge, MA: Harvard Law School.

Ho, S. 2014. Israeli law group accuses Oxfam of funding terrorists. *Times of Israel.*

Honan, E. 2014. Kenya shuts down 500 groups in anti-terrorism crackdown. *Reuters.*

HM Treasury 2017. *National risk assessment of money laundering and terrorist financing 2017.* London: HM Treasury.

Humanitarian Outcomes 2019. *Aid worker security report: Figures at a glance 2019.* London: Humanitarian Outcomes.

Humanitarian Outcomes nd. *NGO Risk Management: Principles and promising practice,* London: Humanitarian Outcomes/InterAction.

Hurst, G. 2018. Oxfam cuts projects and staff in cash crisis after sex scandal. *The Times.*

IRIN 2015. NGOs in Kenya protest threatened deregistration of 959 organisations. *IRIN.*

Jackson, A. and Aynte, A. 2013. *Talking to the other side: Humanitarian negotiations with Al-Shabaab in Somalia.* London: Overseas Development Institute.

Jackson, A. and Giustozzi, A. 2012. *Talking to the other side: Humanitarian engagement with the Taliban in Afghanistan.* London: Overseas Development Institute.

Jones, G. 2018. Two thirds of charities say core functions are under-resourced. *Civil Society.*

Kuznia, R. 2017. Scrutiny over terrorism funding hampers charitable work in ravaged countries. *Washington Post.*

Mackintosh, K. and Duplat, P. 2013. *Study of the impact of donor counter-terrorism measures on principled humanitarian action.* United Nations Office for the Coordination of Humanitarian Affairs/Norwegian Refugee Council.

May, O. 2016. *Fighting fraud and corruption in the humanitarian and global development sector.* Abingdon: Routledge. https://doi.org/10.4324/9781315558301.

Metcalfe, V., Martin, E., and Pantuliano, S. 2011. *Risk in humanitarian action: Towards a common approach?* London: Overseas Development Institute.

Metcalfe-Hough, V., Keatinge, T., and Pantuliano, S. 2015. *UK humanitarian aid in the age of counter-terrorism: Perceptions and reality.* London: Overseas Development Institute.

Modirzadeh, N. 2013. *Counterterrorism and Humanitarian Engagement Project: Enterprise risk management – a new approach to managing the risks posed by counterterrorism regulations.* Cambridge, MA: Harvard Law School.

OFAC 2019. *A framework for OFAC compliance commitments.* Washington, DC: United States Department of the Treasury.

Office of Financial Sanctions Implementation (OFSI) 2016. *For information note: Operating within counter-terrorism legislation.* London: Home Office.

Pantuliano, S., Mackintosh, K., Elhawary, S., and Metcalfe, V. 2011. *Counter-terrorism and humanitarian action: Tensions, impact and ways forward.* HPG Policy Brief 43. London: Overseas Development Institute.

Parker, B. 2018. A Q&A with the pro-Israel US lawyer rattling NGOs on counter-terror compliance. *IRIN.*

Quinn, B. 2018. Save the Children suspends UK funding bids over abuse scandal. *The Guardian.*

Ricketts, A. 2015. Sector condemns Gina Miller's True and Fair Foundation over 'flawed' report into charity finances. *Third Sector.*

Stoddard, A., Czwarno, M., and Hamsik, L. 2019. *NGOs & risk: Managing uncertainty in local-international partnerships.* London: Humanitarian Outcomes/InterAction.

2 The myths

Common misconceptions

Oliver May

One consequence of a poorly-understood, complex issue is that myths and misconceptions build up around it. In this chapter, we explore five of the most common: That preventing diversion is just a matter of screening; that it is a donor and regulatory compliance issue; that any given INGO won't be prosecuted; that no incidents of diversion means no problem exists; and that the humanitarian imperative means that we must tolerate diversion – or even that the anti-diversion agenda itself is contrary to the imperative.

After dismantling these ideas, we suggest alternative ways of thinking and these set the scene for the approach outlined in the rest of this book: A holistic, proportionate, and effective ADP as part of a risk-based approach to tackling diversion in the aid sector.

"Preventing diversion is just a matter of screening."

Knowing who you are really dealing with is a key issue of our time. Perhaps one of the most prominent manifestations of this is in social media, where influencing operations for political ends are allegedly carried out by accounts purporting to be people they are not. Anonymous, automated Twitter accounts ('bots') created one in five of all messages in English about NATO in the Baltics during a 3-month period in 2018. In Russian, bot content represented 49 per cent of all such messages (Fredheim and Gallacher, 2018). The destabilising questions for genuine social media users are, with whom are you really engaging? And are you sure that, by engaging, you are not already meeting their dark purpose?

'Screening,' part of due diligence, is the practice of checking a potential second or third party, such as a person, partner, or vendor, against proscription and sanctions lists. In recent years, this has become the focus of anti-diversion efforts for many INGOs. This prominence is fed by prescriptive donor demands, and by the fact that such processes are relatively easy to adopt, design, and embed – whereas other tools can be more challenging to implement.

But this is misplaced. Checking entities against lists is part of the picture, but it only really helps to affect the risk of engaging an entity on those lists. As we discuss in Chapter 4, there are more ways that diversion manifests itself than this. It does not affect, for example, the risk of engaging entities *linked* to those on the lists – which is arguably the risk more likely to occur. It is very unlikely (though not impossible) that an NGO's local electrician would be a leader of a sanctioned movement, but marginally more likely that the electrician may be a radicalised affiliate of such an entity. Not one of the 19 hijackers in the 9/11 attacks personally appeared on UN or US sanctions lists, for example, though of course they were all affiliated with Al-Qaeda. And even where an entity does appear on a list, there are plenty of ways to mask an identity – especially if you are an individual significant enough to be named on a such a list!

A more sophisticated approach to due diligence through online and offline means, such as that which we outline in Chapter 8, helps – but many INGOs still place more reliance on due diligence than it can bear. Processes can fail or contain gaps, can be vulnerable to de-prioritisation in fast-paced humanitarian emergencies, or be of reduced effectiveness in low-infrastructure environ- ments where public records (and therefore verification opportunities) are limited. In these circumstances, if too much weight has been placed on due diligence, there may be no safety net created by the other parts of an ADP.

Looking to any given single tool as a cure-all to resolve a complex problem is a repeat offence by tidy minds in the sector. Recently blockchain, biometric identification, payment by results, and Cash Transfer Programming (CTP) have all been seen this way. In fact, all these things represent tools in the box, capable of benefit when used correctly and in the right circumstances, and risks when used inappropriately. The key to reducing the risks of terrorist diversion as far as is reasonably possible is to take a holistic approach.

Chapter 5 sets out how this approach might be applied through an ADP, supporting an effective, proportionate, and risk-based way for an INGO to tackle diversion. This includes deterrence, prevention, detection, and response tools – supported and governed by other schedules of work, such as cultural development – that can help an INGO to gain confidence that it really is doing everything reasonable to reduce the risk. It can also help the INGO to be agile, matching the right tools to the right circumstances.

"Diversion is a donor and regulatory compliance issue."

A few years ago, I attended a particular NGO conference in Europe. There was a good turnout of participants, but the breakout session with the greatest attendance was an open-floor discussion on terrorist financing.

Clearly over-subscribed, the hot, small room was packed with nervous- looking faces, and it took a while for delegates to feel comfortable to share. When they did, it rapidly became clear how many saw diversion as principally a matter of complying with donor and regulatory obligations, rather than – for example – as a stewardship, moral, or risk management issue.

This is very common and may stem from a number of places. Perhaps the clearest is that cultural and contextual complexity in country programmes make it easier to talk to stakeholders about 'donor requirements' than 'terrorism,' particularly if the latter is framed as a moral issue. It may also derive in part from a tendency to see such activities as an administrative burden; just one more item on a long to-do list.

If we were to be truly empathetic to the INGO community, however, we would also need to consider that it might be a symptom of fatigue from the exhausting parade of changing donor priorities, in-vogue aid modalities, and public *bêtes du jour* with which INGOs that want to survive must engage. "All right guys, looks like there's another thing that we need to pay attention to," said the jovial host of a 2016 podcast in which I was interviewed about fraud. This entertaining aside captures, in fact, the reality of busy programme staff sentiment worldwide.

Understandable though it may be, seeing diversion as simply a matter of donor or regulatory compliance is inadequate. Were there no donors, charity regulatory requirements, or counter-terror laws, it would still be necessary to take this risk seriously because diversion threatens project and organisational objectives, and contributes to serious societal harm.

Addressing diversion through a compliance-based approach also comes with some significant downsides. These include, for example, that donor require-ments are designed to protect the donor, not the INGO – so simply adopting donor requirements will not necessarily protect the INGO itself. It can also lead to identifying the wrong risks; the risk becomes a breach of obligations, rather than the diversion event itself – setting the INGO up for the wrong controls to reduce incidents. And it misdirects responsibility for managing risks – inclining an INGO to look to its donors, rather than itself. Perhaps this misdirected focus is the origin of the tendency for some INGO staff to complain on the one hand that donor requirements are unclear, and on the other that they are too intense.

In Chapter 5, we describe an alternative – the risk-based approach – and outline its strengths. In a risk-based approach, we start with an assessment of the actual risks faced by the INGO and build out effective and proportionate controls around those. Additional donor or regulatory requirements are then applied on top of this. As we will see, this approach offers some protection against the trend of unbridled risk transfer, and recognises the unique dis-position of each INGO. As many of the activities necessary for a risk-based approach also often support donor frameworks, it also helps to reduce du-plication, improves the speed of programme inception, and promotes more efficient business support.

"We won't be prosecuted."

In 2010, the passing of the Bribery Act in the UK led to a flurry of compliance activity amongst NGOs keen to avoid prosecution for the new offence of failing to prevent bribery. Some managers reported, however, that British officials had apparently indicated that NGOs would not be the focus of the legislation and might not be paid much attention (May, 2016a). This move –

with the best of intentions, no doubt – could have contributed to a dwindling of anti-bribery compliance effort amongst some NGOs.

As we saw in Chapter 1, similar messaging has been made in relation to terrorist financing (OFSI, 2015; Burke, 2017). While these 'get out of jail free' cards may sound reassuring, there is a problem. While 'public interest' may be required before a prosecution can take place, an NGO might engage in a transaction that is not of interest at one point in time, but which later can become as such. Verbal assurances are not the same thing as legal protection.

Those who do feel reassured sometimes also imagine that there is always a threshold of materiality for prosecution too – that minor transactions like the purchase of retail SIM cards from a sanctioned telecoms company, for example, do not count. But as we explore in Chapter 3, many offences do not contain any such threshold – it is the action itself that creates the liability, and the prosecution need not prove any intent. Similarly, it is not just positive action that can create liability, but the absence of action. 'Recklessness' and 'neglect' provisions attached to some offences mean that failing to take reasonable action to prevent and detect diversion – even if an INGO is not covered by a country's AML/CTF legislation in the same way as financial institutions – could also create scope for prosecution. In any event, prosecution decisions are made on the basis of the prevailing circumstances of the case, and it is a gamble to proceed with a potentially unlawful action in the hope that it will never end up in court.

Further, even if a public interest threshold is not met in the country of registration of the INGO or its donor, prosecution may still be a possibility in the jurisdiction of the alleged diversion. Powerful laws exist in places like Kenya, Nigeria, and Israel, and this creates a particular risk for locally-engaged staff or implementing partners, a risk that it may be very unfair for a foreign INGO to embrace. In addition, even if public bodies in any one country are not minded to mount a prosecution, there has been significant growth in private prosecutions and bounty activism. Meanwhile, in Chapter 1 we described the potential adverse impact of flouting the law on internal culture and social licence – even unwieldly laws drafted with inadequate humanitarian engagement.

In the end, proceeding on the basis that infringements of terrorist financing legislation are unlikely to lead to prosecution is unsafe and unsustainable. This book explores the legal environment around INGOs in Chapter 3. Chapter 7 describes the use of an obligations registry to keep track of regulatory requirements, and Chapter 13 discusses the need to maintain dialogue with authorities on the implications of their regulatory regimes.

"No incidents means no problem."

I was once enjoying breakfast in a Bangkok hotel, on the first day of a seminar. INGO country directors from all over Asia were convening to discuss risk, and I was due to speak about fraud. Having just arrived in Thailand, I was blearily hoping that strong coffee would wake me up, and half-wondered if I was dreaming when a cheerful stranger joined me at the table. They turned out to be a country director and here for the seminar, and smiled when I mentioned the topic of my talk.

"Ah," said the director, grandly. "There is no fraud in my country programme!"

I thought of that director again barely a year later when allegations of fraud were made in their country programme and an investigation began.

The assumption that diversion is a peripheral matter that does not occur in any given INGO's operations is common. Tropes that often reinforce this perspective include:

- There have been no 'hits' during screening;
- There have been no incidents reported by staff or partners;
- There have been no relevant findings during any audit or MEL (Monitoring, Evaluation, and Learning) process;
- All books balance, and expenditure is supported by documentation in accordance with procedures.

Deriving too much comfort from these is problematic. I am aware of a case in which local staff allegedly 'protected' senior and international staff from knowledge of access payments, believing that both the payment and the deception was necessary. Meanwhile, confidential reporting ('whistleblowing') can be a fraught process and partner organisations may not be truly incentivised to report. That the books balance, and expenditure appears supported should not necessarily reassure either – the purpose of a fraud, for example, is to deceive; to disguise payments and make processes look to cursory glance like they were followed. Finally, it is not the purpose of audit to detect incidents – only 15 per cent of frauds are detected this way (ACFE, 2018) – and some MEL professionals might not consider the detection of fraud, corruption, or diversion to be part of their work.

In the end, there is a chasm between *detected* diversion and *actual* diversion. The reality is that if an INGO operates in close proximity to a diversionary that has the capability and intent to divert its resources, and its resources are of value to the diversionary, then it is probably only a matter of time before the INGO, its partners, or contemporaries begin experiencing diversion – whether they detect it, or not.

All this reduces the visibility of what is often a high risk. Diversion, as with its cousins fraud and corruption, is a risk that actively hides from management. Given the opportunity, it retreats from view into the shade provided by our human tendency to focus on more prominent risks (availability bias – see Tversky and Kahneman, 1973). These might be those that have captured the public imagination, or which are donor priorities, or which are championed by internal stakeholders that wield significant power and influence. Instead, INGOs have to take positive action to ensure they retain the correct focus. INGOs have to chase this risk.

Keeping diversion in an INGO's sights requires two linked activities: Maintaining visibility of the risk itself and maximising visibility of any materialisation of that risk. In respect of the former, Chapter 6 explores risk assessment, and Chapter 7 considers the discipline of situational awareness. In respect of the latter, Chapter 9 considers some ways that INGOs can improve detection.

"The humanitarian imperative means that we must tolerate diversion. The anti-diversion agenda is contrary to the imperative."

I am aware of a matter in which an INGO was implementing a programme of emergency interventions in a notoriously complex country context. One of these was to provide a relatively hard-to-reach population with access to clean water, and the programme manager had engaged a local transport company to carry out water-trucking.

Against the backdrop of the daily fight to make anything at all happen in that country, he had neither carried out proper due diligence or monitored the work – and may therefore have been defrauded by a substantial sum. When the matter was examined, the investigators challenged the manager's financial stewardship. But with a cigarette hanging from his mouth and a shrug, he simply replied: "I was saving lives."

His response rather begs the question, how many more lives could have been saved if he had stewarded those resources better?

We described the humanitarian imperative in Chapter 1, the important principle upon which aid is both based and protected. But we also described different mental models used by stakeholders in the diversion debate. Some of these models have two features of note. The first is that, for some aid and development professionals, comparatively minor quantities of diversion, by volume or value, need to be tolerated in order to reach certain populations. To do the work of God, runs the old adage, we must dance with the devil. This takes various shapes – at the extreme end a humanitarian director once remarked to me, with resignation, that he thought about 40 per cent of aid was probably stolen in any given emergency. The second is that the anti-diversion agenda itself runs contrary to the imperative; how can anything affecting the free flow of aid be compatible with it?

There is truth in the idea that diversion-free programming is a myth and much of our 'zero-tolerance' thinking is unworkable, reliant on risk management sleight-of-hand. But accepting diversion, or denying the anti-diversion agenda, are equally flawed. After explaining why, we will propose a more productive third way.

The first reason this approach is flawed is because it stands on shaky risk management grounds. The ends do not justify the means, because the means have consequences capable of undermining the ends. While any one tolerated incident of diversion may be low in value, a salami-slicing effect means that they add up in aggregate to substantial sums. Further, in some conflict zones, aid may be one of the only forms of 'foreign direct investment' entering the country – giving misappropriated aid a disproportionate effect on the promotion of corruption and the maintenance of instability there. The ultimate victims of the funding of bad actors in this way may well be an INGO's own beneficiaries.

These considerations may not be foremost in mind for some aid workers because humanitarian need is a powerful driver (May, 2016b). Morality is elastic. The means can stretch to justify the perceived ends, supported by our cognitive errors, biases, and heuristics. One of those errors is to quantify the ethical harm of any one transaction based on its *intent*. We do not always think broadly enough when we consider the precept 'do no harm.' When our aims are pure, all sorts of darkness is justified on the way to achieving them.

In fact, while an action may have positive intent, the consequences are often beyond the full control of the actor and these can be negative – perhaps catastrophically so. I was once present for a tense meeting in which senior finance and audit staff at an INGO reported to British counter-terror police that they suspected an incident of diversion. In response to one participant's observation that the quantum was low, a detective replied that one could buy a lot of bullets with that figure.

A second reason is that the idea that an ADP is adverse to the humanitarian imperative represents a misunderstanding of both. Risk-based anti-diversion is not about impeding aid, it is about directing it in the safest possible way – taking into account mode and approach. It does not negatively affect the principles of humanity, neutrality, impartiality, or independence.

At this point, it is important to avoid confusing onerous counter-terror legislation, or questionable donor decisions regarding whether aid can be provided in certain geographical spaces, with the anti-diversion agenda. They are separate things. From a risk management perspective, it may be appropriate for a donor not to fund projects in places where the risk of diversion is so high that it falls outside its appetite. But this is different to declining funding to geographical spaces on the basis that a diversionary is the de-facto power alone, as there can be options and opportunities to reach populations while managing risks even in those spaces. And even in cases where a licence, waiver, or exemption to counter-terror law exists, agencies still require an ADP.

In fact, it is permissiveness of diversion that can contravene the imperative. Firstly, allowing diversion for the success of one project or programme fails to recognise that there is also an organisational-level value chain to protect. It buys local success at the cost of elevating risks for the agency at large, potentially impeding its ability to execute the imperative in other places in the future. Secondly, there is a negligence in assuming that the imperative has been met without proper visibility of diversion risks and confidence in their management – including having factored this in to decisions about programme design and investment in business support. Which is better – a high degree of confidence that a relatively lower amount of aid actually reached beneficiaries, or reporting that a higher amount of aid was transmitted, but with a relatively lower degree of confidence that it actually got there? One of those options, of course, seems better for fundraising and reporting, but stores up trouble for later.

The third reason is perhaps the most compelling. The origin of these ideas can often be traced to single, extremely complex scenarios, which are then used to generalise across the debate. At the time of writing, for example, these might be Syria, Gaza, and Yemen. But there is a simple cognitive error at work here that itself flies against one of the most important core tenets of all aid work – respecting local contexts. This error is a combination of availability bias – in which we make decisions based on the most readily-available or starkest data – and base-rate fallacy, in which we ignore general data in favour of specific data.

Instead, country contexts sit on a spectrum of risk severity and variance, and operational complexity. In some, the threat is low, the infrastructure to support work to manage it is readily available, and the country is relatively stable. In others, these variables sit at other points on the spectrum. While at the time of writing, Syria polarises sectoral discussion, not all aid work involves the stark, zero-sum choices that might exist in Syria – and not all circumstances in Syria do either. Even in other contexts with intense challenges, these challenges are different. By taking a context-by-context approach, any one agency can reduce diversion risk in the areas within its circles of control, in turn lowering aggregate risk and enabling it to entertain specific risks in more challenging places.

So, how can it be that a level of diversion risk could be within an agency's risk appetite, but that the agency does not accept diversion? This, at least, is simpler than it sounds.

All sector actors must recognise that when the three factors of proximity, capability and intent, and value are in place, the risk of diversion cannot be fully mitigated. To help beneficiaries, a level of that risk must be tolerated. But tolerating *the risk* is not the same thing as tolerating *diversion*. To make the distinction, an INGO and its donors must recognise that incidents might take place, but will not tolerate the circumstances that lead to them. They must commit to tackling the issue through prevention, detection, and response as far as possible, and to the agility required to making changes following incidents the that do transpire.

It also means recognising that, for every INGO, there may be circumstances in which it does not have the capabilities and capacity to respond to the local risk. In a go/no-go decision, 'no-go' does not represent a violation of the imperative, but an honest appraisal of an INGO's capabilities. *Someone* should go, but perhaps it should not be your INGO.

Part II of this book explores the ADP through which an INGO can realise this. In addition to starting with the risk assessment needed to ensure that we engage with the local context (Chapter 6), the book also looks at prevention, due diligence, detection, and response (Chapters 7 to 9). But to dispel the myths, challenge questionable ideas, and foster a pragmatic, more multi-agency operational approach, it is communication, culture, and training (Chapter 10), governance, leadership, and management (Chapter 11), and working in partnership (Chapter 13) that are perhaps most important.

References

Association of Certified Fraud Examiners (ACFE) 2018. *Report to the Nations 2018: Global study on occupational fraud and abuse.* Austin, TX: ACFE.

Burke, J. 2017. Anti-terrorism laws have 'chilling effect' on vital aid deliveries to Somalia. *The Guardian.*

Fredheim, R. and Gallacher, J. 2018. *Robotrolling.* Riga, Latvia: NATO Strategic Communications Centre of Excellence.

May, O. 2016a. Aid diversion to terrorists: 3 things NGOs need to know. Second Marshmallow. https://secondmarshmallow.org/2016/03/24/aid-diversion-to-terrorists-3-things-ngos-need-to-know/.

May, O. 2016b. This is how humanitarian need can enable corruption. The FCPA Blog. https://fcpablog.com/2016/04/28/oliver-may-this-is-how-humanitarian-need-can-enable-corrupti/.

OFSI 2015. For information note: Operating within counter-terrorism legislation. London: HM Treasury.

Tversky, A. and Kahneman, D. 1983. Availability: A heuristic for judging frequency and probability. *Cognitive Psychology* 5(2): 207–232.

3 The rules

International standards and law

Oliver May

This chapter explores the key components of the global CTF system, considering international bodies and the role and artifices of national governments. It examines how legislation and regulation affect diversionaries as proscribed and/or sanctioned entities, and how they affect the organisations and individuals that might deal with them, like INGOs and their staff. We look at the diversity of jurisdictions in which obligations can arise, and the offences themselves. We also consider wider relevant obligations, such as charity regulation, and donor requirements.

The diversity and complexity of national CTF legislation affecting the aid sector is enormous and evolving. It would, then, be both beyond this chapter and futile to attempt a comprehensive guide. Instead, this chapter sets out some of the common features of the regulatory landscape and general trends of which INGOs need to be aware. Similarly, we are concerned with the transfer of INGO assets and benefits into the hands of diversionaries, and so this chapter focusses on counter-terrorist and sanctions law relating to those risks. Clearly, however, a wide range of criminal and civil law might be relevant to the operations of any given INGO. Given this diversity and breadth, it must remain the responsibility of every INGO to obtain advice upon, and understand, the legal environment in any given jurisdiction in which it works.

As a practical guide, this book does not explore the interplay between counter-terror law and IHL, which is designed to protect those who need aid and those who provide it. Much excellent work has already been conducted on the tensions between these two spaces. For helpful introductions to this dimension, see Guinane et al. (2012), Pantuliano et al. (2011), Milatovic et al. (2015), and Lewis (2018).

Key components of the global CTF ecosystem

International bodies

Financial Action Task Force

FATF is an international body with 39 member and observer states and multilateral organisations. It aims to "set standards and promote [the] effective implementation of legal, regulatory and operational measures" for combating threats to the integrity of the international financial system, including terrorist financing (FATF, 2019). It is not a statutory or UN organisation, but functions as an association that "works to generate the necessary political will to bring about national legislative and regulatory reform."

FATF is highly influential and at the heart of the global AML/CTF regime. Member state legislation and regulation reflects FATF's guidance, which is delivered through its *International Standards on Combating Money Laundering and the Financing of Terrorism & Proliferation*. This contains 40 'Recommendations' that function as a global standard for countering terrorist financing, money laundering, and the proliferation of weapons of mass destruction (FATF, 2012–19). In a sense, the term 'recommendations' does insufficient justice to them – in effect, FATF administrates an international standard.

These Recommendations affect INGOs every day as they access the global financial system, but 'Recommendation Eight' especially so. This asks countries to consider laws and regulations relating to NPOs (Non-Profit Organisations) identified as vulnerable to terrorist financing abuse, and apply "focused and proportionate measures, in line with the risk-based approach" (FATF, 2012–19). Together with FATF's other work in this space, and the subsequent work by member states, this has had significant implications for INGOs (see Chapter 12).

United Nations Security Council and the European Union

The UN Security Council prescribes sanctions with which member states are expected to comply, and which are then made into law by each state or the EU. The sanctions are commissioned through Security Council Resolutions, and governed by regime committees arranged geographically or thematically. At the time of writing, the UN consolidated list features more than 1,000 organisations and individuals of which approximately 300 relate to the Islamic State of Iraq and the Levant (ISIL) and Al-Qaeda (UN, 2019). The European Union, meanwhile, both legislates to enact UN sanctions in its member states and creates its own in pursuit of the EU's Common Foreign and Security Policy objectives.

National governments

In addition to legislating for UN sanctions, sovereign governments may have their own autonomous regimes. While US, UK, Australian, and Canadian sanctions may command the most INGO attention, any state might issue sanctions. Further, of course, particular jurisdictions have their own counter-terror legislation also capable of affecting INGOs. A number of devices of state administrate the sanctions and terrorist legislation frameworks with different roles. These include co-ordination bodies, Financial Intelligence Units, and law enforcement and prosecution authorities.

Co-ordination bodies

There will normally be a government department charged with the administration of sanctions, and it is often to this body that applications for permits or licences might be made. In the US, for example, this is OFAC. In the UK, it is the Office of Financial Sanctions Implementation (OFSI). Such bodies might have statutory powers.

Financial Intelligence Units

National Financial Intelligence Units (FIUs) monitor suspicious transactions and support co-ordination. They are usually the place to which a report of a suspicion of terrorist financing should be made (though not necessarily of a sanctions breach). In the UK, for example, this is the UK Financial Intelligence Unit (UKFIU), within the National Crime Agency (NCA). In Australia, it is the Australian Transaction Reports and Analysis Centre (AUSTRAC), and in the USA, the Financial Crimes Enforcement Network (FinCEN).

Law enforcement agencies and prosecution authorities

The bodies that execute criminal investigations into alleged infractions of counter-terror law or sanctions breaches vary between states and are sometimes numerous. In the UK, for example, such offences might be investigated by more than 40 separate policing bodies including the NCA, the Metropolitan Police, local police in England and Wales, the Police Service of Northern Ireland (PSNI), or by Police Scotland.

Proscribed and sanctioned entities

Language differs between jurisdictions but it can be helpful to consider two sets of entities: Proscribed entities, and entities subject to financial sanctions. By proscribed entities we mean those which are banned by law, or which have been identified by a government as a 'terrorist' organisation to facilitate the more streamlined enforcement of criminal anti-terrorist law. An example of the former might be the UK's *List of Proscribed Terrorist Organisations* under the Terrorism Act 2000 (TACT 2000), and of the latter might be what is commonly known in Australia as the 'Attorney-General's List,' under the Criminal Code Act 1995 (CCA 1995). While proscribed organisations are often also the subject of financial sanctions, this is not necessarily so.

Financial sanctions, meanwhile, are restrictions applied by a state or multistate body to achieve foreign policy or security objectives. They target particular entities and prohibit particular financially-related interactions by others with those entities. Sanctions may be created by the UN and implemented by national governments or the EU, by the EU itself, or autonomously by national governments. The purpose of such restrictions might include coercing, constraining, or signalling disapproval of, a target (OFSI, 2018). The complete list of current sanctions for any given state is often known as a 'consolidated list'. Financial sanctions perhaps most relevant to INGOs are 'asset freezes', which prohibit them from dealing with a sanctioned entity's assets or making funds or goods available (directly or indirectly) to them. Restrictions on access to financial services and markets may also be particularly relevant.

Sanctions, then, go beyond CTF. Many organisations and individuals on such lists are not terrorists, even if they may fit the category of 'armed actor.' While the ADP outlined in this book focusses on terrorist organisations, INGOs may find it helpful to consider all sanctions within their own programme's purview to avoid duplication.

People and organisations affected by proscription and sanctions

Counter-terror laws and sanctions affect everybody, but carry different implications for different parties that might interact with proscribed or sanctioned entities. What might be known as 'regulated sectors,' 'designated entities,' or other similar terms might attract the most regulation, but severe penalties for infractions of related laws still apply to other organisations and to individuals.

Regulated sectors and designated entities

Following FATF's lead, national governments often recognise that certain types of organisation are more vulnerable to interaction with money-launderers and terrorists, define these in law, and apply additional legislation and regulation to them. Perhaps the most well-known examples are financial services providers, but 'designated non-financial businesses and professions' might also be captured like lawyers, accountants, and real estate agents.

Legislation and regulation affecting these organisations is usually prescriptive, requiring organisations to abide by a comprehensive set of specific preventative and detective activities. Failure to comply represents an offence for which penalties can be severe and levied upon both individuals (such as Money Laundering Reporting Officers) and the organisations.

Sometimes, INGOs can be captured within a regulated sector. This was the concern generated in the sector by Kenya's Proceeds of Crime and Anti-Money Laundering Act 2009 (POCAMLA 2009), for example. Further, even where a charity might not be captured by virtue of its registered status alone, it is possible that some operations in some contexts – such as micro-finance – could bring it, or part of it, within such a definition. More commonly, however, it is financial services institutions and other privileged 'gatekeepers' that are the target. In the UK and Australia, registered charities are not necessarily captured.

Other bodies, including INGOs and individuals

Where an organisation like an INGO is not captured within a regulated sector, it may have comparatively fewer, less prescriptive obligations – but it retains liability under terrorist financing and sanctions legislation. Further, it is a common and dangerous misconception that terrorist financing or sanctions breaches, committed as part of humanitarian or development aid (and perhaps with the best of intent), are solely a matter of corporate liability for the INGO. Instead, while some offences can be committed by an organisation, some come with a personal liability for the INGO staff or managers involved in the matter – potentially even trustees.

In the UK, for example, while the sanctions breach under the Asset Freezing Act (AFA) 2010 may be committed by a "body corporate", if it is "attributable to any neglect" on the part of a "director, manager, secretary or other similar officer," that individual is also liable to prosecution. The offences to which this applies – including variants on making funds or "economic resources" available to proscribed and sanctioned entities – attract custodial sentences of up to 7 years, or a fine, or both.

Jurisdictions

While there is considerable diversity of CTF laws between jurisdictions, much legislation is extraterritorial. This means that a given state can make and enforce laws relating to conduct beyond its territory (Kamminga, 2012). This CTF has in common with other financial crime like bribery, and it means that an offence does not need to take place within the borders of any given jurisdiction for that jurisdiction's laws to apply. Examples of common triggers for the activation of any given jurisdiction's laws might be:

- Operations of the INGO in the jurisdiction, even if the offence took place in another;
- Registration of the INGO or another contracted party (such as an implementing partner) within the jurisdiction, whether that is charity, corporate, or other registration;
- Registration of the INGO's donor in the jurisdiction;
- Transfer of funds owned by the INGO through the jurisdiction;
- Citizenship of, or residency in the jurisdiction, of a person involved in the matter;
- The INGO's bank or other financial service provider being based in the jurisdiction;
- An entity, such as a supplier or vendor, involved in the project having operations in the jurisdiction;
- Action taken overseas, but which is directed from the jurisdiction.

It should also be noted that not all jurisdictions fully codify their laws, nor that there is always widespread agreement in any given jurisdiction on what the law means and how it is to be applied.

Diversion offences and defences

Although there is considerable overlap, complexity, and interjurisdictional variance, the most relevant diversion offences for INGOs might be best thought of in four groups: Terrorist financing offences, financial sanctions offences, offences of failing to prevent diversion, and offences of failing to report incidents. It should be noted that, in addition to these groups, there can also be offences of travelling to, or being present in, 'declared' or 'designated' areas (see Australia's CCA 1995 and the UK Counter-Terrorism and Border Security Act 2019 (CTBSA 2019), for example). These offences, however, including the Australian and British examples given, may come with humanitarian exemptions.

Terrorist financing offences

As might be expected, the definitions of what cannot be provided, or made available, or allowed to fall into the hands of terrorists vary both between states and sometimes between a state's own counter-terror and sanctions law.

In the UK, for example, financing offences under TACT 2000 rule out "money or other property," while in the USA, federal law proscribes "material support" to designated terrorist organisations. The definition of material support is expansive, being "any property, tangible or intangible, or service, including currency or monetary instruments or financial securities, financial services, lodging, training, expert advice or assistance, safe houses, false documentation or identification, communications equipment, facilities, weapons, lethal substances, explosives, personnel [...], and transportation, except medicine or religious materials" (18 USC 2339A, 1994). Under Australia's CCA 1995, it is "funds," "support," or "resources" that cannot be made available to a terrorist organisation, and neither can the "reckless" provision of training (notably, Australia also prohibits "association" with terrorists, but this is subject to a humanitarian exemption). In Kenya, the Prevention of Terrorism Act 2012 (POTA 2012) forbids the direct or indirect provision of "property, funds or a service."

These insights into the nuance and variety of national laws make it clear that a very broad range of INGO assets and outputs might be captured in the right circumstances. These could include:

- Funds;
- Physical assets and equipment;
- Stock and consumables;
- Programmatic deliverables like food, NFIs or cash;

- Tangible programmatic outputs like buildings or boreholes;
- Less tangible programmatic outputs of value, like training.

Penalties can be severe. The fundraising offences in Sections 15–18 of the UK's TACT 2000 attract custodial sentences of up to 14 years for individuals, or a fine, or both. In Kenya's POTA 2012, the custodial sentence can be up to 20 years.

Breaching financial sanctions

Meanwhile, the variety of financial sanctions means that the list of actions that could constitute a breach is broad. Debarre (2019) describes two examples. In one instance, a humanitarian organisation had to remove nail clippers from hundreds of hygiene kits destined for the Democratic People's Republic of Korea (DPRK), as the importation of metal was subject to sanctions. In another, EU sanctions affected the importation of spare parts necessary for CT scanners in Syria.

UK sentences for breaching EU financial sanctions include a custodial sentence of up to 7 years for individuals in the event of a criminal prosecution, and 50 per cent of the value of the breach (or £1m, whichever is greater) for corporate entities like INGOs. US sanctions legislation is also tough, featuring fines up to $10m (£8m) and a custodial sentence of up to 30 years.

Failing to prevent or detect an incident of terrorist financing

While organisations in regulated sectors may commit offences merely by failing to implement the prescriptions of the relevant laws, INGOs that do not happen to be captured by such legislation must still abide by the 'neglect,' 'negligence,' or 'recklessness' type provisions of criminal law. Provisions like this can be found, for example, in the AFA 2010 in the UK or the CCA 1995 in Australia, and might apply to INGO managers as well as their organisations.

As with all national law these concepts vary, but in essence, these create a liability where an INGO fails to apply reasonable care. This is important, because it means that even where an INGO is an unwilling or unwitting victim of diversionary activity, there may still be some culpability and therefore liability. Intent is not always necessary to complete an offence. It would not be beyond reason to imagine that an INGO which failed, without adequate justification, to apply proper risk assessment and due diligence when operating in a high-risk jurisdiction, for example, could be captured by such legislation.

Failing to report an incident

Some legislation creates a requirement to report a potential incident of diversion to a government. In the UK, for example, TACT 2000 creates an obligation for an individual to make a report to a police officer if they suspect a Section 15–18 offence – and it was this provision that instigated the Metropolitan Police investigation of SCI (Save the Children International) in Somalia (Kerbaj, 2015). The burden of proof threshold for the requirement to report under this Act is low, at suspicion.

Meanwhile, in respect of sanctions, OFSI has issued guidance that requires breaches of financial sanctions to be reported and be 'materially complete.' Whether such a report is made can be an aggravating or mitigating factor in OFSI's determinations in the event of an incident.

The requirement to report, and the consequences of failing to do so, means that an INGO may not have sole discretion. Its bank, suppliers, partners, staff, or other parties may choose to do so unilaterally. Similarly, where INGO managers choose to make a report in one jurisdiction but not another, they should be aware of international co-operation channels that make it possible that the first jurisdiction will alert the other.

Thresholds

As might be expected, different states set varying levels of certainty or foresight that any commodity will be used for terrorist purposes, in order to complete terrorist financing, recklessness, or negligence offences.

These thresholds can be very low. For example, Kenya's POTA 2012 re-quires a person to have 'reasonable grounds to believe' that property, funds, or a service will be for the benefit of a terrorist group. This is a similar level of proof that a police officer might need to seek a search warrant when in-vestigating a crime. But under the UK's TACT 2000, a person need only suspect that "money or other property" will be used for terrorist purposes for them to commit an offence if they provide it. This is a similar threshold to the burden of proof required by a police officer to stop and search an individual for drugs on the street, or to pull over a car on the highway. US counter-terror law also presents a low threshold – a person need only know that they are providing material support to a terrorist organisation. These low thresholds are amongst the factors that has led to unease in the aid sector about 'closed market vendor taxation,' in which an aid worker knows that a vendor is likely to be taxed by a listed entity when they pay them.

Sanctions breaches, meanwhile, are often matters of strict liability. This means that the intent of the INGO or its managers is irrelevant – if a sanction is breached, the offence is complete. Mackintosh and Duplat (2013) found in a review of 14 national state laws that no intent was generally required to be established for the offence to be complete.

While an INGO manager may seek comfort in the idea that a criminal prosecution must prove their breach to a high standard of evidence – some-thing akin to 'beyond reasonable doubt' in Canada, the UK, or Australia, for example – this is not always the case. OFSI in the UK works to a lower, civil standard ('balance of probabilities') in determining whether to apply a penalty.

Defences, exemptions and licencing

It should also be noted that committing an offence, and being prosecuted for the offence, are different things. Law enforcement bodies and prosecuting authorities will often apply a test akin to the concept of 'public interest' in the UK. It may not, for example, be considered a proportionate or sensible use of public resources to prosecute an INGO or individual. All prosecution decisions are taken on a case-by-case basis, but what might not be seen as in the public interest in one case may be in another, or could evolve over time.

Relying on the hope that an INGO's transaction with a diversionary will not be seen as a public interest matter, then, is unsound for both government officials and INGOs. Even so, there are only limited ways in which an INGO could potentially escape from any liability. These might include relying on legal provisions like the common law concepts of 'duress' and 'necessity' or equivalent, making use of a humanitarian exemptions, or obtaining a licence to deal with a sanctioned entity.

Duress and necessity

A helpful definition of the common legal concept of duress might be found in the common law of England and Wales, where 'duress' might be considered a circumstance in which a person is compelled to act in a way that would be an offence because, if they do not, they fear death or serious injury to themselves or another (CPS, 2019). 'Necessity' is a related concept, in which the act might be done to avoid otherwise unpreventable consequences involving "inevitable and irreparable evil" upon oneself or others, that no more is done than is reasonably necessary for this purpose, and that the "evil inflicted by it [is] not disproportionate to the evil avoided" (Stephens, 1887).

A clear example might be that of Tolu in the introduction to this book, who might consider that the repeated demands for hygiene kits, coupled with the mental state of the soldiers and the presence of firearms, constituted such imminent danger. Allowing some hygiene kits to be diverted might, in the circumstances, be considered reasonable by him given the potential alternative of being shot, or of those for whom he was responsible being shot.

While duress and necessity may feel like reassuring possibilities for aid workers in high-risk jurisdictions, this is not necessarily the case. Firstly, not all jurisdictions may have such defences available, and even in those that do, they will not necessarily prevent a prosecution in the first place. Any act must be committed in the hope that, if prosecuted, a court will be minded to see a matter this way. There is no guarantee. Thirdly, not all diversion-related dilemmas are so clear, and take place in such extreme circumstances.

Humanitarian exemptions

The UN operates a humanitarian exemption regime. And while some states have not created humanitarian exemptions to key counter-terror laws, some have. These are not blanket exemptions, however, and identifying and using them can be a fraught legal area. There is no meaningful standardisation (Lewis, 2017). Activities, recipients, and commodities may all variously be exempt. Exemptions may be broad, such as New Zealand's full exemption of humanitarian assistance to designated individuals, or narrow, such as the USA's clear exemption of only "medicines" and "religious materials," leaving the door potentially open to some very stretched interpretations indeed. They may apply globally, or to specific theatres. King et al. (2016) offer a helpful overview.

While some humanitarian exemptions exist to some obligations in some circumstances, it is unlikely that we will see the widespread use of them in relation to counter-terror offences. Although, at the time of writing, such an exemption exists for the 'designated area' offence in CTBSA 2019, the British government has been clear that it considers the risk of abuse of such exemptions too high to warrant wider use and continues to rely on the 'public interest' component of prosecutions to stem disproportionate or unreasonable prosecutions of INGOs (Home Office, 2019).

Licencing

Both the USA (through OFAC) and the UK (through OFSI) boast licencing regimes that can enable humanitarian activity in spite of sanctions. Such regimes may allow INGOs to apply for permission to conduct transactions with a sanctioned entity, such as a foreign telecommunications provider or municipal body, without whom humanitarian aid may be impossible to provide. At the time of writing, for example, OFSI uses the specific examples of purchasing or transporting fuel into Syria in certain circumstances (OFSI, 2018) to explain its humanitarian exemption regime.

Licencing applications typically require specific, evidence-based grounds (including the exact identity of the persons or organisations with whom transactions are intended), the utilisation of specific rules, and urgency. They may come with stipulations – in the UK for example, licencing may involve reporting requirements. Problematically, however, licencing regimes have been seen as slow and unwieldy (e.g. CSN, 2013; CHE, 2013) in responding to urgent and dynamic humanitarian situations. In particular, having to specify ahead of time precisely with whom the transaction will be creates a tension in very dynamic humanitarian situations, where projects change frequently and significantly in response to evolving circumstances.

Charity and non-profit regulations

No two states regulate domestic charities and non-profits in exactly the same way, nor does registration with any given national regulator entitle an INGO to precisely the same privileges the world over. Some states do not register non-profits separately to any private enterprise at all. Others, such as the

United States, create a tax status for such organisations but do not centrally regulate them as a separate category of entity with their own federal or central government regulators, as in the UK, Australia, and Singapore.

Where registration is in place, registered bodies can often expect a unique tax status, access to certain state services, and freedom to operate in line with their objects – likely in exchange for the fulfilment of certain governance obligations on an ongoing basis. Infractions may be investigated by the regulator using statutory powers.

Common obligations and expectations

In more developed charity regulation regimes (England and Wales, and Australia being key examples), requirements are based in law and give rise to core, principles-based standards of governance and behaviour closely linked to the concept of a 'charity' in the jurisdiction. These then often flow into more specific requirements, expectations, and ultimately guidance on how to enact them. As might be expected, these requirements are often important building-blocks in managing diversion risk, and might include:

- Carrying out the purposes for the public benefit, or for the charity's objects;
- Complying with the law;
- Acting in the charity's best interests;
- Managing resources responsibly;
- Ensuring that leaders are suitable and act with reasonable care or skill;
- Engendering accountability.

Sometimes regulators might elevate counter-terrorism commitment to a determinant in whether a charity can exist at all, as in the case of Australia.

Examples of specific obligations and expectations relating to diversion

Despite mounting regulation and guidance over the last 10 years, obligations and expectations that drill down to or isolate diversion – as distinct from other risks or good governance practice – are still relatively discrete. However, in the event of a diversion incident, it is likely that a regulator will examine the relationship of that incident to the high-level obligations of the charity.

Specific obligations might include a requirement to manage diversion risks. In Australia, the External Conduct Standards (ECSs) effectively require many Australian charities and non-profits operating overseas to use risk assessment, for example (May, 2019). And while some jurisdictions depend on the extraterritoriality of counter-terror and sanctions laws to regulate INGOs, Australian legislation now requires that INGOs in some circumstances must now apply Australian fraud, corruption, and diversion law outside Australia.

But perhaps the most common requirement or expectation is to report suspected incidents to the regulator and/or law enforcement. The point at which this should be made varies, and is sometimes unclear, as is what should be reported.

Institutional donors

While donor requirements carry such weight for INGOs that they are often referred to in the same breath as legislative or regulatory obligations, they are not the same. Donor requirements are generally a matter of contract law, even with government donors, bound through the funding agreements or contracts signed by the INGO. Failure to follow the agreed provisions, however, can result in litigation.

Common institutional donor requirements

There has been heavy institutional donor focus on CTF, leading to standards upon which funding is fully contingent and which may not necessarily be clear, feasible, or congruent with other donors' standards (Harvard Law School, 2014). While many in the sector hope for more coordination between institutional donors, and there has been progress here, there could be limits to the achievability of this. In the same way that a range of jurisdictional legislation and regulation applies to any given INGO, so it is for its institutional donors too, and donor risk management activities – including the content of their funding agreements – reflect that.

Adoption of the donor's obligations

A number of institutional donors require their INGO partners to recognise particular definitions of terrorist or terrorism, of diversion to those entities or persons, and to commit that they do not, or will not, allow this to take place. A range of different levels of proactivity might be required, from Australia's 'best endeavours' clause, to an anonymous example of a donor contract that appeared to make diversion a matter of strict liability (NRC, 2015).

Existence of risk management policies, procedures, and systems

INGOs may be expected to demonstrate the existence of better practice tools and activities for the management of risks including diversion, such as 'whistleblowing' systems and anti-fraud and diversion policies. The UK Department for International Development (DFID), United States Agency for International Development (USAID), and the Swedish International Development Cooperation Agency (SIDA) are all examples.

Australia's Department of Foreign Affairs and Trade (DFAT) offers an interesting model. The Australian NGO Cooperation Program (ANCP) uses a prequalification system to create a pool of approximately 60 potential partners. Entry to the pool is dependent on achieving accreditation – an intense assessment of the INGO's capacity and capability to manage DFAT programmes, including its management of key integrity risks like diversion. Partners may then access DFAT funding for specific programmes.

Due diligence

Due diligence for an INGO's own partners, contractors, and other third parties is now frequently embedded in contracts. In some contexts, such due diligence may be very intense and extensive, such as the Canadian International Development Agency (CIDA) approach (Mackintosh and Duplat, 2013), or USAID in Syria (Parker, 2018). The agency that carries out the required due diligence may variously be the INGO itself, or the donor.

Reporting

Institutional donors expect evidence of expenditure, outputs, and outcomes. In addition, there may also be expectations of reporting on risk-management activities, include diversion risk management. Precisely what is to be reported varies (Harvard Law School, 2014), is not always clear, and can even take an 'attestation' form confirming that no issues, incidents, or positive screening matches have arisen – a risky approach for those making the attestation and one which needs to be considered carefully when negotiating contracts.

Multilateral Development Banks

An agreement between the Multilateral Development Banks (MDBs), namely the World Bank, European Bank for Reconstruction and Development, Inter-American Development Bank, Asian Development Bank, and African Development Bank, also applies rules known as 'sanctions.' These, however, are not financial sanctions that carry a legal authority and effectively function as debarment lists or 'blacklists'.

Bounty activism, civil claims, and private prosecutions

In Israel, lawyers and activists have long surveilled the activities of NGOs operating in East Jerusalem, the West Bank, and Gaza with a view to reporting perceived offences to the authorities. In Chapter 1, however, we describe the rise of 'bounty activism,' in which legislation like the US False Claims Act can be used by activists to leverage action against INGOs – and in which the activist can claim a cut of any fine.

Meanwhile, 'private prosecutions' are those brought by an individual or organisation that is not a statutory prosecuting authority. Private prosecutions are common features and occur in many jurisdictions worldwide. Such prosecutions are often brought by the victims of fraud or other offences that were not progressed by the police or statutory prosecutorial authority. In the UK, the Royal Society for the Prevention of Cruelty to Animals (RSPCA) regularly brings private prosecutions against those it believes have committed offences against animals.

Growth in private prosecutions in the UK, potentially as a consequence of an overwhelmed criminal justice system (Baksi, 2019), raises the spectre that the legal activism seen in the USA could cross the Atlantic or be seen elsewhere in the world, or that an aggrieved party may seek remedy against an INGO in this way. A case in which a private foundation, for example, considers itself defrauded by an INGO that allegedly allowed its donor funds to be passed to a terrorist organisation, but which a prosecuting authority declines to progress, could be a speculative example.

References

18 USC 2339A (1994).

Baksi, C. 2019. Private prosecutions: Justice only for the highest bidder. *The Times.*

Charity & Security Network 2013. *A license to aid? How politics delays aid to civilians in conflict zones.* Washington, DC: Charity & Security Network. https://charityandsecurity.org/analysis/license_to_aid/.

Counterterrorism and Humanitarian Engagement Project (CHE) 2013. *OFAC licencing.* Cambridge, MA: Harvard Law School.

Crown Prosecution Service 2019. Duress and necessity. https://www.cps.gov.uk/legal-guidance/defences-duress-and-necessity (accessed 5 August 2019).

Debarre, A. 2019. *Safeguarding humanitarian action in sanctions regimes.* New York, NY: International Peace Institute.

FATF 2012–2019. *International Standards on Combating Money Laundering and the Financing of Terrorism & Proliferation.* Paris: FATF.

FATF 2019. Who we are. https://www.fatf-gafi.org/about/whoweare/ (accessed 3 August 2019).

Guinane, K., Lucas, K., and Holland, E. 2012. *Safeguarding humanitarianism in armed conflict: A call for reconciling international legal obligations and counterterrorism measures in the United States.* Washington, DC: Charity & Security Network.

Harvard Law School 2014. *Counterterrorism and Humanitarian Engagement Project: An analysis of contemporary anti-diversion policies and practices of humanitarian organizations.* Cambridge, MA: Harvard Law School.

Home Office 2019. *For information note: Operating within counter-terrorism legislation.* London: HM Government.

Kamminga, M.T. 2012. Extraterritoriality. In *Max Planck encyclopaedia of public international law.* https://opil.ouplaw.com/view/10.1093/law:epil/9780199231690/law-9780199231690-e1040 (accessed 15 April 2020).

Kerbaj, R. 2015. Met investigated Save the Children after raid. *The Times.*

King, K., Modirzadeh, N., and Lewis, D. 2016. *Understanding humanitarian exemptions: UN Security Council sanctions and principled humanitarian action.* Harvard Law School Program on International Law and Armed Conflict Counterterrorism and Humanitarian Engagement Project. Cambridge, MA: Harvard Law School.

Lewis, D. 2018. Criminalization of humanitarian action under counterterrorism frameworks: Key elements and concerns. *Proceedings of the ASIL Annual Meeting 112*: 268–270.

Lewis, D. 2017. Humanitarian exemptions from counter-terrorism measures: A brief introduction. *Proceedings of the Bruges Colloquium 47*: 141–150.

Mackintosh, K. and Duplat, P. 2013. *Study of the impact of donor counter-terrorism measures on principled humanitarian action*. United Nations Office for the Coordination of Humanitarian Affairs/Norwegian Refugee Council.

May, O. 2019. Risky business: Operating overseas under the new external conduct standards. Pro Bono Australia. https://probonoaustralia.com.au/news/2019/04/risky-business-operating-overseas-under-the-new-external-conduct-standards/.

Milatovic, S., Macdonald, I., and McGrane, K. 2015. *Risk management toolkit in relation to counter-terrorism measures*. Geneva: Norwegian Refugee Council.

Norwegian Refugee Council 2015. *Risk management toolkit in relation to counterterrorism measures*. Geneva: Norwegian Refugee Council.

OFSI 2018. *Financial sanctions guidance*. London: HM Treasury.

OFSI 2018. *Frequently asked questions: Factsheet for charities and other non-government organisations (NGOs)*. London: HM Treasury.

Pantuliano, S., Mackintosh, K., Elhawary, S., and Metcalfe, V. 2011. *Counter terrorism and humanitarian action*. London: Overseas Development Institute.

Parker, B. 2018. US tightens counter-terror clampdown on Syria aid. *The New Humanitarian*. https://www.thenewhumanitarian.org/news/2018/09/21/us-tightens-counter-terror-clampdown-syria-aid.

Stephens, J. 1887. *A digest of the criminal law (crimes and punishments)*. London: McMillan.

United Nations 2019. *Fact sheet: Subsidiary organs of the United Nations Security Council*. New York, NY: United Nations.

4 The risks

How diversion occurs and what it looks like

Oliver May

So far, we have considered some of the factors driving the complexity and challenge for INGOs, and outlined the landscape upon which they operate. But what actually are the risks, and what do they look like?

This chapter sets out a typology of the diversion risks that could arise in the context of the three 'likelihood factors' in Chapter 1. The typology may be especially helpful for risk assessment (Chapter 6), enabling readers to visualise the risks in their INGO's own context. As those contexts vary enormously, it is intended not as an exhaustive categorisation, but more a set of examples to guide risk identification. For some, examples of risk and vulnerability indicators are also provided. Sixteen model risks sit across four categories:

- Direct transfer;
- Misappropriation;
- Fees and taxation;
- Value chain diversion.

Direct transfer

In direct transfer, an INGO voluntarily transfers resources or material benefits to a diversionary, irrespective of whether the INGO knows that the recipient is one. These risks cover staff remuneration, transactions with third parties, and gifts and other transfers.

It is important to count two risks each for staff remuneration and transactions with third parties: The risk of transfers to *listed entities* and to *non-listed entities*. Key controls for each will differ, as non-listed entities will not be detected by traditional list checks but can still be affiliated to, or controlled by, listed entities.

Staff remuneration

Staff enjoy substantial access to INGO funds and resources. In this risk, members or associates of a diversionary may be directly employed by the

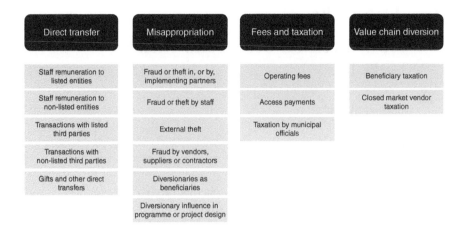

Figure 4.1 Model diversion categories and risks.

INGO on a formal or casual basis and then channel legitimately-received assets or funds to the diversionary. An example might be salary.

It can certainly be in the interests of diversionaries for 'their people' to work with INGOs, and they can take steps to arrange this. Jackson and Giustozzi (2012) reported that in Kandahar, Afghanistan, the Taliban expected NGOs to employ persons who the Taliban 'trusted'. Al-Shabaab required the same in Somalia (Jackson and Aynte, 2013).

Interestingly, Jackson and Giustozzi also reported that many aid agencies were unwilling to discuss this with their researchers. Those that did suggested that this was "in line with existing approaches that focus on recruiting local community members," though while there are benefits to working with and through local communities, employing an individual suspected to be a member of a listed entity can have severe consequences.

Meanwhile, the presence of members or associates of diversionaries in an NGO might occur even without the knowledge of the diversionary's leaders. In a case of which I am aware in Asia, an allegedly-retired member of a listed entity had found work with an INGO.

Risk indicators for staff remuneration might include:

- Environments in which adequate background checks on applicants cannot be reasonably conducted;
- Places in which diversionaries have a history of requiring the employment of nominated individuals on projects;
- Places in which specialist local knowledge is required to operate, and in which the INGO has a deficit and may need to obtain local assistance;
- Places in which diversionaries also operate as political entities and in which membership or association is common.

Transactions with third parties

Examples of an INGO's third parties might include suppliers, vendors, consultants, contractors, and implementing partners. A direct transfer risk materialises when one is associated with, beneficially owned, controlled by, or contains persons working with diversionaries. In effect, entering into a transaction with such an entity may immediately place funds or resources in the hands of a diversionary. It was this area of concern that was at the heart of allegations in 2012 by Shurat HaDin. Here, Shurat HaDin alleged that an Australian Aid funded Palestinian civil society organisation, the Union of Agricultural Work Committees, employed members of the Popular Front for the Liberation of Palestine (Murphy, 2012). An Australian statement responded robustly to those allegations.

Direct transfer is also, to an extent, about value rather than physical assets. Training might also be captured, for example. And so for many INGOs, the key control for this risk is due diligence. Indeed, in a number of suspected incidents involving such third parties of which I am aware – including telecommunications providers, money transfer organisations, and government officials – due diligence could have potentially helped to prevent the alleged incident.

But this is not always the case, of course. Direct transfer risks arise not only from contracting, but also from the use of cash – like petty cash and floats – for which due diligence is often impractical. And in some country contexts and crises it can be very challenging indeed – Peter Clarke (formerly of both the CCEW (Charity Commission for England and Wales) and the UK's counter-terror police) has described it as a "fog of war issue" (Hope, 2013). Not only can background checks be difficult to execute, but the presence of 'false positives' can drown useful data in white noise.

Further, dialogue, contact, or even – to an extent – sympathies with a diversionary does not immediately signify that the third party is owned, controlled by, or contains such persons; daily contact with such entities may be necessary or inevitable in some contexts, and during due diligence it can be challenging to dissect this nuance.

Risk indicators here might include operating spaces in which diversionaries:

- Have a great deal of influence, control, or popular support;
- Are large and sophisticated entities with a portfolio of fundraising interests;
- Are part of, or linked to, wider movements, political parties, or other entities that are not listed, and which may work closely with aid agencies or receive funding from them.

Gifts and other direct transfers

In the course of achieving and maintaining a working relationship with a diversionary, other opportunities or requests for the transfer of funds, resources, or other benefits may arise. Jackson and Giustozzi (2012) explain that NGOs might have been expected to buy vehicles for the Taliban as part of the conditions under which they operated. And further, that a Taliban commander told them that an NGO had provided some kind of gift upon commencement of a new project.

Jackson and Giustozzi's paper shows the diversity of responses amongst NGOs operating in the same spaces. At one end of the spectrum, one agency told them that it did not pay "bribes" but made "donations to local mosques," and "some staff made individual donations and provided support to madrasa students." At the other, a different agency said that it refused to provide anything that could be viewed as a bribe and threatened to withdraw if placed under pressure, because "if you start paying, it will get worse and worse."

Risk indicators that such transactions may take place might include operating contexts:

- Where diversionaries have been known to make such demands, or where other agencies have been known to comply;
- Involving relational cultures in which gifts are expected as part of interaction;
- In which relatively unsophisticated diversionaries may operate, and therefore the extent of 'command-and-control' over them cannot be assumed.

Misappropriation

Misappropriation risks arise when the traditional methods of dishonesty are used to benefit diversionaries – including fraud, theft, deception, and manipulation.

Fraud or theft in, or by, implementing partners

Good partnership working is important because it provides access to local expertise and networks, helps to build the civil society sectors of host countries, and addresses the global structural power imbalance. In some places, it might also be the only way that an INGO can achieve programme outcomes. These aims are laudable, and the fear of diversion amongst institutional donors and INGOs can have catastrophic effects on partnerships. This, and what can be done about it, will be explored further in Chapter 13, but here we set out some of the experiences from which that fear arises.

Fraud in (or by) implementing partners is distinguished from other third parties as a consequence of their privileged position, access, distinctive status in the sector, and common mechanisms of engagement. In a sense, this mechanism of diversion is the same as any other fraud by an implementing partner – the difference being that the ultimate beneficiary of the assets, funds, or stock is a listed entity.

Perhaps the fraud type most in the public consciousness here is the notion that a diversionary could establish a fake local NGO for the purpose of extracting funds from INGOs. Certainly, in relation to Syria, Peter Clarke told journalists that it was "perfectly feasible for charities to be established as a sort of cover" (Hope, 2013).

But maybe the more common type occurs where multiple motivations for the existence of an organisation exist, one of which may be diversion, or in which originally noble motivations are eclipsed, or the local partner is abused. A leaked UN report, dated May 2014, described that more than $600,000 (£456,000) was "either fraudulently claimed or unsubstantiated" by a Somalian partner of the United Nations Office for the Coordination of Humanitarian Affairs (OCHA). The report described evidence of "a system of fabricating documentation" to "misappropriate and conceal [...] diversion." While OCHA told CNN that it had "no indication" that any funds had been diverted to terrorists, Fox News claimed to have seen a 2012 e-mail from a UN contractor asking for funds and mentioning that a colleague was being "pressed" by Al-Shabaab to make payments "as quickly as possible" (Russell, 2015).

As with staff, a 'noble intent' may exist amongst some implementing partners. Leveraged by the need to deliver to demanding contracts, and perhaps interpreting a wilful blindness on the parts of the INGO who want their hands to be clean, they may make and conceal payments that are considered inevitable.

Examples of fraud carried out by implementing partners, in which diversionaries are the ultimate beneficiaries, might include:

- Paying fees and taxes to diversionaries, which are accounted for as 'logistics,' 'security,' or other deceptive line items. This may be with or without the knowledge of the INGO itself;
- Theft by a partner's own staff or leadership, in order to pass funds to a diversionary's cause with whom they sympathise;
- Collusion between partners to conceal diversion; for example, between those engaged separately for beneficiary selection, delivery, monitoring. and audit.

This final form can be particularly challenging. In a matter of which I am aware, a local consultancy acting as a third party monitor for an aid agency made allegations that beneficiary taxing had taken place. After the agency requested further details, the firm initially dragged its feet in responding to the queries and then ultimately ceased communication altogether. When dealing with armed diversionaries, co-operating with international aid agencies can come at some risk.

Fraud or theft by staff

Here, staff deceptively channel funds or resources to diversionaries. This form of occupational fraud or abuse may be executed by an insider themselves, in concert with other insiders, or in collusion with third parties such as implementing partners or contractors.

While many of the risks in this chapter relate to delivery at country-level, this risk extends all way back through an INGO's value chain through regional offices, headquarters, and countries of registration. Areas traditionally perceived as vulnerable include procurement, expenses, payroll, and delivery – but any area in which a transaction can take place is potentially at risk. Perhaps the most commonly considered risk early in the value chain is the diversion of fundraising, in which fundraisers at legitimate charities might skim money raised from supporters.

There are at least three 'human factor' drivers of the risk of fraud by staff or volunteers, each requiring different approaches to control it. The first two are perhaps the most obvious: That persons already affiliated with a diversionary may infiltrate an INGO for this purpose, or that existing staff or volunteers may become ideologically aligned with, or sympathetic to, a diversionary.

But the third requires consideration. In this scenario, staff without any ideological support for a diversionary may deceptively provide resources to them, motivated by the imperative to rapidly access beneficiaries but mindful of proscriptions against such actions. At a basic level, this may involve hiding payments in the records with vague or false descriptions. At a more sophisticated level, it could involve complex fraudulent methodologies.

A potential example from Asia of which I am aware occurred during a rapid-onset humanitarian emergency. A logistician allegedly used deception to swing a tender process to a particular supplier not for personal gain, but to expedite the process in the face of urgent humanitarian need. A critical problem, of course, is that if proper selection and diligence controls are not applied, the supplier could turn out to be in the control of a diversionary.

External theft

In Somalia in 2012, Al-Shabaab raided the premises of SCI, taking equipment and supplies to a value of approximately £200,000 (Kerbaj, 2015). Theft by external actors may occur at any stage in a supply chain, and perhaps this overt, armed robbery is the simplest and most visible form of diversion.

Somalia provides a litany of such complaints about Al-Shabaab. MSF supplies were interdicted three times between 2009 and 2013 (Belliveau, 2015), while British aid worth £480,000 was stolen in thefts from warehouses between 2011 and 2012 (Burke, 2017). Medicines were also stolen from World Health Organisation (WHO) offices in 2011 (Ni Chonghaile, 2011) amid angry statements from Al-Shabaab about foreign aid and interference.

Those statements are important. Motivations for such attacks are not necessarily solely pecuniary; sophisticated diversionaries can have a range of objectives including punishment for perceived non-compliance, retribution for perceived challenge (Murdie and Stapley, 2014), or to send messages to individuals and groups wider than the NGO itself.

Indicators of rising risk might include:

- The presence of armed diversionaries in the vicinity and wider security indicators, such as the reduced presence of legitimate security or policing forces, remoteness of a location, and intensity of local conflict;
- Tone and trajectory of political relationships between the INGO and local diversionaries, their representatives or associates, and the populations from which they draw their support;
- Declining interest amongst beneficiary or other local populations in engagement with the NGO;
- Likely conditions that will be demanded of the NGO to permit their working, but which will be outside their risk appetite.

Fraud by vendors, suppliers, or contractors

Aid programming is often carried out in collaboration with private contractors. This is particularly the case in remote programme management; in Syria, for example, for one agency almost all water and sanitation health work was being carried out this way (Harvard Law School, 2014). And as with any other sector, INGOs must also procure a range of services in order to function – utilities, media, telecommunications, premises, fuel and consumables, information technology, and so on. In this risk, providers defraud the INGO and pass the resources or benefits to diversionaries.

Perhaps one of the most well-known examples of this type was the allegation that the Tigray People's Liberation Front (TPLF) diverted aid intended for victims of the Ethiopian famine in the mid-1980s. A member of the TPLF claimed to have posed as a merchant selling sacks of grain, but these really contained sand, and through tricks like this they were able to obtain \$100m (£76m) from aid groups (Plaut, 2010). It is hard to imagine that modern, professional INGOs could be fooled by such a trick – but even the most cunning frauds involve a sleight of hand like this somewhere along the line.

Risk indicators here might include:

- Reduced ability in an operating context to verify service outputs or validate the delivery of goods;
- Reduced ability to carry out due diligence processes on a prospective supplier, or non-compliance by a prospective supplier with such a process;
- Operating contexts or sectors with a history of fraud against aid agencies.

Diversionaries as beneficiaries

As in any value chain, the recipients of the value present risks to the provider. In this set of risks, diversionaries gain access to project outcomes as beneficiaries, whether this is through deception (such as fraud), a breakdown in due diligence, the influence of diversionaries in beneficiary targeting, or some other method.

Speculative examples might include where a diversionary is able to use a newly-constructed school as a headquarters, or diversionaries are amongst those trained in a technical or semi-technical skill, like media relations, during advocacy programming. The range of 'material benefit' potentially in-scope can be broad.

Perhaps that breadth was behind the events reported by Pantuliano et al. (2011) in Gaza, following the electoral victories of Hamas, when some aid agencies felt compelled to cease training programmes for public officials.

Clearly, irrespective of their legal obligations, INGOs seek to alleviate the suffering of their beneficiaries with independence and impartiality. This can be a particularly challenging set of risks, as the complex relationships of vulnerable and excluded populations with diversionaries can mean that those with enormous humanitarian need might appear associated with diversionary groups. Clarity and care are needed in determining the specific risks in each project, and expertise in understanding the legal dimensions.

Risk indicators that diversionaries could pose as, or become, beneficiaries might include:

- Carrying out distributions (such as food, NFIs or CTP) in areas controlled by diversionaries;
- Inability to collect sufficient data to determine beneficiary identities and detect diversionary presence in the target group;
- Instances where an INGO allows delivery to be influenced, directed, or carried out by diversionaries.

Diversionary influence in project or programme design

Incorporating local perspectives, knowledge, and experience into the programme and project design phases is critical to successful interventions. Further, when the diversionaries are armed actors controlling the space in which an NGO seeks to assist beneficiaries, some form of engagement is a matter of safety and security.

Dialogue with armed actors, even those who are listed, is not necessarily illegal. Historically, however, this has been a subject of confusion and mixed messaging. Different donors, national governments, and other bodies have taken various stances on the permissibility of contact (Pantuliano et al., 2011; Egeland et al., 2011).

The involvement of diversionaries in establishing, executing, and assessing projects becomes a diversion issue when their influence enables them to obtain access to resources or benefits, perhaps through determining aid modalities, target beneficiary populations, or locations. In Somalia, Longley et al. (2012) reported that both the transitional national government and Al-Shabaab attempted to influence the beneficiary targeting and registration process. Al-Shabaab also sometimes refused to allow aid operations unless its own partners were used in the implementation.

Further, conditions imposed by Al-Shabaab could include them executing the distributions themselves (Jackson and Aynte, 2013). But where aid agencies entered into this arrangement, an individual from Baidoa told them that Al-Shabaab "kept half or maybe two-thirds to give to their fighters." They also describe another interviewee reporting that Al-Shabaab distributed food intended for one area in another, and quote an aid worker stating, "you see someone with extra food or some other items and you ask how he got it, and the answer is 'he is enlisted with Al-Shabaab' ".

These Somalian examples may seem straightforward, but there is plenty of complexity here. In local consultations, for example, while it may be clear to whom the INGO is speaking, it may not be clear whose interests are being relayed to it. Not all local power actors are directly affiliated to diversionaries, of course, and INGOs may work with clan chiefs, village elders, landlords, municipal leaders, and others to identify beneficiaries and appropriate interventions. But diversionary networks and influences can be nebulous; Al-Shabaab for example did not have formal member lists, could often appear like a collective with constantly changing boundaries, and its influence could filter through a range of local actors. Further, as well as the challenge of access described in Chapter 1, there is always a little grey in any planning cycle over the extent to which an INGO is being guided by local interests, the true sources of those interests, and the extent to which it is carrying out an independent assessment.

Risk indicators that diversionaries may attempt to influence programme design may include operating contexts in which:

- Diversionaries have a nuanced relationship with aid agencies, and are known to have a corresponding agenda;
- Open dialogue is held between aid agencies and diversionaries, and through which access is negotiated;
- Limited dialogue takes place between aid agencies to compare and moderate diversionary demands.

Fees and taxation

Operating fees, access payments, and taxation by municipal officials are perhaps the most common risk types of all. The distinction between operating fees and access payments is one of formality – operating fees might be those required at relatively high levels, or with an elevated degree of sophistication, for an INGO to operate in a particular place. Access payments are more informal, comprising chiefly of roadside tolls. Taxation by municipal officials occurs where the municipality enjoys permanence or legitimacy, but in which diversionaries are involved.

Operating fees

Operating fees are payable to diversionaries in order for INGOs to obtain 'authorisation' to operate in areas controlled, to a greater or lesser extent, by the diversionary. These may be demanded as part of a regular series of payments, or sporadically and without warning. There is a similarity here to extortion; failure to pay can open INGOs to violent attack if their operations continue. Fees may be demanded through a representative or co-ordinator. They do not have to be in cash, and could be with the tacit acceptance of donors. Menkhaus (2010) reported that "aid workers [...] noted that relief agencies in Somalia have long worked out arrangements in rebel-held areas and donors have quietly supported the deals they have struck for access, knowing a percentage of aid was being diverted."

Fees may be part of a broader raft of conditions applied to NGOs operating in areas controlled by diversionaries (as many as 11 demands were reported in the Bay and Bakool regions of Somalia by Belliveau, 2015). This was described by Jackson and Giustozzi (2012) in their case studies in Faryub, northwest Afghanistan, though they also described some flexibility for "trusted" (usually Afghan) NGOs to operate under relaxed conditions. They also described a sliding scale of taxation; projects considered by the Taliban to be a matter of "public welfare" were exempt, other NGO projects were taxed at 10 per cent, and projects by private contractors at 20 per cent. A range of aspects of an NGO's operations might attract taxation, whether structured or ad-hoc. In Somalia, for example, Al-Shabaab levied registration fees, tax on employee salaries, and tax on goods and materials to be used in projects (Jackson and Aynte, 2013). One UN-associated agency allegedly allocated 10 per cent of its project budget to Al-Shabaab in 2009 (Vilkko, 2011).

The same application of restrictions and taxes have been seen in the Syrian conflict, according to Dettmer (2014), who was told by an anonymous aid coordinator that convoys had to be approved by the Islamic State of Iraq and Syria (ISIS) and payments were necessary – disguised as transportation costs and paid directly, or through locally contracted transportation companies.

Access payments

Access payments are the more informal cousin of operating fees, payable on a per-transaction or per-visit basis, often through road checkpoints or other means. This form of diversion may be the most common of all.

In Iraq, for example, IRIN found that Islamic State combatants took an opportunistic approach: "If someone has a truck of aid on the street, they will ask for money from them to allow them to pass" (Svoboda, 2014). Access payments may not of course involve cash transactions – where food or NFIs are being distributed, diversionaries may skim a proportion of the goods.

Access payments can be lucrative. The UN estimated that in 2010, Al-Shabaab could have been making more than £140,000 a year from roadside tolls (Burke, 2017). For INGOs, however, it can be hard to detect. Local staff, forced to bridge the gap between the expectations of powerful armed actors, the refusal of INGOs to pay, and the intense pressure to deliver to donor-mandated timelines, might pay out of their own pocket.

Taxation by municipal officials

While a government or municipal authority may not be listed in itself, there may be entities with access to its resources and capabilities that are. Political actors or parties holding office may be, or there may be departments, agencies, or other entities that are.

Unpicking the webs of control and influence in public authorities can be very difficult. Gaza is an example of such a scenario in which NGOs agonised over the question of whether paying a registration fee to the Hamas government was unlawful.

Burniske et al. (2014) offer a sobering insight into the difficulties of operating in a context like this, where the designation of Hamas has meant that aid organisations operating in Gaza have to bypass central and local government officials. Some agencies, they report, have been unable to work in municipalities with a Hamas-affiliated mayor, or have to withdraw following the success of Hamas candidates in mayoral elections.

Value chain diversion

While many of the risks described so far have relatively clear opportunities for control, there are risks that may be harder to address. These reflect the wider value chains of INGOs and the ripples they create: Beneficiary taxation and closed market vendor taxation.

Beneficiary taxation

Even if an INGO successfully completes a distribution, diversion can still occur. Beneficiary taxing takes place when a local power takes a 'cut' of the commodity delivered to beneficiaries. This is common, and was widely reported in Somalia (Longley et al., 2012), including in displaced person camps (Dunn et al., 2013). Whether a beneficiary considers the tax voluntary or legitimate is often irrelevant; the reality is that for many beneficiaries consequences exist for failing to cooperate, and local powers are not the intended recipient of the commodity.

Historically, not all aid workers have recognised beneficiary taxing as a form of diversion. In the view of some senior aid officials, such incidents are not a matter for agencies' concern – the payments have already been made and therefore the money is the responsibility of the beneficiaries.

This view is problematic. At a basic level, this hand-washing would not give much comfort to the public, were they to see armed diversionaries literally waiting for the INGO staff to leave before they collected their cut. And critically, a transactional perspective like this fails to recognise the wider implications of distributions being used to maintain potentially exploitative power relationships. And, depending on the foreseeability of the taxing, of course, such a view may not offer a legal defence.

An example of a risk indicator for beneficiary taxing might be where beneficiaries are subject to localised power structures like gatekeepers or block leaders in formal or informal displaced person camps, or landlords. This may especially be the case where there is a history of those actors requiring formal, informal, regular or irregular payments from beneficiaries.

Closed market vendor taxation

As with beneficiary taxing, where funds expended by an INGO and then later paid to diversionaries by (for example) vendors might not be seen a diversionary problem, the difficulty arises when it may be reasonably suspected, even reasonably believed, that these resources will be passed to diversionaries. We might define this risk as the provision of assets, funds, stock, or other items of value to a party which, although no suspicion exists that they are a proscribed or sanctioned entity, a suspicion does exist that the value or part of the value will be passed on to such an entity.

Belliveau (2015) effectively describes the accrual of resources by Al-Shabaab as impossible to avoid in areas under its control between 2009 and 2013. Al-Shabaab taxed not only local NGO staff but the local businesses from whom they procured services. Trying to prevent any funds from ending up in Al-Shabaab hands, then, was arguably futile; even procuring overseas and shipping goods in would not have helped, according to Belliveau, as Al-Shabaab also taxed port and land transport movements.

This picture reflects one painted by Kiley (2018), following a visit to the Baidoa camp for internally displaced persons and conversations with aid workers and former Al-Shabaab combatants. Kiley's report inferred that cash transferred to beneficiaries by the UN was being used by the beneficiaries to buy goods from local merchants, but that these merchants would in turn pay their dues to Al-Shabaab. For every sack of rice, a former combatant told Kiley, Al-Shabaab would require about $3 (about £2.30) on top of an annual tax paid to the group.

In addition, Kiley also described the requirement for local merchants to pay tolls at roadblocks to and from the camp, and reported interviews with former members of Al-Shabaab who described that tolls applied at roadblocks were "one of the biggest sources of money" for Al-Shabaab. Kiley also referenced a UN estimate that a single toll-extorting roadblock on the way to the Baidoa camp could extract as much as $5,000 (£3,800) a day.

This is a concern for many sector workers: That the way that certain counter-terror legislation is articulated means that if they make payments to suppliers and vendors – and reasonably consider that those suppliers and vendors will make payments to diversionaries – then this may make the workers themselves liable.

Imagine you are an aid worker in Gaza City, supporting people in what has been described as the "largest open-air prison in the world" (Høvring, 2018). As aid workers do their work, they must eat, wash, and sleep. This requires transactions with local vendors. While they may have no reason to suspect that any of these vendors are beneficially owned or operated by diversionaries, those business must pay taxes. And the governing authority in Gaza is, at the time of writing, Hamas. The dilemma many find themselves struggling with is whether they have reasonable grounds to suspect that their vendors will pass on a portion of their payment to the municipal government, placing it under the control of members of Hamas. The same is even true of items available on the black market in Gaza, smuggled from Egypt – Hamas licences and taxes smugglers (Burniske et al., 2014).

And yet, governments and institutional donors have exhibited dogmatic responses to this risk when humanitarians have raised concerns about it, emphasising that knowing, direct transfer is the object of legislation and that closed market vendor taxation is unlikely to result in humanitarian prosecution.

The risk indicators here might be very simple, being where:

- A diversionary enjoys de-facto control over the space in which an INGO's third parties are operating;
- The diversionary extracts rates and taxes from the INGO's third parties;
- The extraction is known and regular.

References

Belliveau, J. 2015. *Red lines and Al-Shabaab: Negotiating humanitarian access in Somalia.* Oslo: Norwegian Peacebuilding Resource Centre.

Burke, J. 2017. Anti-terrorism laws have 'chilling effect' on vital aid deliveries to Somalia. *The Guardian.*

Burniske, J., Modirzadeh, N., and Lewis, D. 2014. *Counter terrorism laws and regulations: What aid agencies need to know.* London: Overseas Development Institute.

Dettmer, J. 2014. U.S. humanitarian aid going to ISIS. *The Daily Beast.*

Dunn, S., Brewin, M., and Scek, A. 2013. *Cash and voucher monitoring group: Final monitoring report of the Somalia cash and voucher transfer programme Phase 2.* London: Overseas Development Institute.

Egeland, J., Harmer, A., and Stoddard, A. 2011. *To stay and deliver: Good practice for humanitarians in complex security environments.* New York, NY: United Nations Office for the Coordination of Humanitarian Affairs.

Harvard Law School 2014. *Counterterrorism and Humanitarian Engagement Project: An analysis of contemporary anti-diversion policies and practices of humanitarian organizations.* Cambridge, MA: Harvard Law School.

Hope, C. 2013. Charity cash 'going to Syrian terror groups'. *The Telegraph.*

Høvring, R. 2018. *Gaza: The world's largest open air prison.* Oslo: Norwegian Refugee Council.

Jackson, A. and Aynte, A. 2013. *Talking to the other side: Humanitarian negotiations with Al-Shabaab in Somalia.* London: Overseas Development Institute.

Jackson, A. and Giustozzi, A. 2012. *Talking to the other side: Humanitarian engagement with the Taliban in Afghanistan.* London: Overseas Development Institute.

Kerbaj, R. 2015. Met investigated Save the Children after raid. *The Times.*

Kiley, S. 2018. Funding Al-Shabaab: How aid money ends up in terror group's hands. *CNN*.

Longley, C., Dunn, S., and Brewin, M. 2012. *Monitoring results of the Somalia cash and voucher transfer programme: Phase I*. Humanitarian Exchange 55, September 2012. London: Overseas Development Institute.

Menkhaus, K. 2010. Stabilisation and humanitarian access in a collapsed state: The Somali case. *Disasters 34* Suppl. 3: S320–341. doi: 10.1111/j.1467–7717.2010.01204.x.

Murdie, A. and Stapley, C. 2014. Why target the "good guys"? The determinants of terrorism against NGOs. *International Interactions 40(1)*: 79–102.

Murphy, N. 2012. *Palestinian Territories – UAWC*. Canberra: Australian Agency for International Development.

Ni Chonghaile, C. 2011. Al-Shabaab bans aid agencies in Somalia and raids offices. *The Guardian*.

Pantuliano, S., Mackintosh, K., Elhawary, S., and Metcalfe, V. 2011. *Counter-terrorism and humanitarian action: Tensions, impact and ways forward*. HPG Policy Brief 43. London: Overseas Development Institute.

Plaut, M. 2010. Ethiopia famine aid spent on weapons. *BBC*.

Russell, G. 2015. Millions in UN Somalia aid diverted; hints that some went to terrorists. *Fox News*.

Svoboda, E. 2014. *Aid and the Islamic State*. London and Geneva: Overseas Development Institute/IRIN.

Vilkko, V. 2011. *Al-Shabaab: From external support to internal extraction*. Uppsala: Uppsala Universitet.

Part II

5   Principles and approaches
Introducing an Anti-Diversion Programme (ADP)

Oliver May

The first part of this book considered the nature of the problem, tackled some myths and misunderstandings, explored the legal landscape, and unpacked the diversion risks themselves. This second part turns to potential ways forward, and describes a framework through which an INGO can manage the risk of diversion. After exploring the advantages that a risk-based approach to diversion has over a compliance-based approach, this chapter sets out the framework which will also be the subject of the rest of this book – the ADP. It also includes a case for investment in an ADP, given the frequent complaint of the rising cost of delivery amongst INGOs.

Risk-based versus compliance-based approaches

'Risk' and 'compliance' appear in both risk-based and compliance-based approaches. Adopting one does not mean abandoning the other. But each represents a different profile of priorities, focus, and application. This section describes first the issues with what might be termed a 'compliance-based approach,' and then outlines the strengths of the risk-based approach that is the foundation of this book.

A compliance-based approach to diversion

In a compliance-based approach, diversion is seen primarily as a matter of complying with donor, legislative, and regulatory obligations. Anti-diversion activities are often seen as expensive compliance costs observed in order to unlock funding and the ability to operate.

Characteristics of a compliance-based approach

A range of indicators may suggest the presence of such an approach. The first cluster around the dialogue between an INGO partner and its donors; the INGO demands clarity from donors on precisely what its obligations are, perhaps with a supplicant tone akin to 'just tell us and we'll do it'– but suffers from fatigue as intensive requirements build up across multiple donors.

Table 5.1 Advantages and disadvantages of risk–based and compliance–based approaches

	Advantages	*Disadvantages*
Risk-based approach	• Respects the disposition of each INGO, country context, aid modality, and project • Embeds proportionality • Results in controls that may often harmonise with legal and donor requirements • Offers some protection against legal opacity and alternative agendas • Supports advocacy and public engagement • Encourages a focus on humanitarian opportunity	• Risk-management capacity and capability in the sector is still developing • Low visibility of diversion risks for many INGOs • Requires investment
Compliance-based approach	• Compliance is a mature business discipline • Subcontracting is a tried, tested, and lower-cost way to help manage risk in third party relationships • Perhaps the main contemporary mode of participation in the global aid system	• Donor requirements protect the donor, not necessarily the partner • Can misdirect risk assessment • In diversion incidents, can underemphasise the consequences that should be an INGO's priority • Misdirects responsibility for managing diversion away from the INGO • May contribute to a 'chilling effect'

Some of those donors issue ever-more onerous and directive requirements and guidance, particularly around screening.

Internally, armies of donor accountants, donor reporting officers, and donor relationship managers command the attention of programme staff. The issue of diversion is jealously guarded by the legal department, and the surest way to generate action from both business support and programme functions is to leverage the law. When that activity does take place, it represents the minimum effort, at the last possible moment, to comply.

Dry, legalistic training for staff focuses on quoting laws, donor rules, and definitions. Participants leave sessions uneasy, none the wiser, and on course to have forgotten most of it by the following week. Should an incident actually occur, there is hand-wringing up and down the management chain at the prospect of notifying the donor, and when that does happen it can result in suspensions, emergency remedial controls, and lengthy investigations. After all, it is potentially a breach of both the law and the donor's requirements – a liability the INGO is carrying alone.

Disadvantages of a compliance-based approach

It should be clear from this picture that while a compliance-based approach is a matter of choice for an INGO, it is also encouraged by the global development system at large. Institutional donors, for example, do need to manage the risks associated with their own funds, and are accountable to other government actors. As both 'compliance' is a well-established and broadly positive business discipline, and contracting a key lever and safety net in business relations, passing on billowing contractual requirements to implementing partners is an attractive way for donors to protect themselves. But in this sector, even the word 'compliance' seems inadequate, suggesting that we steward resources properly only because a donor or law requires it.

The approach is not entirely negative, nor should INGOs decline to comply with donors or the law, but it presents some significant disadvantages. Firstly, institutional donor requirements are often designed to protect the donor, not its partner. The controls prescribed do not necessarily derive from the risks borne by the INGO, but the donor. Following the donor's controls alone, then, can blind the INGO to its own actual diversion risks. Merely executing the donor's screening requirements, for example, might satisfy an INGO's contract but unless *all* risks have been properly considered by the INGO, it may lead to a false sense of security. It also damages the link between risk and control, as donor requirements rarely elucidate the risks that each control is designed to address. Inviting INGO staff to carry out onerous procedures without a clear understanding of the relevant risks fosters bureaucracy.

Secondly, a compliance-based approach can misdirect risk assessment. Where INGOs identify a diversion risk it might be articulated as 'legal non-compliance,' for example, rather than focussing on diversion typologies. Legal non-compliance may indeed be a business risk, but controls to modify it may be different from those which would modify the risks of diversion incidents. And as we explored in Chapter 4, diversion can occur in many different ways – a compliance-based approach may not successfully identify all of them in any given programme, may misidentify them, or could lead to those risks being structured ineffectively.

Meanwhile, in diversion incidents, a compliance-based approach can underemphasise the consequences that should be of the greatest focus to an INGO – the implications for its beneficiaries and its operations. Incidents become alarming donor management and legal issues rather than opportunities to improve and adapt for the benefit of the INGO's mission.

Fourthly, the approach can misdirect responsibility away from the INGO and towards donors, regulators, and lawmakers. INGOs lose agency, and become implementation engines and the objects of legal leverage for donor agencies. Worse, many INGOs will perpetrate this systemic dysfunction by passing on equally over-specific requirements to their own implementing partners. As the sector wrestles with how to be more localised, it is not helped by this practice.

Finally, perhaps the most compelling issue is that compliance-oriented thinking might contribute to the 'chilling effect' (Debarre, 2019), in which counter-terror and sanctions laws are allowed to discourage humanitarian and development programming. In this context, it is a starting point that can emphasise hazard management, rather than the more difficult but exhilarating practice of focussing on humanitarian possibility, and the negotiation, in-novation, and collaboration necessary to seize it.

Introducing the risk-based approach

In a risk-based approach, we start with the specific diversion risks faced by an organisation, programme, or project, and respond to those. Our primary objective is to minimise incidents of diversion. This is delivered through a schedule of work, the ADP, whose focus, activities, and resourcing are directed by risk assessment.

A risk-based approach does not mean that compliance with donor requirements or the law is not important. It means that it is not the sole purpose, or even the focus, of the ADP. The risk-based approach can also be applied by donors, through avoiding lengthy, detailed screening obligations and instead requiring the existence of a risk-based ADP in their partners.

Advantages of the risk-based approach

A risk-based approach is the only way to fully respect the unique disposition of the INGO, each country programme, different aid modalities, and every project. Assessing the specific risks faced by each can ensure that they are relevant, and controls are effective and proportionate. It is also pragmatic – procedures or systems that do not have a clear link to a risk can be removed. This pragmatism puts an INGO in a stronger position to manage complexity, especially in dynamic situations.

This touches on a second key advantage – that it embeds proportionality, the minimum disruption to business in order to reduce risks to an acceptable level. Identifying risks and determining their priority and severity guards against two equal but opposing errors – ineffective or non-existence controls, on the one side, and overbearing bureaucracy at the other.

A third advantage is that a well-designed risk-based ADP should result in a range of policies, procedures, systems, and activities that may well harmonise with donor and legal requirements, reducing duplication. With such policies, proce-dures, and systems in place, an INGO may not need to 're-invent the wheel' with every new contract, for example, but can draw from a pre-existing collection. Gaps can then be filled through obligations management (Chapter 7). Much financial crime legislation expects elements of a risk-based approach, and there is now considerable consistency of expected practice. Another form of efficiency arises in the ADP's relationship to other risk management programmes – there may already be policies, procedures, and systems from which to draw.

Fourthly, the approach offers some protection against legal opacity and alternative agendas. Where there are tension points with unwieldy legislation, disharmony between different government departments, or bounty activism, a risk-based approach can help INGOs to reduce aggregate risk by focusing on minimising the incidents that exacerbate or give succour to these issues in the first place. A risk-based approach can also support advocacy and public engagement; being able to articulate a well-designed ADP can reassure donors, both when assessing an INGO's funding bid, and should an incident take place. Having a clear and documented picture of the risks an INGO faces also supports its wider engagement with the sector, banks, regulators, and legislators.

Finally, just as compliance-oriented thinking might contribute towards a 'chilling effect,' a risk-based approach is positive and constructive. It focuses not on what we must not do or must avoid, but on what we *can* do. Good risk management is about enabling the safe pursuit of opportunity – and for aid organisations, that is the opportunity to save and improve lives. With a clear understanding of the risks and a functional ADP to manage them, INGO boards can enjoy confidence that they are able to operate as safely as possible in highly challenging places.

Key principles

The principles of an ADP are important because country contexts vary so enormously. This constantly generates unique and complicated situations, and no organisational framework can reasonably be expected to provide clear direction at all times. Principles, then, provide guidance in moments of ambiguity. A model ADP should be proportionate, transparent, accountable, predicated, holistic, and risk-based.

These principles should be seen in conjunction with wider principles of humanitarian and global development work, such as the four humanitarian principles (humanity, neutrality, impartiality, independence), and conversant with the wider principles of a counter-fraud and corruption framework (May, 2016).

Proportionality

Proportionality is about incurring the minimum disruption to business in order to modify diversion risk to an acceptable level. Proportionality is perhaps amongst the principles most commonly overlooked by the sector. But if we do not consider it, we end up with insufficient means to deliver objectives safely, or overbearing bureaucracy that prevents us from delivering them at all.

This is very important when considering the activities in an ADP. The guidance in this book must be considered in the context of the risks and circumstances of each organisation. For some INGOs, that will mean a need for substantial investment. For others, it may even mean cutting back on anti-diversion activities that are not, in fact, necessary or effective.

Transparency

Transparency is the clear and forthright disclosure of relevant material, such as policies, procedures, and records. Transparency is important because it is one of the ways in which we facilitate accountability, helps to reduce the risk of fraud, corruption and diversion, helps donors and partners to manage their own risks, and helps to improve learning and reflection.

Transparency is reliant on three things –creating records; processes to ensure that these are not lost, destroyed, or hidden; and processes to ensure that they are disclosed. A guiding principle for the execution of transparency is the 'four Rs': Record, retain, review, and reveal.

Accountability

In the context of an ADP, accountability is the responsible execution of duties, in line with clear, agreed parameters, coupled with a readiness to explain the rationale for the manner in which those duties were executed, and the presence of a scrutinising function to facilitate that explanation.

Lawfulness

An ADP should operate according to the legislation and regulation of the jurisdictions in which it does so, and from which its funding derives, except where such laws or their enforcement represent clear violations of human rights.

This can sometimes be subject to the perception of conflict with some of the humanitarian principles. How can an INGO be acting independently if it complies with counter-terror regimes that, by definition, are established by one side of a conflict to erode the other? But this can be a less helpful argument than it might appear, because it moves us into a zero-sum discussion. Just as one side may perceive that an INGO fails to act neutrally and independently because it complies with a counter-terror regime, the other may perceive the same if it does not. Instead, through the application of the principles, a risk-based approach, and the components of the ADP, some such situations may in fact be avoided.

Predication

All actions and decisions should be as evidence-based as possible. In a space dominated by misconception, ideology, and politics, we must be pragmatic and factual if we are to actually reduce the risk of diversion incidents. There is no space for 'fake news,' cognitive errors, beliefs, and impressions – decisions must be based on facts. Where clear facts are unavailable, the best information or estimate possible should be used.

Holistic

An ADP should consider the full range of options to minimise diversion across deterrence, prevention, detection, and response approaches, and within wider enablers such as cultural development and leadership. A holistic ADP provides the tools and systems from which a practical approach at programme and project level can draw.

Some INGOs may find the extent of work described in this book daunting. But it is entirely scalable; the key to scalability is breadth. Every INGO for which diversion is relevant should ensure that it addresses all dimensions of an ADP, though the depth and extent of each will vary according to the circumstances of each organisation. The ADP of a large INGO working in 100 countries should not be the same as a comparatively small INGO working in ten. For many organisations, while the ADP itself is broad, it may be operationally relatively modest.

Introducing the ADP

This model aims to provide an INGO with the means to take a risk-based and principles-based approach to tackling diversion.

Components of the ADP

Situational awareness and risk assessment

Awareness of the space in which an INGO is working is critical, and there is a huge range of volatilities – sometimes risks and issues change overnight, sometimes they are static for years. An INGO must appreciate its environment on tactical and strategic levels. We explore situational awareness in Chapter 7.

Similarly, all anti-diversion work must be grounded in a clear and, as far as is possible, objective assessment of the risks (Chapter 6). In turn, diversion risk assessment should sit within a coherent, organisation-wide risk-management framework supported by appropriate capability (Modirzadeh, 2013; Milatovic et al., 2015).

Together, situational awareness and risk assessment keep us pragmatic and practical – they keep us focussed on the INGO's actual operations, in its actual environment.

Deterrence

Deterrence is the starting point for our control of threats and risks. Ideally, a threat can be deterred. If it cannot, then perhaps the risk it creates can be prevented from materialising. If it cannot be prevented, then perhaps the incident can be detected, and of course, if it is detected then we must respond to it.

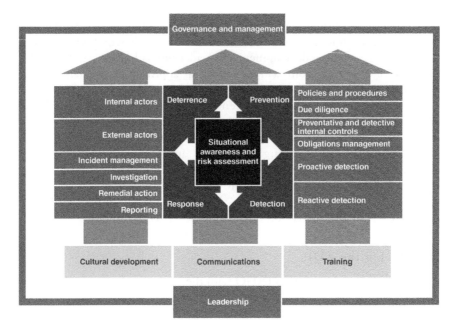

Figure 5.1 A model ADP.

To deter diversion is to discourage potential perpetrators from participating in it. It is the psychological battlefield – how do we stop, as far as possible, both inside and outside parties from engaging in diversion?

To deter internal parties, such as staff and volunteers, we can use the 'fraud triangle' model of dishonest behaviour, in which dishonesty arises from the right level of pressure, perception of opportunity, and ability to rationalise the action. May (2016) outlines a range of activities INGOs can deploy to tackle these three factors, and which are also relevant to diversion.

But reducing the risk of diversion also means deterring external parties. This is more challenging, but can be possible – as long as INGOs are permitted to engage with diversionaries. Options can include:

- Obtaining acceptance without transactions through careful dialogue with diversionaries (see Milatovic et al., 2015);
- Taking collective action with other INGOs to avoid transactions;
- Engaging independent researchers to understand the circumstances of local contexts and act as vehicles for sharing information that facilitates deterrence strategies;
- Building and maintaining a reputation for refusing to make payments or provide 'gifts';

- Leveraging local relationships and interlocutors to build trust (see Egeland et al., 2011);
- Using passive physical security measures.

Prevention

Prevention represents reducing the likelihood and consequence of diversion through limiting the opportunities for it. For our ADP, prevention has four components:

- Anti-diversion policies and procedures;
- Due diligence;
- Preventative and detective internal controls (subject to management oversight and independent review);
- Obligations management.

These components share much in common with other risk management programmes such as fraud, Prevention of Sexual Exploitation and Abuse (PSEA), and security. This book considers due diligence in Chapter 8 and the other parts of a prevention work in Chapter 7.

Detection

Detection is the identification of suspicious matters that could be incidents of diversion (Chapter 9). This book considers this in two parts: Proactive detection, which is work dedicated to spotting the red flags of diversion; and reactive detection, which are means to ensure that where concerns arise, they can be readily captured.

Response

If a suspicious matter is detected, then an INGO needs to respond to that in a way which not only manages the risk represented by the matter itself, but which manages the risks generated by the response. This book explores four components to response in Chapter 9:

- Incident management;
- Investigation;
- Remedial action;
- Reporting.

Culture, communication, and training

Internal culture is the great enabler or disruptor of incidents, and we explore how to develop an anti-diversion internal culture in Chapter 10. How an

INGO communicates about diversion with its staff, volunteers, and third parties to support that culture and manage the risks is also important. This includes training and development.

Governance, leadership, and management

Finally, all the work within an ADP must interact with the governance and management structures of an INGO, be subject to clear anti-diversion leadership, and be properly audited and assessed. An approach is set out in Chapter 11.

Key stakeholders and dependencies

The ADP outlined in this book is dependent on several systems already being in place. It complements, rather than replaces:

- A performance and disciplinary management system for staff and volunteers;
- A robust framework of financial controls;
- An existing risk-management framework;
- A structure of governance, management, and reporting lawfully aligned with the regulatory requirements of the INGO's jurisdictions.

Challenging the cost narrative

A common narrative in the aid sector that generates friction with the anti-diversion agenda is that anti-diversion costs – such as obligation management, monitoring, and reporting – can risk prohibiting aid operations in particular environments. Underlying this may be a sense that 'compliance' is an unfair and unnecessary cost, one that might be seen as more readily applicable to the private sector rather than one that saves and improves lives. Stakeholders in the aid sector should be sympathetic to INGOs here. INGO work is intensely risky and extremely complex, and yet is often misrepresented through an outmoded Victorian concept of 'charity,' carrying a sense of volunteerism and amateurism. There are a lot of risks and challenges for INGOs today. Diversion is just one.

But in this sympathy is also a difficult truth. It is because aid work has high inherent risk levels that it attracts regulation, and we need to re-think the way that we resource business support like risk management. Industries with high inherent risk levels, and the capability to significantly affect people, become regulated. Financial services most readily comes to mind, perhaps, but consider accounting, aerospace, construction, defence, extractives, human services, pharmaceuticals, utilities, and so on.

Humanitarian work should not be excluded on the basis of its valuable mission – healthcare, for example, also saves and improves lives but is highly regulated. Sometimes regulation is the only lever that truly results in an organisation spending more on the necessary systems. And spend they do –

organisations in these industries pour billions into compliance. The aid sector, by comparison, is remarkably under-regulated.

When we take a compliance-based approach, these costs can seem burdensome. But sophisticated operations do not take place without business support costs like anti-diversion activities. The greater the risk, the greater the cost. Most people probably accept that some business support costs are necessary, but *how much* is where we become mired in cognitive errors, heuristics, and biases. We begin to experiment with ratios – blunt expressions of the value of assistance versus the costs.

The idea that the value of aid or development outputs should be at a certain ratio to that which is spent on business support is without sound basis. It is rooted in a general concern that the public would object to fat ratios, a belief that lean ratios are associated with more generous giving, and pressure to reach more and more beneficiaries. But we know how public perceptions can be starkly fact-free, that the exotic accounting that delivers lean ratios is troubling at best, and that no one agency will ever reach all potential beneficiaries – it is far more likely that overstretch will dilute the quality of delivery, or that the holes that open in the stretch will allow diversion to occur.

The application of a zero-sum lens to INGO resources is one of the most pervasive and harmful errors ever to be applied in the sector. INGOs, institutional donors, and the public are all responsible. A penny spent on business support is not a penny unspent on beneficiaries. This simplistic idea is a major blockage to the sector's proper management of risk across a range of domains.

A risk-based approach is a way forward. The principle of proportionality helps to ensure that spending on business support is as little as possible, while risk assessment ensures that it is as much as necessary, spent as effectively as possible. But it requires managerial courage. INGOs must adequately resource their ADPs, and donors must improve grantee access to business support funding.

References

Debarre, A. 2019. *Safeguarding humanitarian action in sanctions regimes.* New York, NY: International Peace Institute.

Egeland, J., Harmer, A., and Stoddard, A. 2011. *To stay and deliver: Good practice for humanitarians in complex security environments.* New York, NY: United Nations Office for the Coordination of Humanitarian Affairs.

May, O. 2016. *Fighting fraud and corruption in the humanitarian and global development sector.* Abingdon: Routledge. https://doi.org/10.4324/9781315558301.

Modirzadeh, N. 2013. *Counterterrorism and Humanitarian Engagement Project: Enterprise risk management – a new approach to managing the risks posed by counterterrorism regulations.* Cambridge, MA: Harvard Law School.

Milatovic, S., Macdonald, I., and McGrane, K. 2015. *Risk management toolkit in relation to counter-terrorism measures.* Geneva: Norwegian Refugee Council.

6 Risk assessment

Oliver May

There was a British charity facing large-scale theft from its clothing collection bins. In the UK, second-hand clothes are big charity business – charity shop revenue reached £578m in 2016 (Statista, 2019). This income is a vital source of unrestricted funds – but the wider 'rag' trade is valuable too, and after the charity's supporters dropped their donations into the bins, organised criminals were stealing entire binloads.

One sunny afternoon, I travelled to an anonymous depot on an English business park to learn about the charity's response. It had hit upon the novel solution of putting electronic GPS trackers inside garments in the bins, which the criminals would then gather up as they raided the contents. The charity workers would set off in their own cars and follow the GPS. Once the criminals' vehicle was parked up, the charity would phone the local police to report the crime and effect arrests. Charity workers were driving all over the country, tearing up the motorways in hot pursuit of organised, potentially violent criminal gangs!

"You need a risk assessment," I told the person running the project. "There's a lot that could go wrong here and you need to make sure you've taken account of it."

"Ah, well, to me a risk assessment is just a tick-box exercise," they replied.

Risk assessment and the aid sector

This charity's uneasy relationship with risk assessment was not unusual. Many organisations struggle. While risk management capacity and capability are growing in the aid sector, maturity can still be comparatively low for many INGOs.

There are a range of reasons for this. Perhaps a root cause is that risk assessment is not necessarily instinctive. We have evolved to evaluate the lethal threats and visible opportunities around us – when threats, outcomes, and opportunities are harder to perceive, it is more difficult to weight it all up. Paul Slovic at the University of Oregon summarises it well. "Risk is an inherently complex concept and is an invention of the human mind to help people deal with things that can be harmful and dangerous. Once we start to characterise events in life with the word 'risk' and then try to quantify the level of risk, we are entering the domain of subjectivity and emotion," he says (Heires, 2017).

Another is access to human capability. Diversion risk assessment requires a diverse array of skills and experiences that are not necessarily found together, for example:

- Analytical skills, but also creativity and imagination;
- Local contextual understanding, but also the ability to see the big picture for the programme and the INGO;
- Ability to work conceptually, but also to keep outputs practical;
- Familiarity with the principles of control and control systems, but also an appreciation of human factors.

Thirdly, good risk assessment requires time and space that is not often made available to it. It is not complicated, but it must be methodical, and the volatility of the sector's work – both from year-to-year and day-to-day – makes this a perennial challenge. It is a somewhat self-sustaining problem, of course, because the fewer who know what 'good' looks like, the more likely 'bad' is to proliferate.

Despite the challenges, risk assessment remains a powerful management tool. Executed well, it enables us to:

- Identify things that could go wrong;
- Determine how best to respond proportionally to those events;
- Prioritise our focus and determine our resourcing between them;
- Operate transparently and accountably.

This is, of course, in pursuit of humanitarian and development opportunities – if we can identify and manage our risks, we can seize opportunities to improve and save lives.

A challenge of execution

Risk assessment is a process upon which each step is reliant on the successful completion of its precursor. In this respect, it is like cooking – much can go wrong at any stage which will significantly affect the quality of the final product. And as risk assessment is the foundation of the risk-based approach, mistakes here can have a disproportionate effect on the INGO's ability to stop diversion.

Common examples of issues that can undermine diversion risk assessment in INGOs include:

- An over-complicated approach that makes the assessment too fragile to be of use in a volatile context, or too demanding for busy programme staff to use;
- Insufficient time, or access to necessary information or stakeholders to fully inform the assessment;
- Articulating risks at the wrong level of specificity for the subject of the risk assessment;

- Improperly defining a risk, or framing it in the wrong context (for example, articulating fraud risks as compliance or reputational risks);
- Framing control issues as if they were risks;
- Failing to account for the differing variability of risks, some of which might be static for the life of a project and others of which might change daily;
- Flawed identification or assessment of controls, such as the use of those that do not properly address the risk, over-weighting a particular control, or failing to match the proportionality of the controls to the risk;
- Failing to document the risk assessment, reducing transparency and objectivity;
- Confusion between inherent risk and residual risk.

This chapter sets out a constructive approach to identifying and evaluating diversion risks for INGOs, and helping to avoid these issues. This is important, because the nature and operation of the entire ADP derives from the decisions made here. Assuming that the INGO has a risk-management framework with which diversion risk assessment should align, the chapter outlines three core products: The organisational (or 'enterprise') risk assessment, the country programme ('business unit' or 'jurisdictional') risk assessment, and the project risk assessment. Some INGOs will have need of all three, others of just one.

Diversion risk assessments

Diversion represents just one set of risks that INGOs must manage – there are plenty of others, many of which are related across several axes such as wider fraud and corruption, security, and legal risks. Indeed, while this book focusses on diversion risk, every organisation must take a holistic view. I have seen many risks across a range of domains – diversion, fraud, sexual abuse, security, health and safety – materialise with common vulnerability denominators around culture, accountability, transparency, and risk mindset. Arriving at proactivity may require some organisations to re-think their approach to risk.

The challenge is to establish an organisational approach to risk management that enables the INGO to stay on top of the risks, appreciates the specificities of each risk domain, but which recognises the points of contact to support integrated approaches.

In respect of diversion, then, the purpose of risk assessment is to:

- Inform the design and operation of the ADP;
- Support ERM;
- Determine whether to tolerate, terminate, transfer, or treat diversion risks at any given level;
- Ensure that activities to deter, prevent, detect, and respond to diversion are present, effective, and proportionate.

As a management tool, the levels at which risk assessment should be conducted would normally follow the structure of the INGO. Any given INGO may wish to understand its exposure as a whole, at the core business unit level (such as country programme, or functions such as finance), and at the operational level (usually projects). This section introduces three examples of risk assessment, roughly analogous to what might be known in other sectors as 'enterprise,' 'functional' or 'jurisdiction,' and 'process' assessments respectively: Organisation, country programme, and project. Each has a different but linked purpose.

The Institute of Risk Management's 2014 *Risk management for charities* is a helpful introductory guide, but in essence, risk assessment is a basic sequence of activities that enable managers to appreciate the environment in which they are working. Diversion risk assessment involves the same core steps as all other forms:

- Identification of risks;
- Assignment of inherent likelihood and consequence to risks;
- Prioritisation of risks;
- Identification and assessment of controls;
- Review of residual risk.

Identification of risks

At the highest level, there is substantial consistency between diversion methodologies. This means that organisational risk assessment might be able to consider risk in terms of the four risk categories in Chapter 4, and business unit or country risk assessments in terms of the 16 model risks. But as assessment zooms in on processes and unique contexts, it becomes more important to use those risks as *starting points* to identify how diversion can occur in specific circumstances. Mapping relevant risks for any given scenario is the critical first step.

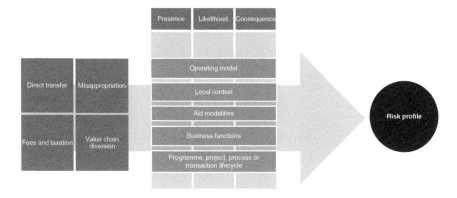

Figure 6.1 Towards risk profiles.

Inherent likelihood and consequence of risks

The likelihood of a diversion risk is a judgement on the chances that it could materialise, while the consequence represents a judgement on the likely events should it do so. Ideally, diversion risk assessment will be able to draw on an enterprise risk framework that allows these judgements to be made consistently with the management of risk elsewhere in the organisation.

At this stage, the likelihood and consequence of the risk should be considered without factoring in controls. This can be very challenging, and a range of vectors can affect the presence, likelihood, and consequence of diversion risks (and will affect the nature of the controls used): Local context, operating model, aid modality, project and programme lifecycle, and business function.

Local context

Huge diversity exists between contexts, and the inherent risk of diversion can be affected not only by the three likelihood factors (Chapter 1) at the core of diversion, but also by:

- Local infrastructure;
- Local need;
- Cultural factors;
- Scale of diversionary capacity and capability;
- Power dynamics;
- Proximity to protective authorities;
- Environmental crime and disorder levels.

Operating model

The risk profiles of different ways in which INGOs carry out work vary both between models, and within those models, including:

- Partner-based (with differing profiles between partner types);
- Consortia and other joint ways of working;
- Direct delivery;
- Rapid on-set humanitarian emergency;
- Remote programme management.

Aid modality

The resources that can be affected by a diversion event reflect the differing resourcing profile of aid operations, with variance between (for example):

- Distribution (both NFI and food);
- Cash transfer programming;

- Construction;
- Agriculture;
- Advocacy;
- Modalities involving training.

Programme, project, process or transaction lifecycle

Risks vary in their likelihood and consequence at different points in the lifecycle of an operation, whether it is as broad as a programme, or as specific as a transaction. For example, at the inception of a project, fees and gifts may be of an elevated likelihood. Towards conclusion, the risk of staff theft might rise. Risk assessment should reflect this dynamism.

Business function

Diversion risks also affect different parts of an aid operation in different ways, including:

- Procurement;
- Logistics;
- Finance;
- Programme management;
- HR and payroll;
- MEL.

Prioritisation of inherent risks

Having considered the likelihood and consequence of the risks, this should allow the risk assessment to rank the risks – to determine the priority of the risks for focus and action. Throughout the risk assessment process, the INGO may choose to tolerate, terminate, transfer, or treat any given risk.

In its truest sense, tolerating the risk means taking no further action to modify it. While technically this is, of course, an option for diversion risks, it may only be defensible to stakeholders when the levels are perceived to be at the lowest ends of likelihood and consequence.

The best option for some INGOs will be to terminate the risk. INGOs for whom this is the case may be those:

- That do not have the capacity or capability to manage a diversion risk adequately in that country context or programme modality, or to ensure that an implementing partner can;
- With insufficient time, prior to the commencement of a project, to adequately invest in their capacity and capability to elevate them to the correct level.

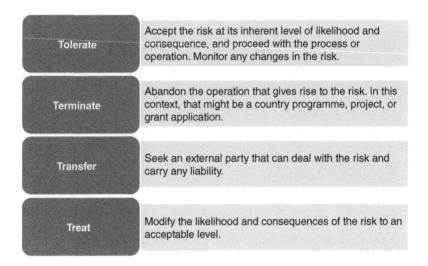

Figure 6.2 Responses to risks.

An honest and informed assessment of capacity and capability must take into account the resources not only of the INGO, but the complexity and volatility of the jurisdiction.

The third option, transferring the risk, is common – but as discussed in Chapters 1 and 13, should be treated with caution and without the expectation that it alleviates all the INGO's actual or moral liability. But it is the treatment of risks that will be the most common approach for INGOs with the resources to operate in these places.

Identification and assessment of controls

In this context, 'controls' are the policies, procedures, and systems that an INGO can deploy to modify the risks – to reduce them to a manageable level of likelihood and consequence. Controls can affect one, or both, of those aspects, and it can be helpful to consider them across deterrence, prevention, detection, and response. They may be controls that help to:

- Deter a threat from manifesting the risk;
- Prevent the risk from materialising;
- Detect the incident if it has materialised;
- Respond to the materialised risk, reducing its consequences and managing any onward risks generated by the materialisation.

Residual risk

Residual risk is the inevitable balance of risk which remains after controls ('treatment') have been applied to modify it. In the case of diversion, it is not a credible position to imagine that controls can reduce all residual risk to zero.

Qualification questions

Not all INGOs may need a diversion risk assessment, so it might be helpful to consider three key questions before deciding to proceed with one. These might be:

- Does the INGO or its implementing partners operate in countries in which diversionaries also operate or fundraise?
- Does the INGO operate in countries identified by FATF, or other bodies on the basis of evidence, as containing an elevated risk that INGOs will be subject to diversionary interference?
- Does the INGO provide services or outputs that, while not necessarily geographically co-located with diversionaries, are known to face abuse by them?

If the answer to any of these questions is 'yes,' then a risk assessment may be valuable. Organisational risk assessments can be useful for medium and large INGOs that carry out programmes in a number of different countries. A small INGO with, perhaps, only one or two programmes may wish to jump straight to a country or project risk assessment.

Organisational Risk Assessment (ORA)

ORAs are the highest level of risk assessment, and of direct value to boards and senior leadership teams. ORAs are important because the total risk facing an INGO is not an aggregate of project, programme, and business unit risks – there are risks, and consequences, at an organisational level that might not appear in such assessments. For example, while the diversion of food aid may not attract an existential level of consequence to a programme, it may entail consequences of severity for the INGO as an organisation.

Features of an ORA

An ORA has the following objectives:

- To identify and prioritise at-risk business units (usually countries and programmes);
- Inform the scale of investment required in an ADP;

- Direct the focus, resourcing, and priorities of the ADP at an organisational level;
- Provide senior management with visibility of the organisational risk profile;
- Align with programme and business-planning cycles, and look forward.

Because an ORA operates at a high level, the risks it assesses might be best articulated broadly. These might only be the categories of model risks in Chapter 4: Direct transfers, misappropriation, fees and taxation, and value chain diversion.

Country Risk Assessment (CRA)

This is a jurisdictional or core business unit risk assessment. We use the term 'country' as, for many INGOs, the country programme is that business unit – though there are plenty of cases in which other functions or units might merit an assessment like this. These might be regional centres, procurement hubs, finance departments, and others, for example. Similarly, the risks carried by a business unit can extend beyond the country – if the business unit has a supply chain extending abroad, for example, this should also be considered.

CRAs are important because we must not homogenise. The reasons that anti-diversion work is challenging in Syria, Yemen, Nigeria, and Kenya differ. Part of the CRA process needs to be understanding the particular local complexity and allowing the flexibility to respond to it.

Features of a CRA

The objectives of the CRA are to:

- Contextualise the ADP, adapting and focussing its tools in the country context;
- Ensure that proportionate and effective controls exist for treated risks;
- Inform project and programme planning;
- Ensure that key control systems are available for projects to draw upon.

While the ORA works at a high level, the CRA might compare the business unit against more specific risks. It can be supported by further risk assessment of projects, initiatives, or programme processes (such as payroll, personal expenses and floats, or procurement) where there is concern about specific risks. While at least an annual assessment will assist, it should be revisited in the event of any major business unit or environmental change. A useful ORA might:

- Use the model risks in Chapter 4;
- Draw upon and adapt the organisational ADP provisions, and other

existing controls such as those governing financial, HR, and procurement processes;

- Articulate controls in a deterrence, prevention, detection, and response format, best preparing the business unit for any eventuality.

Project Risk Assessment (PRA)

The PRA is the most granular of our three levels. Its objectives are straightforward:

- To identify the specific risks facing a project or process;
- To identify the controls to modify those risks;
- To enable management to make decisions on the residual risk.

Subsequently, a key difference between a PRA and our other two assessments is that while they assess against predetermined risks, the PRA uses the model risks as a starting point.

Features of a PRA

A research process will be needed to identify the risks, perhaps involving workshops with key staff, engagement with local experts, and liaison with other agencies working in the locale.

Risks might be best articulated using a SEA model, which ensures that it considers the Source of the risk, the Event itself, and the Asset affected. For example, a 'beneficiary taxing risk' might be identified as follows: 'Immediately following a cash [asset] distribution, armed parties [source] extract some or all of the cash from beneficiaries [event].'

Controls might be expressed through the deterrence, prevention, detection, and response categories. These will be procedures, systems, and specific actions. For example, one response control for the above risk might be to establish a line of communication with local armed groups in order to try to influence, persuade, or leverage them not to conduct such taxation.

Improving diversion risk assessment

Truly useful diversion risk assessment requires focus, and there are some key things that we can do to elevate this. But perhaps the most important is recognising that risk is a state of mind, and assessment a discrete process. Having a risk assessment document is not the end of the matter, it is the start of the process. It must sit within a cycle of regular review. It must also become a discipline of management, a way of thinking about how we manage resources. Managers must consider whether the likelihood or consequences of the risks identified in their project or programme are rising or falling on a daily, weekly, monthly, or annual basis.

Simplicity and specificity

Risk assessments should not be complicated. In fact, the more steps and more nuance involved, the more likely that the diversity and volatility of local contexts will break it. In particular, beware of control descriptions which:

- Are generalised;
- Overreach with meaningless adjectives like 'robust' or 'strong';
- Cannot be audited;
- Do not have clear owners, monitoring, or means by which they could be measured (and therefore might not, in fact, exist).

Similarly, be cautious of very complex risk assessments and associated processes, perhaps with lots of tiers, ratings, and numbers. Numerical thresholds and quantifications are very vulnerable to disruption.

Practicality

Because risk is conceptual, risk assessments can drift off into abstraction. This is easy for a sector where headquarters' functions are often physically far away from the relevant projects. A risk assessment needs to generate action, not just tidy up minds. If it does not tell you anything you do not already know, or does not result in the removal, modification, or introduction of any controls, this should be a warning sign.

A practical diversion risk assessment is a diagnostic tool to support decision-making. It is not:

- A document for the sole purpose of securing donor funding;
- For primarily demonstrating compliance;
- A stylised representation of policies, procedures, and systems;
- A laborious process for its own ends.

Realism of expectation

Risk assessment is not a fully objective exercise – it is an imperfect science, vulnerable to human factors, that involves a best judgement. We can minimise subjectivity through ensuring a robust process and access to as much data as possible, but we must not expect razor-sharp accuracy.

Further, we should not assume that we can identify and neutralise all risks. This urge might often derive from our grasping need for certainty, but unless we terminate a risk by simply not operating in a particular place, or providing services in which diversionaries have no interest, we cannot reduce the risk to zero. In the aid sector, there will be diversion incidents that could not reasonably be avoided. There are plenty of incidents that can, of course, and by dealing effectively with those, we can reduce – but probably not eliminate – our total exposure.

Proportionality

Risk assessment should not result in the prescription of a fresh set of controls that stifle programming. It should be rationalising and enabling – determining precisely the minimum controls needed to modify the risks acceptably in order to facilitate programming. There are a number of ways to avoid the equal and opposing errors of over- and under-control.

For example, draw on existing controls, where available. And not every risk requires its own special controls; one control can serve many things, for example – this might make it a 'key control.' Similarly, take the opportunity to eliminate controls that are unnecessary or ineffective. If an INGO has a diversion control for example that clearly does not sufficiently affect a risk, or a more efficient control exists, remove it. Risk assessment can help INGOs to be leaner.

Consistency

The scale of risk management variance between aid actors is problematic. Despite moves in recent years towards harmony, not all practitioners speak the same language. Hopefully, an INGO has a risk management framework that defines precisely the approach to be followed; how the tiers of likelihood and consequence are to be determined, for example, or what is meant by terms like inherent and residual risk, or attributes, vectors, and factors. But even if not, ensure that the approach to carrying out risk assessments and the language used to facilitate this, are consistent.

It is also important to be consistent through the stages of risk assessment. Problems often derive from failing to properly assess inherent risk *first* before moving on to controls. People often struggle to consider risks in the absence of key controls, for example, skewing inherent risk assessment – or fail to treat control assessment with the same probing analysis. I find it can take up to 20 minutes in risk workshops to properly explore how to think about inherent risk with participants, prior to starting any rating exercises!

Consistency is also needed within the risk domain being assessed. For a diversion risk assessment, focus should be on the risk of incidents, not on other risks like donor non-compliance or reputational impact. Incidents are the root issue and require their own specific activities to deter, prevent, detect, and respond to them. Donor non-compliance in this context is a consequence, not a risk – there is space for considering wider risks like these elsewhere in a risk management framework.

Access the right skills, knowledge, and information

Who will carry out the risk assessment, with whom will they engage, how will they find relevant information, and how will they use it? Risk assessment should only be carried out by those with the capacity and capability to do so. It might require a range of participants, including staff from risk and compliance functions, finance, audit, programme, legal, and those with local contextual knowledge, or training or experience in diversion prevention.

Ensuring that the exercise taps the best of participants' knowledge and experience also means making sure it is as engaging and stimulating as possible. Throw out the boring workshops in which participants sit around a table agreeing ratings, chugging coffee to stay awake, and waiting for the session to end. Introduce exercises that make use of space, get people sharing, and unlock their creativity and imagination.

Similarly, the best risk assessments derive from a structured and broad approach to collecting information globally and locally. What are the experiences of other INGOs, of donor agencies, of beneficiaries, for example? What is the latest published research? What qualitative and quantitative data can be used to inform risk identification and rating?

Account for human factors

Of all the things to bear in mind when running a risk assessment exercise, human factors must be at the forefront. These represent the interplay between the individual, the task, and the workplace (HSE, 1999). For us, this is particularly important in the context of human psychology and sociology. All our endeavours are affected by the messy, fallible, complicated, and exhilarating creatures that we are. There are three key implications for risk assessment.

The first is to be aware of agendas. Because risk assessment is subjective, it is vulnerable to intentional or unintentional manipulation by those whose interests might be affected. One of the main sources of pressure to lower risk ratings or elevate control ratings, for example, can be senior management, donor management or funding teams, programme teams, and partner management teams – but frankly all stakeholders have potential here. This must, of course, be held in tension with the fact that those who may have perceivable agendas may also be the genuine experts in the country context. So, collect information from stakeholders, but assess it in the round. Risk assessment is not a democracy – assessment by consensus is how we end up with useless, middling ratings for all risks and controls.

The second is to be aware of the cognitive biases, errors, and heuristics that derail our efforts to be as objective as possible. There is a long roll-call of effects here, but one of the most common might be the availability bias we encountered in Chapter 2, in which we ascribe disproportionate importance to information that is more readily recalled. We might rate the risk of diversion, for example, as higher if an incident was recently detected, but lower if the INGO has never detected one. Another might be optimism bias, which leads us to see our own INGOs as less likely to sustain a diversion event than others.

Finally, we must not underestimate the impact of organisational culture. If there are facets to the INGO's culture that can create friction with careful, informed risk assessment, these must be considered during planning and execution. INGO cultures that might struggle with risk assessment can include those that are highly action-oriented, those with poor accountability or in which the consequences of poor risk management are not keenly felt by relevant stakeholders, and those which insufficiently value business support functions.

Document it

'If it's not written down, it didn't happen,' is the golden rule that criminal investigators often follow to ensure that they make full records of their actions. Documenting risk assessment is important so that other internal stakeholders can understand what is being done, and to provide to any later audit, investigation, or donor compliance review. Whether a matter of financial crime regulation or not, if something goes wrong, amongst the first questions asked will be: Was there a risk assessment?

References

Health and Safety Executive (HSE) 1999. Reducing error and influencing behaviour. *Structural Survey 17*(3). http://dx.doi.org/10.1108/ss.1999.11017cae.007.

Heires, K. 2017. The psychology of risk. *Risk Management*. 1 September.

Institute of Risk Management 2014. *Risk management for charities*. London: Institute of Risk Management.

Statista 2019. Second hand retail in the United Kingdom. https://www.statista.com/topics/4593/second-hand-retail-in-the-united-kingdom-uk/ (accessed 19 January 2019).

7 Prevention

Oliver May and Paul Curwell

Prevention is the art and science of reducing the likelihood and consequences of diversion through tackling the opportunities for diversionary threats that cannot be deterred. Within a fraud and corruption framework, prevention might encapsulate policies, procedures, and systems, with management oversight and independent review, coupled with a system of risk management and a supportive culture (May, 2016).

For the ADP, the components of the prevention workstream are similar:

- A policy framework that includes a code of conduct, an anti-diversion policy, and a diversion response plan;
- Integration with wider risk control policy areas;
- Due diligence (see Chapter 8);
- A framework of effective, proportionate, risk-based preventative and detective controls, especially in relation to staff lifecycle management, asset management, high risk role management, vendor and supplier management, partner management, and programme management;
- An obligations register and associated processes.

Policy framework

As with all integrity risks, a code of conduct is the cornerstone of the INGO's framework for managing behaviour. The code should, of course, clarify the corporate values of the INGO and how they relate to the conduct of its staff, volunteers, and third parties. Values alone however, are insufficient. The 'protected values' of individuals may be at variance to those of the organisation (Gibson et al., 2016), or could be interpreted in ways that the organisation would actually prefer they are not. So, the code should describe specific acceptable and unacceptable behaviours, and name the transacting of resources with diversionaries as amongst the latter.

Anti-diversion policy and response plan

The provisions of anti-diversion policy might sit within a dedicated policy document, or within a wider policy depending on the scale and complexity of the INGO. Whether in its own document or incorporated into a wider policy, written and appropriately authorised anti-diversion policy provisions should:

- State that the INGO will not tolerate diversion and commits to a risk-based approach to reducing the likelihood and consequence of incidents;
- Link the purpose of the anti-diversion policy to the mission of the INGO;
- Determine the principles by which the INGO will tackle diversion;
- Clearly set out the responsibilities of key persons and functions, such as the board, the Senior Leadership Team (SLT), country directors, and all managers and staff;
- Authorise and set out the aims of the ADP, and create a responsibility for all managers and staff to implement and support it;
- Define key terms such as 'diversion' and 'terrorist financing';
- Establish incident reporting requirements and procedures to facilitate them;
- Take account of the diversion risks relevant to the INGO;
- Be compliant with legal obligations in all relevant jurisdictions.

The risk and complexity associated with handling a suspected incident of diversion should be managed through a clear anti-diversion response plan (see Chapter 9).

Integration with wider integrity risk policies

The close relationships between the risks and controls associated with diversion, and those associated with other integrity risks like fraud, corruption, and sexual exploitation, mean that none of these policies should be developed in isolation. In particular:

- Ensure that diversion risks are considered during the drafting of such policies. Is there overlap? Are there provisions or systems being developed from which the ADP should benefit, or which could affect diversion risk management?
- Consider the end-user. Are there ways to harmonise policy provisions or procedures, such as through single whistleblowing mechanisms, for example?
- Explore a single language for integrity risk management. Consider using single definitions of 'incident,' reporting thresholds, principles, and even procedures and mechanisms such as a single response plan.

Due diligence

Due diligence is the collection of information in order to assess the risks presented by an entity. This is discussed more fully in Chapter 8, which presents three key sets of entity that should be subject to an INGO's review:

- Partners;
- Vendors and suppliers;
- Staff.

Most INGOs draw the line at beneficiary screening as a matter of humanitarian ethics, and so does this book. While this has been challenged, those who do so do not necessarily take account of some key factors:

- Beneficiary screening could be open to challenge under IHL;
- The process of targeting and selecting beneficiaries incorporates risk, environmental, and impact assessments – and is therefore a form of aggregated due diligence;
- The likelihood of an individual in a crisis population being a listed entity may be low, presenting a poor level of return for investment in screening as a control;
- Large-scale screening of crisis populations in humanitarian emergencies – where infrastructure may be destroyed or inaccessible – is unlikely to be reasonable.

There has been some challenge to the concept of due diligence in aid operations. Certainly the concerns of Pantuliano et al. (2011) as described in Chapter 1 are real, and some necessary governance, stewardship, and transparency practices are subject to very different cultural interpretations (see Maranz, 2001). But this is cause to take care over their implementation, not to abandon them. Proportionate due diligence is a critical component to preventing diversion.

Developing effective and proportionate controls

Policies, procedures, and systems are a primary way in which we protect business units from diversion. They must be documented so that they can be communicated, enforced, and reviewed, and be clearly identified as mandatory. Whether manual or systematic, a wide array of control types are available for use. These might include:

- Due diligence;
- Access controls and physical security;
- Reconciliations, enabling the identification of differences between accounts, or stages of a process;
- Inventories;

- Authorisations, aligning the level of risk involved in a decision with the right level of seniority;
- Supervision;
- Monitoring, spot-checks, and evaluation, including independently of the management line (such as external organisations);
- Documentary evidence, such as receipts;
- Use of standardised documentation, enabling the rapid identification of anomalies or inconsistencies;
- Segregation of duties, preventing any one person from completing a transaction;
- Third party contracting, setting out expectations and creating a safety net should they not be met;
- Risk-based internal audit.

As we have seen, however, there is considerable variance between diversion risks. That variance includes from whom the threat arises, how it might be carried out, and what might be diverted. This is why it is important to ensure that controls directly modify specific, identified risks.

Risk and controls in dynamic and challenging contexts

A key difficulty in the development and application of anti-diversion procedures and systems is the types of context in which diversion is typically an elevated risk; conflict zones, fragile states, rapidly-changing situations, and places with low infrastructure and accessibility. All too often, auditors might diagnose that an INGO 'needs a good control environment,' but this is like a doctor advising that a patient 'needs to be healthy.' The challenge for INGOs is not whether they recognise that they need effective and proportionate controls, but how that effect and proportionality is achieved in difficult operating circumstances.

Recognise and respond to changing risk indicators

The practice of situational awareness can assist a country programme to spot and react to the changing diversionary environment around it, particularly in relation to diversionary threats themselves. But programmes also need to recognise ways of working that contain particular vulnerability too, especially remote programme management, rapid onset emergency, working in partnership, and faster disbursement in greater volumes. Agility is important during the programme or project, not just at inception. Challenging environments can throw carefully-designed plans and procedures out of the window. Situational awareness, continuous programme review with a diligent risk mindset, and a readiness to make changes to operations is needed.

Determine minimum standards

INGOs can define 'bare minimum' stewardship procedures governing people, assets, funds, and stock, and the circumstances in which a control framework might be pared back to these standards. Generally, these should be a temporary measure, and should be linked to the INGO's risk appetite statement – there may be locations, aid modalities, and operating models that are outside that appetite.

Local contextualisation versus global consistency

While global consistency of policies, procedures, and systems is important, but so is it that controls appropriately modify the risks in any given business unit. Attaining global consistency with sufficient space for local contextualisation is the ultimate challenge for all international organisations.

Achieving this is demanding, requiring an ongoing process of consultation and review, but in the context of any individual business unit, accessing deep local expert knowledge and understanding is key. It is rare, for example, that a place is truly 'lawless.' Even warzones have rules, and while these may not be codified in the way that northern eyes expect, sophisticated forms of local accountability may be available that local actors can help INGOs to access. INGOs need to engage with trusted local staff and stakeholders in the design, execution, and review of their anti-diversion policies, procedures, and systems. Such engagement can be supported with analytical tools, such as 'red teaming' or process mapping.

Technology

A range of technologies are either already available, under trial, or in the pipeline. The revolutionary growth in connectivity, even in some of the most remote or challenging places on earth, has meant that INGOs may be able to choose from a long menu of innovations to improve diversion control. These might include:

- Distributed ledger technology, such as blockchain;
- Digital currency;
- Mobile money;
- Artificial intelligence;
- Virtual and Augmented Reality;
- Drones;
- Digital identity technologies, such as biometric identification;
- Data analytics;
- Smartphone technologies, including apps and tablets;
- 3D printing;
- Digital photography.

While technology unquestionably offers new possibilities for control of diversion, it is not the cure-all that commentators sometimes imply. Diversion risk mutates, so while a technology may help to control one risk, INGOs should be on the lookout for others that may develop in response. In a case in Mexico, for example, the use of electronic cash-cards introduced a new risk of card cloning (*The Economist*, 2017). Biometric technology may improve verification, but can create a reserve of data open to loss, misuse, and exploitation.

The fight against diversion must be enabled by technology, not led by it. Introducing technology into diversion control, then, requires careful consideration of:

- How the technology will affect a specific diversion risk;
- The capability and capacity of the INGO to manage the technology;
- The specific, local contextual circumstances in which the technology will be deployed;
- An assessment of the risks introduced by the technology, and how the INGO will manage these.

Considering human factors

I once assisted an NGO experiencing poor compliance with its procurement processes. In particular, its manual new vendor form was amongst the controls exhibiting the lowest compliance. When I saw the form itself, it was written in Comic Sans – that informal, cartoony font originally intended for children's documents (Beaumont-Thomas, 2017). It was hardly surprising, then, that staff were not taking the form seriously, when the form did not even appear to take itself seriously!

The policies, procedures, and systems most likely to enjoy adoption, use, enforcement, and iterative enhancement are those designed with human factors in mind. For diversion, there are several things to consider:

- Controls should be accessible and easy to use. Busy people default to the quickest and most efficient path;
- Find ways to incorporate the 'why' into the control. Compliance rises when people understand why they are required to do something;
- Ensure that policies, procedures, and systems are enforced. People prioritise according to their manager's priorities;
- Take account of the array of cognitive errors, biases, and heuristics that can affect the successful operation of a policy, procedure, or system.

Designing with human factors in mind is about considering the end-user. Busy programme staff have programmatic objectives, not necessarily compliance-oriented ones – so how can these ordnances be as intuitive as possible, minimise friction, and contribute to programmatic success as visibly as possible?

Alignment and integration with existing control frameworks

In addition to finance and logistics, several functions are particularly key for diversion management. These are:

- Staff lifecycle management;
- Asset management;
- High risk role management;
- Vendor and supplier management;
- Partner management;
- Programme management.

Staff lifecycle management

Staff lifecycle management is about recognising the role that staff play in enabling or limiting diversion, and that both the risks posed by individuals and their tendency to enable or limit it varies, according to the point at which they sit in their individual lifecycle with an INGO. This is best achieved through a risk assessment, and this may result in the ADP affecting such controls and initiatives as:

- Due diligence;
- Staff assistance programmes;
- Contracting and agreements;
- Risk-based induction and briefing;
- Supervision, monitoring, and evaluation;
- Exit procedures and interviews.

Asset management

Clear policies and procedures are required to identify and track assets that may be of interest to diversionaries. This includes fixed assets, stock, consumables, and data. Value, condition, location, and security must be monitored. Robust systems must be used to maintain data regarding the assets, and clear principles of control such as inventories, reconciliation, and segregation of duties must be applied. Spot-checks, include surprise checks, should be carried out.

High risk role management

High risk roles are those which have an elevated level of opportunity to participate in diversion, to detect it, or are prescribed in law as having particular relevant responsibilities. INGOs require a procedure to identify high risk role holders on an ongoing basis, and apply additional controls to those roles identified, such as due diligence, enhanced training, leave requirements, and enhanced auditing or proactive checks.

Vendor and supplier management

The nature of due diligence and selection procedures for vendors, suppliers, consultants, and contractors should be developed according to the risk level inherent in that potential relationship, in that particular location. Subsequently, a useful approach to developing the right anti-diversion controls can be in two strokes:

- Use a risk assessment to determine different categories of third party, and assign particular tiers of due diligence or selection according to the risk;
- Assess the changing diversion risks across the vendor lifecycle, as they will vary across needs identification, supplier selection, engagement, monitoring, and relationship closure.

Particular key controls for diversion will likely include:

- Audit clauses in contracts;
- Sharing of, and requiring compliance with, anti-diversion policies and procedures;
- Attestation;
- Agreement to anti-diversion statements;
- Requirements to report suspicions.

Partner management

It is vital that a risk-based approach, in which the activities rise in intensity and scrutiny according to the risk level, is applied to partner selection and due diligence, monitoring (including financial monitoring such as spot-checks), and post-implementation assessment.

These processes require consistent, documented methodologies informed by risk assessment – it is only with consistency that deviation can be identified, and continuous improvement can be facilitated. This should be accompanied by a genuine commitment to building the capacity and capability of partners through documented capacity-building plans, aligned to their initial assessment. Meanwhile, INGOs must also monitor the partnership for the warning signs of elevated diversion vulnerability. For example:

- Partners are given more funding than they were assessed for;
- Partners are not assessed at all;
- Programmes are changed, but no fresh risk assessment is conducted;

- Diversion risks in an environment change, but the programme does not – particularly if there also no review of the risk assessment.

Programme management

The design of projects and programmes themselves can sometimes be over-looked as a key opportunity to limit diversion by design. This can include the avoidance of particular geographical areas or routes, particular aid modalities, or particular relationships. It can also involve building in diversion monitoring to key programmatic activities – both in terms of risk indicators and red flags.

Obligations management

Keeping track of the extensive legislative and regulatory requirements with which an INGO must comply requires a Business Obligations Register (BOR), which records each obligation and supports its management. Depending on the nature of the INGO's relationship with institutional do-nors, some INGOs may wish to incorporate donor obligations into the BOR.

A BOR can be as simple as a spreadsheet, or for large organisations dealing with extensive obligations, a Governance, Risk and Compliance (GRC) soft-ware platform may be required. There are four key benefits to using a BOR:

- It provides a single 'source of truth';
- It can promote harmonisation, allowing the use of a single control to meet multiple obligations;
- It keeps a record of the rational for a particular control, informing any process reengineering or change management;
- It supports regulatory risk management.

Using a BOR

There are three key stages in the effective use of a BOR: Developing the BOR, mapping the obligations, and updating the BOR.

Developing the BOR

There are four steps to developing a BOR:

- Ensure that the correct capabilities are in place, such as legal advice or access to expert peak bodies;
- Identify applicable legislation, regulation, and other relevant obligations, recognising the breadth of jurisdictions in which obligations might exist (see Chapter 3);
- Review and extract each specific obligation. Key information for inclusion in the BOR might include a reference number, functional category (such as

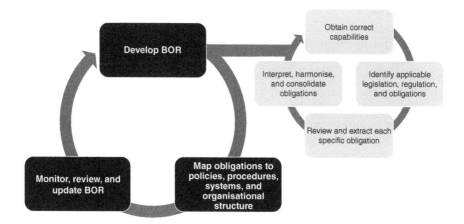

Figure 7.1 The Business Obligations Register process.

'sanctions'), the verbatim obligation, additional interpretation guidance, affected jurisdictions, legislative reference, issuer, and date of issue;

• Interpret and harmonise the obligations, determining what it means and what is required – consolidating similar obligations.

Mapping the obligations

Having built the BOR, map each obligation to the INGO's policies, procedures and systems, and the organisational structure. A gap analysis exercise can help to identify where existing ordnances are capable of meeting the obligation, and where new policies, procedures, or systems might be required. Controls may be needed at enterprise, functional and business unit, or process level.

Monitoring, reviewing, and updating the BOR

Legislation and regulation are best seen in the context of continual change. Maintaining visibility of this evolution can be very challenging for in-house functions, and may require the INGO to engage commercial compliance services that provide automated alerts, or external legal counsel that can manage the process on the INGO's behalf. Every change requires the cycle to begin again, as existing controls may require modification, become redundant, or even become unlawful.

Situational awareness

While many in the sector will recognise the need for situational awareness in conflict zones, fragile states, and rapid-onset emergencies, the reality is that it is required in any scenario in which diversion represents anything more than a negligible risk.

Building on the definition of Clarke and Mitchell (2015), situational awareness for us might entail ensuring that an INGO has the 'right level of knowledge to contextualise new data and information in order to make rational decisions, and take appropriate actions.' In practical terms, it is the stance that enables the collection and processing of information to inform both dynamic and documented risk assessment, the procedures used to steward people and resources, and project and programme decisions in real time.

Dynamism in risk assessment is increasingly expected by regulators, not least as it enables organisations to revise procedures or engage stakeholders in sufficient time to manage an evolving situation. Close engagement between risk and compliance, programme, and security staff is crucial. The information used, whether qualitative or quantitative, should be observable and collectable, relevant, reliable, and stable – observable actions, conditions, facts, or events whose simultaneous occurrence would suggest that a phenomenon is present or very likely to occur (Heuer and Pherson, 2011).

Sources of such data might include:

- Local consortia;
- Security reports;
- Security consultancies;
- Local knowledge and experience;
- Peak bodies;
- Trusted-source government information services.

The breadth of diversion risks, and the wide arrange of drivers and enablers affecting them, mean that such information should not be limited to physical security matters such as the presence of armed groups or attacks on aid actors. Anticipating fundamental changes to the local context requires awareness of:

- Priorities and political agendas of key actors, including governments, other political operators, and diversionaries themselves;
- Movements of armed actors;
- Historic actions taken by key actors and the relationships between them;
- The context of the wider local milieu.

References

Beaumont-Thomas, B. 2017. How we made the typeface Comic Sans. *The Guardian*.

Clarke, R.M. and Mitchell, W. 2015. *Target-Centric Network Modelling: Case studies in analyzing complex intelligence issues*. Thousand Oaks, CA: CQ Press. http://dx.doi.org/10.4135/9781483395807.

The Economist 2017. Defrauding the do gooders. *The Economist*.

Gibson, R., Tanner, C., and Wagner, A.F. 2016. Protected values and economic decision-making. In Brosch, T. and Sander, D. (eds), *Handbook of value: Perspectives from economics, neuroscience, philosophy, psychology and sociology*. New York, NY: Oxford University Press, 223–241.

Heuer, R.J. and Pherson, R.H. 2011. *Structured analytic techniques for intelligence analysis*. Thousand Oaks, CA: CQ Press.

Maranz, D. 2001. *African friends and money matters: Observations from Africa*. Publications in Ethnography, Vol. 37. Dallas, TX: SIL.

May, O. 2016. *Fighting fraud and corruption in the humanitarian and global development sector*. Abingdon: Routledge. https://doi.org/10.4324/9781315558301.

Pantuliano, S., Mackintosh, K., Elhawary, S., and Metcalfe, V. 2011. *Counter-terrorism and humanitarian action: Tensions, impact and ways forward*. HPG Policy Brief 43. London: Overseas Development Institute.

8   Due diligence

Paul Curwell

This chapter introduces due diligence concepts and explores what due diligence might look like for INGOs in relation to diversion. It encompasses partners, vendors, and staff in relation to questions of their identity and their background or character, enabling a risk and values-based judgement on whether further association is in the INGO's interests.

According to the Nordic Investment Bank, 'integrity due diligence' involves "gathering specific information and identifying risks in connection with the reputation and integrity of counterparties" (2018). This chapter adapts the principles of 'integrity due diligence' to managing the risk of diversion. Anti-diversion due diligence, then, is the practice of gathering information to inform risk-based decisions on the engagement of other parties. This task can be conducted in isolation from financial, legal, and operational due diligence.

The importance of this has increased with global anti-corruption and sanctions legislation, and greater awareness of reputational risk, with better practice being typically defined by MDBs, the OECD, World Economic Forum, and the AML/CTF community (OECD, 2009, 2014; Uniform Framework, 2006; Votava et al., 2018).

'Check-box' due diligence, performed after a decision has already been made, is the cause of many poor business outcomes (Yong, 2013; Loughman and Sibery, 2012). Thorough due diligence adds value to decision making by challenging inherent human biases and providing a mechanism to test hypotheses and assumptions, particularly around risks and benefits, in a structured manner. One example might be where risks associated with an activity are initially considered high and above risk appetite, but due diligence demonstrates the risk is actually lower and within appetite, creating opportunity.

In all types of due diligence, finding an issue or risk indicator does not necessarily mean an INGO cannot proceed. Rather, it means the INGO needs a plan to mitigate the risk within its appetite. These processes must be consistently applied across an INGO, and this chapter outlines three key models:

- Know Your Partner (KYP);
- Know Your Vendor (KYV);
- Know Your Staff (KYS).

Due diligence fundamentals

Due diligence is a tool to inform decision making, evidence the exercise of 'reasonable care and skill' in terms of a decision maker's fiduciary obligations, and to provide a basis for legal defence if required (CCEW, 2016; Lajoux and Elson, 2011). It starts with understanding the risks and issues in question, before converting these questions into a scope.

Scoping

Scoping typically determines what is reasonable, proportionate, and possible under the circumstances. It is a function of legal considerations, risk appetite, and the risks themselves. The scope should clearly articulate the questions to be answered, and the high-level information required to answer those questions (OECD, 2009). In respect of diversion, the model risks in Chapter 4 can help to inform the scope.

It is important to take a broad, collaborative approach to scoping. Legal teams can advise on how regulators could challenge scope, rationale, approach, findings, and actions taken in response to an incident, while locally engaged staff can advise on contextual matters that will affect the activity.

Developing a research plan

Once the scope is approved, it can be converted into a research plan which divides it into discrete tasks. This involves looking for risk indicators of potentially unlawful or high-risk activity (Loughman and Sibery, 2012). The ability to properly identify them requires an understanding of what to look for – which is not always obvious and may require experience.

Conceiving risk indicators

Prior to commencing the diligence, it is worthwhile to compile a list of risk indicators. Sources may include:

- Training courses;
- Research;
- Case histories;
- Interviews;
- Collaborative discussions with local contextual experts;
- Other INGOs working in similar spaces;
- Media reports.

One current challenge is that it is not easy to obtain reliable 'off the shelf' software tools to automate identification of these risk indicators.

Undertaking due diligence

Policies and guidelines associated with an INGO's due diligence practices should be thoroughly documented, including when and how diligence should be performed, review and escalation processes, and internal diligence committee mechanisms (OECD, 2009). Typical due diligence exercises involve following leads to verify information against multiple sources and consolidate these results into a single viewpoint, to inform risk assessments and management decisions.

The way in which an INGO's due diligence procedure works should be informed by proportionality, and its sophistication by volume and complexity. For example, smaller organisations with lower case volumes may be able to use a spreadsheet as a case management system whilst large organisations typically utilise a system or database.

Specialised systems are particularly useful where 'continuous evaluation' (see Know Your Partner) is undertaken as they can streamline management and oversight. Irrespective of the outcome, due diligence requires those performing it to document the following for each case:

- The reason for the diligence;
- The steps taken to validate any identified red flag and substantiate the results (where possible);
- The rationale for any conclusions and subsequent action taken.

Tools such as peer review are useful but often overlooked, and can help ensure adherence to common standards. Where red flags are identified through the diligence process, follow-up inquiries should be performed to attempt to validate their accuracy. Quality assurance processes should be overseen by appropriate risk committees.

Due diligence and opacity

The nature of due diligence is such that it is not always possible to substantiate a finding, especially if the other party is unwilling or unable to provide the required information, raising the question of when to cease the research. Prescribed rules are uncommon in due diligence, so a guiding principle can be to stop when there is enough information for the risk owner to make a risk acceptance decision.

Organisational approaches to managing incomplete or unsubstantiated information in a due diligence report is typically dependent on materiality, risk appetite, available time, and budget. There is nothing wrong with presenting preliminary findings, suggested next steps, and associated cost estimates for guidance from a risk owner, lawyer, or diligence committee before amending the scope.

In some cases, organisations may accept the risk posed by incomplete or unsubstantiated information and monitor the relationship a closely or impose 'approval conditions' (see Know Your Partner), whilst in more serious cases they may terminate the relationship, exercise mandatory reporting obligations, or undertake further inquiries. In the case of partners and donors, the extent of diligence performed (and associated costs) often varies by case, whilst staff due diligence is more standardised.

Information sources

The research plan should identify what information is required to address the scope and where it might be obtained. Sources are typically selected based on relevance, accuracy, availability, and reliability.

Information sources can be internal or external to the INGO or its partners with external sources including:

- Public records;
- Non-public records (potentially accessible through legal authority);
- Commercial databases (e.g. credit ratings, Watch Lists);
- Internet and social media searches;
- Human sources.

The nature of external sources, including commercial Politically-Exposed Person (PEP) and sanctions databases, means buyers typically have limited visibility into their accuracy, reliability, and versioning. Good practice requires considering a source's provenance, biases, and accuracy prior to relying on it (Van der Does de Willebois et al., 2011; Nam et al., 2017).

Watch Lists

Watch Lists promulgated by bodies like the UN, regulators, and law enforcement agencies are key sources and contain names of individuals and entities potentially involved in unlawful activity. PEP Lists contain names of public officials and their families potentially at greater risk of exposure to corruption by virtue of their position (Greenberg et al., 2009).

Most government Watch Lists are freely available online although aggregated Watch Lists can be purchased from information brokers who maintain currency of the information, which is onerous given the update frequency and absence of a common global data model (Joint Money Laundering Steering Group, 2017).

Processes to manage Watch Lists should be documented and periodically reviewed, including deciding which Watch Lists to screen against for initial due diligence. Watch List selection is typically based on criteria including (The Wolfsberg Group, 2019):

- Applicable jurisdictions – the INGO's registered office, countries of operation, and potentially origin and transit countries for aid shipments;
- Applicable regulators;

- Nature of business activity. MDBs and the US government publish lists of allegedly fraudulent suppliers which are examples of potentially useful industry databases;
- Values. Every INGO will need to make a risk-based judgement on whether to use a particular country's Watch Lists, and the extent to which it considers these to be accurate and respectful human rights.

Due diligence in LMICs

There are parts of the world where public records are unavailable, inaccurate, or unreliable. (Van der Does de Willebois et al., 2011). For example, in countries with high rates of corruption, it is not uncommon for people to pay to have public records falsified (Bureau van Dijk, 2013).

This is challenging, but options might include:

- Seeking guidance from local staff or third parties (such as lawyers) on potential avenues of research;
- Seeking information from, or lawfully sharing information with, other INGOs and partners;
- Seeking information directly from the subject, such as requiring documentation, on-site inspections, and interviews;
- Engaging local due diligence service providers, though INGOs should be alert to the risks that information is obtained illegally (Gracie, 2015) or that such research may lead to accusations of spying.

Due diligence and diversion risks

Due diligence is not just carried out for diversion risk, but in accordance with the risk-based approach, all anti-diversion due diligence activities should be linked to specific, identified risks. Without this, due diligence can rapidly become bureaucratic, and leave actual risks uncontrolled.

Know Your Partner

There is no globally-accepted standard of anti-diversion due diligence for INGOs. The model KYP due diligence process at Figure 8.1 is based on better practices typically employed for working with various types of partners across a range of industries. It uses partner due diligence questionnaires as the foundation. These provide an opportunity to collect a comprehensive range of public and non-public information from the partner including:

- Contact points;
- Legal entity details and details of key persons;
- Copies of incorporation documents, trust deeds, charters etc, as well as other relevant public record filings;

- Financial Statements and financial viability;
- Details of litigation, adverse publicity, or regulatory incidents;
- Bank, personal, and industry references;
- Details of related parties and business affiliations;
- Description of the partner and its activities;
- Details of suppliers, sub-contractors, or its own partners ('fourth parties');
- Details of relevant risk and compliance frameworks, policies, procedures, and controls.

KYP inquiries can be incorporated into the application, assessment, and selection stages of the partner engagement cycle. In addition to the questionnaires, INGOs may also wish to use:

- Interviews with key staff at the partner;
- Reviews or inspections of premises, operations, and documentation;
- Recent references from other partners and donors.

Initial assessment and scoping

Initial enquiries, and the INGO's assessment of its operating contexts, might lead the KYP process to begin with a preliminary risk rating. This can inform what type of questionnaire is issued; proportionality may demand that low-risk partners provide a lower quantity of material to high-risk partners. They should be issued to a person at the partner with sufficient knowledge and delegated authority to make legal representations on behalf of the prospective partner (i.e. an 'Authorised Officer') (World Economic Forum, 2013; Loughman and Sibery, 2012).

The questionnaire also provides an opportunity to obtain warranties, attestations, and certifications from the partner to help evaluate their risk rating. Other supporting evidence, such as letters of good standing or bank references, can also be requested. Upon receipt, the INGO should review the response for evidence requiring any change in risk rating. This is important as it informs the extent of due diligence appropriate to the case.

The KYP research plan

A proportionate, risk-based approach will result in the preliminary risk rating for a partner determining the intensity of due diligence. KYP checks can grouped into 'levels' corresponding to the scale of the perceived risk. Table 8.1 outlines suggested checks for each risk rating and its corresponding level of due diligence.

The checks should be modified as required to suit specific circumstances, and the rationale for such decisions documented. Where reliable 'primary' sources, such as verified government documents, are unavailable common practice is to try and obtain the same information from three separate parties ('triangulation') to help confirm accuracy and reliability.

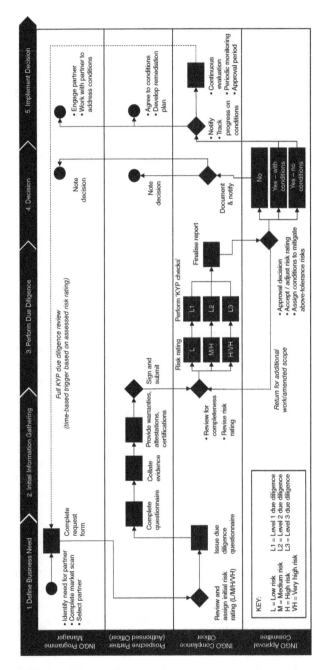

Figure 8.1 Model KYP due diligence process.

Table 8.1 Illustrative partner due diligence checks by risk rating and level

Risk rating	Due diligence level	Suggested partner due diligence checks related to diversion risk
Low	L1	• Confirmation of Legal Entity registration • Obtain names and biographical details of the partner (e.g. directors, trustees) and key management positions • Perform individual Proof of Identity Verification
Medium – High	L2	Level 1 plus: • Watch List screening of entities and individual names • Review any governing documents or charters • Understanding of the partner's integrity, competence, reputation, and track record • Adverse media searches • Company records and director searches • Identification of undisclosed business interests which could create a conflict of interest • Regulatory enforcement searches; • Other checks as appropriate based on applicable jurisdiction or any specific diversion risks
High – Very High	L3	Level 2 searches, plus: • In-country site inspections or audits of the partner's premises and operations • Inspection of partner's books and records • Evaluation and sample testing of partner's internal controls • By exception, use of specialist service providers to perform other inquiries to corroborate facts and events

Beneficial Ownership – identifying individuals behind a legal entity

Beneficial Ownership is a core concept in both sanctions and AML/CTF and involves 'lifting the corporate veil' to determine who runs a legal entity. A Beneficial Owner can be defined as "the legal person (individual) who owns (directly or indirectly) or controls a legal entity" (FATF, 2014). Legal definitions, which are generally expressed as a 'shareholding' percentage, vary by jurisdiction. Determining Beneficial Ownership gets complicated where legal entities are owned by other legal entities across jurisdictions ('chains of ownership') and where trusts, foundations, and partnerships are involved (FATF, 2014).

Closely linked to the concept of Beneficial Ownership is the concept of 'control,' which applies where there is no clear owner, or where ownership is intentionally concealed. Ultimately, one objective of KYP should be to identify the individual(s) behind the partner's legal entity. Once identified, these individual(s) should be incorporated into the research plan.

The KYP report

Once the checks have been completed, the case file should be reviewed to identify risk indicators, and a report prepared. A factual report that links the findings to applicable risks can simplify deliberations in respect of materiality, final risk ratings, and management plans. Assumptions, judgements, or assessments should be clearly distinguished from facts, with information that cannot be corroborated being clearly caveated.

Review, affirmation, and approval

Once the report is finalised, the assigned risk rating is affirmed and the entity formally approved as a 'partner.' This final step involves the approval by an accountable manager or committee with the correct authority. In considering the report, approvers may adjust the partner's risk rating based on the findings. Typically, organisations approve partners or suppliers for a given 'approval period', such as 1 to 3 years, based on the assigned risk rating and the nature of activity being undertaken.

Incomplete information

An effective Know Your Partner (KYP) process is dependent upon information being available to facilitate the diligence. Where information is unavailable or incomplete, INGOs must make a risk-based decision on engagement. Two factors to consider might be whether the information gaps are material to making any decision, and whether the situation might expose the INGO to diversion risk. A partner may be approved, but in the circumstances rated 'high risk.'

Approval conditions

In any due diligence it is rare to find a counterparty which meets the often-comprehensive partner criteria set by the engaging party. As terminating a relationship is not always necessary or practical, 'approval conditions' are increasingly being used, such as a capacity-building plan that enables the partner to uplift its capabilities.

Continuous evaluation and periodic monitoring

Once approved, risk-based due diligence does not end. Depending on the risk rating and the circumstances, low-risk partners might receive a periodic desktop review throughout their approval period, whilst high-risk partners may be more closely monitored through field visits, audits, and inspections, and hold a shorter approval period.

Continuous evaluation

Continuous evaluation is a term increasingly used to reflect the use of 'near real-time' monitoring tools in business processes to identify and evaluate the risks posed by a partner on a frequent basis. The feasibility of continuous evaluation is accelerating in the light of recent technological developments, and an increased emphasis on such functionality by software vendors.

Examples of continuous evaluation tools relevant to INGOs include:

- Use of automated alerts on a partner's name (search keyword) in media, social media, and PEP and sanctions Watch List systems;
- Customised dashboards which track a partner's warehouse and distribution metrics to identify potential diversion using tools such as Tableau or Microsoft's PowerBI using real-time data feeds;
- Automated alert flags for director or ownership changes, creditor watch, or other records relating to conflicts of interest and commercial viability.

Periodic monitoring

Period monitoring is used where it is not feasible to undertake continuous evaluation, with one example being data that change infrequently (e.g. annually). Used here, periodic monitoring refers to the Level 3 activities including inspections or audits of a partner's facilities or books and records, evaluation and sample testing of partner's internal controls, and updates to in-country background checks. Depending on the partner and the risk involved, periodic monitoring could be performed in conjunction with continuous evaluation, or in isolation.

The purpose of both continuous evaluation and periodic monitoring is to provide early warning of risk indicators, or potential issues throughout the life of any relationship, enabling timely response and remediation. New risk indicators arising during the approval period should be validated for accuracy. Validated indicators may trigger a due diligence review, as well as internal escalation.

KYP in exceptional circumstances

In circumstances like rapid-onset humanitarian emergencies, partners may need to be onboarded rapidly, at short notice. Such scenarios reduce the scope for anti-diversion due diligence, despite the often higher inherent risks. Options include:

- Pre-determined, risk-based 'minimum standards,' using basic due diligence checks most likely to affect most diversionary risks, together with clearly assigned conditions in which the minimum standards are to be used and when they are to be ceased in favour of standard operating procedures;

- The use of a bank of preferred suppliers and partners known to the INGO, and which have already been through a standard KYP process;
- Dynamic KYP, where the partner is approved on the basis of minimum standards, but with the approval condition that the INGO will continue the standard due diligence checks while programming is underway.

Know Your Vendor

Vendors and suppliers are a category of third party which can also include local agents and government facing representatives acting on the INGO's behalf. As with partners, vendors should be subject to appropriate due diligence checks, including the identification of any known or possible links to diversionaries. The diligence principles previously outlined in this chapter, including for KYP, also apply to vendors. Whilst they are similar in many ways, in the aid sector vendors may not receive as much scrutiny from a diligence perspective as partners, despite posing similar risks.

The purpose of any 'Know Your Vendor' checks should be to identify, to the extent possible, the likelihood of these scenarios occurring before any supplier agreement is signed. In determining what diligence checks are appropriate, INGOs may wish to consider:

- What role/function is the vendor performing? Is it a small, one-time task or will the task be performed over an extended period of time?
- Is the vendor owned or controlled by PEPs sympathetic to a diversionary agenda or are they proscribed individuals?
- Where is the vendor performing the work?
- How mature is the vendor's general governance, risk, and internal control environment (including its own KYE programme)?
- How much oversight may the INGO or other independent parties (e.g. auditors) have of the vendor?
- How long has the vendor been established? Do they have a good track record and the capacity to deliver the required goods or services? Have they been set up overnight in response to a market opportunity?
- What diversion risks from Chapter 4 are applicable for the vendor and need to be considered?

Answers to these questions are likely to be derived from a combination of investigative research (e.g. public records, media searches), Watch List checks, verification of identity for both legal entities and key employees (e.g. beneficial owners, controllers, senior management), and local background or character enquiries, amongst others depending on the vendor's risk profile and materiality. As with KYP, KYV should be proportionate to the vendor's inherent risk. These considerations may help inform choices around the scope of any diligence performed on a vendor.

Making cash payments to vendors

In many parts of the world, cash payments remain the norm. The risk of course, is that cash can be stolen, unintentionally given to an imposter purporting to be the vendor's legitimate recipient (who subsequently diverts it), or given to a vendor's employee who is linked to a diversionary.

Some of these scenarios are addressed through better practice financial controls; however, for higher risk suppliers or high-risk scenarios, INGOs should consider the following before any contracts are signed:

- Performing due diligence on the vendor's employee who will receive the cash payments to minimise the chance of the INGO physically handing cash to a known diversionary;
- Procedures to limit the number of a vendor's employees to whom the INGO is prepared to physically hand cash to a small number of people who have been appropriately screened, and ensuring appropriate receipts for any cash exchange;
- Before any cash is exchanged, reviewing the cash handling procedures for the vendor to minimise the risk of diversion between payment by the INGO and any bank deposit. In the event cash is diverted in the future, such diligence helps evidence the INGO has given the risk due consideration.

In the above situation, the minimum due diligence checks which an INGO might consider undertaking should include identification and verification (of that identity) for the respective individuals and legal entities; Watch List and adverse media searches for name matches; and in LMICs or areas of diversionary activity, local character enquiries into the parties concerned.

When to stop and the availability of information

Previously in this chapter we discussed the principle of stopping due diligence when you have sufficient information for the risk owner to make a decision, and also that there will be situations where the INGO may never be able to fill information gaps to a satisfactory degree within the timeframe available. This advice also stands for suppliers.

There are four basic choices for INGOs in this scenario, which is most likely to arise in LMICs:

A   Use a local vendor that can be appropriately screened;
B   Do the work of a local vendor yourself;
C   Use a supplier from another area which can be appropriately screened;
D   Use a local supplier that cannot be appropriately screened and accept the risk.

Options A–C are likely to be the most preferable to option D in many cases. However, where an INGO needs to contemplate option D, this decision should be informed by any insights that can be gained into levels of diversionary activity or sympathy in and around the area concerned. This information might be obtained from other INGOs, through conversations with local and foreign government representatives and embassies, reviews of media reporting, and even sources such as think tanks or other research bodies. Where there are indications that diversionaries are operating in the area, INGOs may consider option D unacceptable and seek alternative options until the local environment changes.

Know Your Staff

The importance of KYS has been seen in the wake of public cases in which candidates have falsified qualifications, misrepresented their experience, possessed known criminal affiliations, or have a track record of exploiting or abusing vulnerable people.

For diversion, KYS is about minimising the risks in Chapter 4 that relate to our people, whether they are trustees, directors, managers, employees, or volunteers.

KYS typically involves:

- Identity verification;
- Obtaining information from the candidate as well as public records;
- Obtaining references;
- Verifying that information is correct and complete.

Candidates typically provide written consent for these inquiries, and where adverse information is identified, candidates are often given opportunity to comment or challenge such findings (Standards Australia, 2006; Information Commissioner's Office, nd).

The design of the KYS programme should be risk-based and reflect an assessment of the role. High-risk roles should see a greater level of due diligence, but even more routine roles should still be considered for their risk footprint. For example:

- Do they provide a high degree of access to IT systems?
- Do they have financial or physical access privileges, such as unrestricted warehouse access?
- Is it a position of authority?

The KYS process

KYS should be carried out not only on application or entry, but also promotions and lateral moves. Many KYS checks can be incorporated into the recruitment process. A matrix for the checks that will be carried out for standard roles, and for high-risk roles, can ensure consistency and that the checks are risk-based.

KYS should be completed prior to the issuing of an employment contract. Common risk indicators include lying, omitting material information, or

Table 8.2 Illustrative KYS checks for medium–high risk roles

Domain	Illustrative checks
Identification and verification	• Name, date of birth, and biographical details • Current and previous residential addresses • Nationality • Verify the candidate's identity against a reliable source
Professional qualifications and work history	• Education certificates, transcripts • Document and verify employment history • Validate occupational licences
Business interests	• Identification of conflicts of interest
Civil and criminal history	• Civil litigation history • Police check • Working with vulnerable people accreditation (e.g. children, elderly)
Reputation and integrity	• Adverse media and internet searches • Government and commercial Watch Lists • Regulatory penalties/disqualifications
Financial history	• Bankruptcy status • Credit rating/credit history

positive name matches with known diversionaries. Material risk indicators should trigger an adjudication process prior to any hiring decision.

References

ASIS International 2006. *Preemployment background screening guideline, ASIS GDL PBS 09 2006.* Alexandria, VA: ASIS International.

AUSTRAC 2019. Determine whether a customer or beneficial owner is a PEP. In Part B of an AML/CTF program (customer due diligence procedures). http://www.austrac.gov.au/part-b-amlctf-program-customer-due-diligence-procedures.

Australian Prudential Regulatory Authority (APRA) 2008. *APG 520 – Fit and proper, Prudential practice guide.* Canberra: Commonwealth of Australia.

AUSTRAC 2018. *Politically Exposed Persons (PEPs).* http://www.austrac.gov.au/key-terms-used-amlctf-rules-definition-peps (accessed 13 December 2019).

Bureau van Dijk (2013). *Lack of due diligence in emerging markets putting firms at risk of fraud.* Salford, UK: Bureau van Dijk.

Charity Commission of England and Wales (CCEW) 2016. *Chapter 2: Due diligence, monitoring and verifying the end use of charitable funds. Compliance Toolkit: Protecting charities from harm.* London: CCEW.

FATF 2014. *Transparency and beneficial ownership.* Paris: FATF.

Gracie, C. 2015. Investigator Peter Humphrey warns over GSK China ordeal. *BBC News.*

Greenberg, T.S., Gray, L., Schantz, D., Latham, M., and Gardner, C. 2009. *Politically Exposed Persons: A policy paper on strengthening preventive measures.* Washington, DC: The World Bank Group.

Information Commissioner's Office nd. *Right to object in guide to the General Data Protection Regulation.* https://ico.org.uk/for-organisations/guide-to-data-protection/guide-to-the-general-data-protection-regulation-gdpr/individual-rights/right-to-object/ (accessed 13 December 2019).

Joint Money Laundering Steering Group 2017. *Prevention of money laundering/combating terrorist financing: Guidance for the UK financial sector, Part I.* London: Joint Money Laundering Steering Group.

Lajoux, A.R. and Elson, C.M. 2011. *The art of M&A due diligence: Navigating critical steps and uncovering crucial data.* New York, NY: McGraw-Hill.

Loughman, B. and Sibery, R.A. 2012. *Bribery and corruption: Navigating the global risks.* Hoboken, NJ: Wiley Corporate F&A. doi: 10.1002/9781118386620.

Nam, H., No, W.G., and Lee, Y. 2017. Are commercial financial databases reliable? New evidence from Korea. *Sustainability 9*: 1406.

Nordic Investment Bank 2018. *Integrity due diligence policy.* https://www.nib.int/filebank/a/1523013238/5cf49b75504cd5f09482784aa3dba954/7704-Integrity_due_diligence_policy.pdf (accessed 12 December 2019).

Organisation for Economic Co-operation and Development (OECD) 2009. *Good practice guidance on internal controls, ethics and compliance.* https://www.oecd.org/daf/anti-bribery/44884389.pdf (accessed 12 December 2019).

OECD 2014. *Responsible business conduct matters, OECD guidelines for multinational enterprises.* Paris: OECD.

Standards Australia 2006. *AS4811–2006: Employment screening.* Sydney: Standards Australia.

The Wolfsberg Group 2019. Wolfsberg guidance on sanctions screening. The Wolfsberg Group. https://www.wolfsberg-principles.com/sites/default/files/wb/pdfs/Wolfsberg%20Guidance%20on%20Sanctions%20Screening.pdf (accessed 30 April 2020).

Uniform Framework for Preventing and Combating Fraud and Corruption 2006. Signatories include the African Development Bank, Asian Development Bank, European Bank for Reconstruction & Development, European Investment Bank, Inter-American Development Group, Nordic Investment Bank, International Monetary Fund and the World Bank.

Van der Does de Willebois, E., Halter, E.M., Harrison, R.A., and Park, J.W. 2011. *The puppet masters: How the corrupt use legal structures to hide stolen assets and what to do about it.* Washington, DC: The World Bank Group.

Votava, C.L., Hauch, J.M., and Clementucci, F. 2018. *Licence to drill: A manual on integrity due diligence for licensing in extractive sectors.* Washington, DC: World Bank Group.

World Economic Forum 2013. *Good practice guidelines on conducting third-party due diligence.* Geneva: World Economic Forum.

Yong, K.P. 2013. *Due diligence in China: Beyond the checklists.* Singapore: Wiley Corporate F&A.

9 Detection and response

Oliver May

We cannot always deter and prevent diversion, despite the assumption that we can lurking beneath the incendiary media articles that accompany diversion scandals. It is no surprise that often-misinformed public reactions to such incidents are alarming and destabilising events for INGOs. Even so, where a responsible INGO is unable to deter or prevent an incident, then it must try to detect it so that it can manage – and ideally minimise – the risks associated with it.

Handling such matters from inception to closure is complex and risky, and demands a structured and methodical approach, integrated with wider incident management. After exploring the value of detecting diversion and the use of detection planning to overcome obstacles, this chapter sets out the detection and incident response components of the ADP.

Detection

There are a plenty of reasons to invest in good detection systems. Early detection, for example, correlates with lower overall losses in fraud incidents (ACFE, 2018), and in some cases INGOs may even be obliged to have such systems.

A key benefit is that detection informs good risk assessment and control planning. When a risk is complicated – even invisible, in some respects – incidents become a particularly important contributor to the INGO's picture of its threats and vulnerabilities. But a second benefit is important too – and this is that it can help an INGO to get out in front of a public engagement disaster.

In early 2019, 22-year-old job applicant Olivia Bland e-mailed a tech company in northern England to turn down the role they had offered. She posted the e-mail on Twitter, and in it accused the company's CEO of abusive behaviour during her interview (Bland, 2019). In less than a week the tweet had tens of thousands of 'likes' and retweets, had been covered by media outlets like *The Times* and the BBC, and social media creaked under the weight of angry messages directed at the beleaguered company and its CEO.

Bland is far from the only person to use social media to raise a complaint. MSF, hospitals, Uber, Telstra, and others have all been the subjects of alarming blog posts by angry employees and ex-employees. Public allegations like this can be made in an instant, by anyone, travel far and fast and carry the power to shame organisations into oblivion. Meanwhile, many news outlets offer their own confidential means through which to make allegations.

If INGOs do not proactively detect an issue before it can become the subject of a public complaint, or make the means to report concerns available to stakeholders, or fail to create systems in which those stakeholders can have trust and confidence, then there are plenty of other places a worried person can go. It is important, then, to ensure that detection systems exist, are easy to use, and that the response framework is credible.

Such a detection framework comprises two parts:

- Proactive detection, incorporating proactive review, independent transaction testing, and electronic review;
- Reactive detection, incorporating overt reporting, confidential reporting, and information-sharing agreements.

The challenge of detection

In one scheme of which I am aware, an INGO's local and partner staff al-legedly colluded to make regular access payments to a diversionary, and used a local print shop to create documents that masked the transactions. The scheme rather fell apart when the local INGO staff came to account for the money – and named the diversionary in the INGO's accounting records!

Sadly, most diversion is not this easy to detect, and the sector under-detects fraud and corruption in general. There are a number of possible causes for this: Loud 'background noise' that obfuscates the signs, limited use of electronic data analytics, disincentives for staff and third parties to make an overt or confidential report, and the tendency of INGOs to operate at stretch – thus reducing both detective resources and opportunities (May, 2016).

These factors all play a role in relation to the under-detection of diversion, but there are other reasons that may be at play, too:

- The ambiguous circumstances in which red flags arise can enable alternative explanations to diversion that are never fully tested;
- In humanitarian operations or remote programme management, an INGO's overall visibility of funds downstream can be comparatively low;
- Low awareness of the tell-tale signs of diversion;
- Low accountability of business units for low or no detection, including at its extreme, a form of 'ask no questions, tell no lies';
- System failures, such as the absence of a beneficiary feedback mechanism, or the handling of beneficiary feedback containing diversion allegations by the wrong team, or the failure to connect a beneficiary feedback mechanism with the system for handling such allegations;

- Failing to take beneficiary allegations as seriously as those raised by staff, partners, or donors;
- Ingroup–outgroup behaviour, in which an overseas NGO or donor to whom a report should be made is seen as the outgroup, and local actors as the ingroup.

Improving detection in these circumstances can be difficult, but the various dimensions of an ADP can help significantly. Particularly important is careful, risk-based detection planning.

Risk-based detection planning

Red flags, and where best to look for them, vary between diversion risks. The indicators that staff are paying fees at checkpoints are very different to those of vendor fraud, for example – which is why taking a risk-based approach is crucial.

This approach can help senior managers to have confidence that all reasonable steps are being taken to detect diversion. It involves three simple steps:

- Consider the diversion risks facing the organisation, programme, or project;
- Ensure that sufficient means of proactive and reactive detection are in place;
- Direct proactive activities, and orient reactive systems, towards these risks.

An array of available proactive and reactive detection means is described below, while the risks facing an organisation, programme, or project will derive from risk assessment. Our model risks are a starting point. The red flags for each, the functions in which they might arise, and the likelihoods that they might do so vary – so this step involves imagining *where* diversion red flags might arise and *what* they might look like. Generally, higher risk areas include procurement, payroll, personal expenses, and programme transactions (like distributions).

Having established detection mechanisms, and determined what they should be detecting and where, the final step is to calibrate them to do so. For example:

- Where electronic analytics of structured and unstructured data can be deployed, incorporate diversion risk red flags into the rules being applied;
- Issue managers in high-risk programmes or functions with guidance on red flags relevant to the specific risks carried by those programmes or functions – to reflect upon when designing programmes or authorising procurement operations or transactions;
- Focus staff training on the risks present in any given programme and explore the point at which they are expected to make a report;

- Promote the confidential reporting system in the highest-risk programmes through focussed internal communication campaigns. Share anonymised 'success stories' to elevate confidence in the system;
- Introduce a schedule of diversion risk meetings with partners, other consortia members, or key strategic suppliers to ensure that they understand their contractual obligation to report concerns to your INGO and give them a space to do so.

Red flags

Detecting diversion is an arms race. The other side constantly looks for a vulnerability in our processes, systems, or operations to exploit, while with equal urgency we shore up our work. One way in which we do so is to consider the 'red flag,' an item of information that could indicate the presence of diversion. It is possible that it may have a rational and innocent explanation, but it is important that diversion is considered as a possibility.

Jim Ratley, former president of the Association of Certified Fraud Examiners (ACFE), identifies four broad categories of red flags (2012). These are operational anomalies (which we might think of as programme anomalies), accounting anomalies, internal control weaknesses, and behavioural anomalies.

Programme anomalies are unusual events, relationships, and approaches in the life of an INGO or a particular country programme – perhaps transactions with unexpected people or companies, or odd trends. Accounting anomalies are more specific – deviations from standard financial and logistical practices. Internal control weaknesses are persistent or significant failures of programme controls. These might indicate a deliberate control gap to enable diversion, or represent red flags of diversion that are wrongly being seen solely as control failures. Examples might be frequent management overrides, or repeated non-compliance with procedures.

Behavioural anomalies, meanwhile, are a very broad category of the behaviours demonstrated by individuals that may indicate the presence of diversion, or at least a heightened vulnerability to it. That might include sympathies with particular diversionary causes, for example, but equally, evidence of attitudes at variance to good diversion risk management. Some examples of different types of red flags are provided in Table 9.1.

When reflecting on red flags, it can help to consider an incident and work backwards. If one were to carry out this form of diversion, how would it be done, and what tell-tales might that leave behind? Sources of information on possible diversion risks and methodologies might include:

- Media articles about incidents;
- Conferences, seminars, and symposia;
- Previous incidents, audit reports, and MEL assessments;
- Other INGOs, donors, implementing partners, or sector actors;
- Information about similar fraud or corruption methodologies;

Table 9.1 Example red flags of diversion

	Direct transfer	Misappropriation	Fees and taxes	Value chain diversion
Programme anomalies	• Evidence of meetings with diversionaries that were not reported internally or to donors • Use of novel means to move funds • Opaque references to mysterious partners in reporting • Sudden or unexplained recruitment of individuals during project inception, particularly if documentation for the recruitment process is inadequate	• Staff describe a culture of fear and suspicion • Turnover of staff in high-risk functions like logistics or finance is very high, or very low • Inexplicably close relationships between certain staff and partners or vendors • Vague, unconvincing, or absolute assurances by programme managers that such transactions are not made, without reference to the strategies used to prevent them; • Branded items appear in local markets	• Municipal bodies transparently require registration fees for NGOs, and the party of government is subject to sanctions • Incidents reported in or by other NGOs, but not your organisation • Limited engagement and mutual advocacy with other NGOs • Lack of transparency between local offices and regional or HQ functions on spending, particularly petty cash and incidental expenses	• Allegations on local language social media • Programme procures locally in a closed market • Key words and phrases are used in communications which are often associated with diversion • The experience of other agencies working concurrently with the INGO in the same context
Accounting anomalies	• Entities in Human Resources (HR) or Accounts Payable (AP) files appear on sanctions lists, or in media as	• Anomalies in records of distributions, such as poor fingerprinting on receipts • Incomplete, inadequate, or non-existent records of delivery	• Vague costs like 'logistics' and 'security', particularly in the absence of supporting documentation • Lack of receipts or justifications in petty cash	• Conflicting accounts in feedback from beneficiaries on the value and nature of distributed commodities

(Continued)

Table 9.1 Continued

Direct transfer	Misappropriation	Fees and taxes	Value chain diversion
connected to diversionaries • Unexpected unrestricted spending on restricted contracts • Vaguely-described or unsupported transactions • Supporting documents do not align with transactions	• Extreme variance in budget items between aid modalities in different country contexts, or values and frequencies of certain items seem unusual or unexpected • Anomalies in project evaluations, such as unexplained variance between planned beneficiary numbers and actuals • Bank accounts, names, or addresses appear in both HR and AP files • Reconciliation issues between sets of documents • Missing, incomplete, non-compliant, or inconsistent transaction documentation such purchase orders, goods received notes, invoices, and receipts	• Vague or unexplained items in the Miscellaneous account	• Anomalies in selection processes for third party monitors • Same third party monitor, which is not the best value option, used repeatedly • Failure to claim all costs from the donor to which the programme is entitled

(Continued)

Table 9.1 Continued

	Direct transfer	Misappropriation	Fees and taxes	Value chain diversion
		• Contradictions between project documentation from different sources, such as numbers of beneficiaries reached, beneficiary lists, numbers and locations of distributions, timelines, and persons involved		
Internal control weaknesses	• Inadequate due diligence • Errors or inconsistencies in project documentation used to track due diligence • Absence of documented partner selection criteria or process	• Absence of reconciliation between steps in supply chains (e.g. between delivery and distribution records) • Poor identity verification controls in distributions • Unexplained divergence from tender processes with vague or inadequate justification, or with rationales that only those with deep local knowledge would be able to challenge;	• Strong internal controls in all partners of a consortia except one • Detail in donor reporting in most areas except some • Absence of certain records, or the requirement for records, such as vehicle logs and travel diaries	• MEL absent or inadequate • Absence of a policy position on beneficiary taxation or local procurement in closed markets

(*Continued*)

Table 9.1 Continued

	Direct transfer	Misappropriation	Fees and taxes	Value chain diversion
		• A third party's incomplete compliance with due diligence requirements, or the presence of anomalies, gaps, or inconsistencies in its documentation or narrative, or that of its principals		• Application of inappropriately high burden of proof to suspicion reports • Evidence of attitude that INGO liability ends upon beneficiary receipt in distributions • Managers conflate the motive of overt or confidential reporters with the veracity of their information
Behavioural anomalies	• Managers resistant to audit or external review • Managers don't answer direct questions and appeal to local contextual complexity • Concerns, not necessarily voiced or documented, by other local staff around an individual • Evidence of ideological alignment or regular contact with diversionaries	• Managers evasive or circumspect about the role of local actors in programme design • Over-reliance on one partner, vendor, or donor • Logistics or programme staff protective and defensive about a particular vendor or partner • The presence of references to connections of the third party, or persons at the third party, online • The ability of a third party to gain access, or provide certain key	• Managers unwilling to engage in frank discussion of risks • Evidence of 'ends justify the means' mentality in managers • High engagement with issue in general, but low transparency about own programme • Unresponsiveness to requests from audit or compliance teams	

(Continued)

Table 9.1 Continued

Direct transfer	Misappropriation	Fees and taxes	Value chain diversion
	services, when hardly any other providers are able to do so without making payments • Failure to comply – either within reasonable timeframes or at all – with requests for documentation, evidence of transactions, and project outcomes • Directors of a partner never seeming to be present during an inspection		

- Academic studies, peak body reports, books, and online 'thought leadership'.

It is important not to imagine that a 'complete directory' of red flags could be developed, as every methodology and context is different. But learning to understand them is an important part of training managers and staff in how to manage diversion risk on a day-to-day basis.

Proactive detection

In proactive detection, we set out to spot the red flags of diversion. This is not the same as maintaining a general level of vigilance, or looking for them as we go – that is the preserve of reactive detection. Proactive detection represents making deliberate efforts to find them. There are three broad categories of activity: Proactive review, independent transaction testing, and electronic review.

Proactive review

Proactive review might be carried out by programme, business support, or audit functions. Ideally, however, it should be carried out by all these parties at different stages of the programme cycle and in different ways. In proactive review, we regularly and retrospectively examine:

- Higher-risk business processes, such as procurement, expenditure, petty cash, and partner selection;
- Accounts, such as the commonly-abused 'miscellaneous' account or other high-risk accounts – like those associated with diverse transactions in high volumes, or with low consistency between items or values, period-on-period;
- Transactions, including beneficiary distributions.

A proactive review, at a minimum, involves a desktop examination but will be of greater value if reviewers engage with the staff responsible for the process. An example might be the engagement of a third party monitor in a remote programming context. A proactive review may, for example, examine Request-for-Quotation (RfQ) or tender processes for compliance with procedures, whether any pattern of non-compliance could represent a sequence of red flags, and whether any anomalies are potentially consistent with the relevant diversion risks.

In high-risk contexts, proactively looking for potential diversion must be a matter of business-as-usual. Planned, transparent reviews may generate some deterrent effect, but the best scope for actual detection belongs to surprise or spontaneous review. Another form of regular review is to re-screen staff and third parties on a regular basis (see Chapter 8).

Independent transaction testing

In addition to proactive review by local managers, a second stage of transaction testing carried out independently can be particularly important in high-risk jurisdictions. This might involve similar activities, but be carried out by a regional or headquarters function and reconciled with local records.

Electronic review

Electronic review is the exploitation of data to identify diversion red flags, or areas of greater risk requiring further – potentially manual – review or investigation ('hotspots'). Electronic review can be used across structured data (such as databases and accounts) and unstructured data (such as e-mail or documents on corporate hard drives). Even in chiefly paper-based programmes, and fragile states and conflict zones, the reliance of operations on technology can still create opportunities to detect potential diversion.

The sector's comparable under-use of data analytics means there are plenty of opportunities. Those in structured data might include:

- Identifying red flags in AP, payroll, supply chain, and distribution data;
- Isolating unusual trends between operations and geographies;
- Monitoring unusual login times or activity on key systems, such as accounting packages, or swipe card access to buildings.

Opportunities to use it with unstructured data might include:

- Filtering e-mails for keywords or terms associated with diversionary activity;
- Filtering documents on corporate hard drives for characteristics potentially associated with fraud or corruption, such as 'invoices' in editable Microsoft Word format;
- Identifying references to sanctioned entities.

Caution must be applied in the use of electronic review. Not everything that is possible is lawful, and nothing is without risk. For example, in the case of workplace monitoring, many states have strong privacy and staff protection regimes with which any monitoring programme must comply. Further, there can be restrictions on the movement of data across borders – a significant consideration if an agency plans to review data centrally. Meanwhile, the collection and generation of insights from data – especially beneficiary data – can create its own risks of exploitation and abuse.

Reactive detection

Reviewing documents and data for the footprints of diversion can only take us so far. Humans are still the best detective tool, with 40 per cent of occupational frauds identified by overt or confidential reporting (ACFE, 2018). And so, in reactive detection, we expect our stakeholders to look out for red flags as they go about their business, implement systems they can use to report them, and we build their confidence to do so.

To harness an 'honest majority' who both look for diversion and report it, then, INGOs need to:

- Involve all stakeholders – staff, volunteers, third parties (including donor agencies, implementing partners, consortia partners, vendors and suppliers, contractors and consultants, beneficiaries, and the public) and ensure that they have the means to report;
- Provide guidance and training in what to look for;
- Invest in improving the confidence of stakeholders in reporting systems, whether overt or confidential;
- Encourage stakeholders to report – including creating a clear and non-negotiable requirement to report suspicions of diversion for staff, volunteers, and third parties;
- Ensure that the workflow for reports from all sources is robust and integrated. Beneficiary feedback mechanisms, for example, should not be completely disconnected from the main 'whistle-blowing' system;
- Monitor the performance of reactive detection systems on an ongoing basis, as problems, deviations, or failures can disproportionately damage stakeholder confidence in them and, therefore, future detection.

Reactive detection has three broad categories of activity: Overt reporting, confidential reporting, and information-sharing agreements.

Overt reporting system

The primary way that an INGO should aim to collect a report is through the management line. This heightens the chance that it will be made early, often provides more investigation opportunities, extends the INGO's ability to protect the reporter, and contributes to an anti-diversion culture.

To facilitate an overt reporting system, an INGO should:

- Create clear and contractual requirements that any staff or volunteer must report a reasonably-held suspicion of diversion;
- Develop and provide practical guidance to those who might receive such a suspicion about what they should do;
- Ensure that the means to report overtly is available to the full range of stakeholders;
- Ensure that a robust workflow follows every raised suspicion, through a diversion response plan.

Confidential reporting system

Anonymous reporting, sometimes known as 'whistleblowing,' is common. This is understandable, as many potential reporters do not fully trust organisations to protect their interests. Diversionaries, by their nature, are often many more times capable of violence than INGOs are to protect overt reporters.

A confidential reporting system provides a greater degree of information security around a reporter, scope to report if the reporter does not trust their management line, and of course the opportunity for anonymity. To help to create an effective system, considerations should include:

- Language;
- Breadth of mode of capture. Phone lines, e-mails, text messages, and even apps are now used;
- Breadth of user. The best confidential reporting systems offer a range of options to a range of parties;
- Caution with the use of physical 'suggestion box' type arrangements. These can be particularly open to abuse;
- The workflow system behind the point of capture. How will an INGO ensure that it is robust, effective, timely, and secure?
- Compliance with local law – many jurisdictions now have specific legislation relating to 'whistleblowing'.

Information-sharing agreements

Third party organisations with information about potential diversionary threats or incidents, or which would benefit from an INGO's own information, include donor agencies, local implementing partners, vendors and suppliers, contractors and consultants, and other sector actors working in the same spaces (such as private contractors, other INGOs and CSOs, and multilaterals).

This is an avenue for collaboration, solidarity, and risk mitigation that is frequently underused. INGOs can:

- Incorporate requirements to report suspicions involving the INGO's work into partner agreements, and contracts with suppliers and vendors;
- Develop formal agreements with other INGOs, as other means outside of MOUs (Memorandum of Understanding) may be necessary;
- Participate in regular fora with other agencies to share information and perspectives.

Detection as a whole-organisation responsibility

I once ran a fraud workshop for the local staff of a large INGO in the Middle East. Most participants seemed content with most of the material we covered, but when we arrived at the need to report suspicions, one programme officer became animated. "But if we have to report every suspicion of fraud, we'll be doing nothing but filling out fraud reports all day!" they opined.

A 'not-my-job' mentality can be common, especially in busy or stretched functions, or those in which staff may perceive future challenges for their work if they report a suspicion of diversion. Similar objections to the programme officer can sometimes be heard from MEL and internal audit functions, for example.

It is true that detecting diversion may not be the purpose of a particular function's work. But it is a key responsibility of all functions, and some are better positioned to do so than others. Internal audit is a good example – it is not the purpose of internal audit to detect malfeasance, but 15 per cent of occupational frauds and abuses are identified this way (ACFE, 2018).

Leveraging these resources involves clear responsibilities articulated in policy, adequate training, and clear guidance. Detection diversion may not be the purpose of a particular function's work, but doing so is a key responsibility.

Response

Response represents the management of diversion suspicions and, therefore, potentially materialised diversion risk. In this part of the ADP, an INGO undertakes activity to manage risks:

* Presented by the suspected incident itself;
* Created by how it responds to that incident;
* Generated by the actions taken by other stakeholders, such as implementing partners or donor agencies.

It is also a workstream that is critical to the effectiveness of the other components of the ADP, giving an INGO an opportunity to use case data to support more informed preventative and detective controls, for example, or to better target training and communication. It is, therefore, broader than simply 'investigation,' which is just one component of response. The others are incident management, remedial action, and reporting.

Alarming as suspicions of diversion might be, responding well to a suspected incident can significantly strengthen an INGO. In addition to informing better risk management, system improvement, and elevating the awareness and confidence of internal stakeholders, a good response also provides the opportunity for robust advocacy and engagement. It provides a few moments in a news cycle to explain the complex reality of aid work to donors, regulators, and the public.

A poor response, however, can leave a seemingly limitless trail of disaster in the INGO's wake. Damaged international reputation, underperforming programmes, and disallowance from bidding for donor grants are just the starting point. Negligently failing to prevent further incidents, criminal charges, abused beneficiaries, dead witnesses, and donor funds financing murder and exploitation are all plausible effects.

Incident management

The backbone of successful incident management is a diversion response plan. This plan should be at least conversant with other incident management protocols (such as those governing security incidents), if the components of the response plan below are not directly incorporated into a generic incident management plan. Two further attributes of incident management are key: The response manager and the stakeholder panel.

To ensure the best outcome, a single response manager should be accountable for:

- Administrating the response, driving it through the stages of the response plan;
- Co-ordinating stakeholders;
- Ensuring the creation of adequate corporate memory of actions taken, their rationales, and outcomes.

Meanwhile, diversion incidents often affect multiple stakeholders at various levels. These might include, for example, multiple tiers of programme management, donor management, general counsel, audit, risk and compliance, finance and logistics, counter-fraud, public relations, and HR. This many voices, each with differing priorities and viewing the matter through different lenses, generates risks of its own.

A helpful way to ensure collaboration and consultation, but also a structured and agile approach, is for each incident to have a stakeholder panel – the role of which is determined in the response plan. That role might include:

- Informing decision-making;
- Providing guidance on the basis of their areas of expertise;
- Identifying and helping to control risks.

The response plan

Whether diversion is incorporated into an existing response plan, or a separate procedure is developed, the response plan should have the following characteristics:

- A description of the role of the response manager and stakeholder panel, and guidance on selection of personnel;
- A simple, phased workflow that begins at the point of suspicion and ends with confirmation that remedial action has been taken, all requisite reporting has been completed, and all risks have been successfully managed;
- A 'triage' stage early in the workflow, which enables the INGO to align the capability, capacity, and priority of its response with the risks, complexity, and urgency of the matter;

- An 'initial response' or 'initial investigation' stage, in which the INGO can collect further information to enable decision-making – but without necessarily progressing to a full investigation, should there be no predication for it after all;
- Clear responsibilities allocated to specific roles at each stage, including the identification of decision makers, the decisions they will make, upon the basis of what information, and the point at which these decisions will be taken.

Investigation

In a sense, the purpose of an investigation is to create an evidentially-robust file of information, containing the available facts, to support onward administrative, civil, or criminal action. Investigations bring clarity to ambiguity, facilitate the decision-making process, and are a business improvement tool. They are not inherently punitive.

Whichever function carries out the internal investigation into diversion, it should be carried out consistently and represent a broad enquiry, incorporating:

- Fact-finding into whether diversion has taken place, what level of confidence can be applied that it has, and the value (quantum) of any loss;
- An exploration of control gaps or failures;
- The possibility of management or staff negligence, enabling diversion.

Investigations are technical activities that involve the management of a range of risks and should not be undertaken lightly. For the INGO's own investigation, the response manager and stakeholder panel must determine the right resource to carry out the work. Available resources might include internal parties, such as internal audit, risk and compliance, dedicated investigation teams, or even regular programme or finance staff with appropriate qualifications or experience. Alternatively, the INGO could engage an outside specialist forensic investigation company. To make the decision, the principles of capability, capacity, and independence can be applied.

Investigative capability

Factors that can be used to assess whether a resource has the requisite capability include:

- Knowledge and experience in the execution of reliable investigation procedures;
- Sufficient understanding of relevant civil, criminal, and labour legal frameworks;
- Sufficient understanding of, and ability to manage, the full range of risks;
- Adequate knowledge of diversion methodologies, indicators, and issues;

- Expertise in the functions affected, such as finance, logistics, or controls;
- Expertise in the investigation tools required, such as forensic accounting, data analytics, specialist interviewing, or the application of forensic technology (e.g. reviewing hard drives and e-mail);
- Understanding of the programme modality affected, local context and culture, and the unique environment of the aid sector;
- Appropriate behavioural competencies to successfully deliver the investigation, such as stakeholder management, strategic thinking, and communication skills.

Investigative capacity

Understanding whether a resource has the necessary capacity requires an informed assessment of the scale of the investigation. Matters that may seem small can blossom to include many interviews, dozens of interrogations of hard drives and e-mail accounts, and weeks (even months) of painstaking analysis of accounts and commodity flows.

Investigative independence

Finally, to be sufficiently independent, an investigation resource should be:

- Outside the management line in which the incident has occurred;
- Free of interests in their working relationships with those in that management line;
- Demonstrably independent – not only objective and impartial, but seen to be objective and impartial.

Third party investigations

Donor agencies, regulators, and criminal justice agencies commission their own audits and investigations into diversion incidents. This creates some complexity for an INGO, because it will likely also be carrying out its own internal review. In particularly serious incidents, it would not be unusual for multiple investigations to occur, perhaps originating from more than one country. INGOs in receipt of USAID funds can, for example, expect the Office of the Inspector General (OIG) to carry out an investigation upon reporting a diversion incident to that donor. British INGOs reporting a matter to the CCEW, for example, might be more accustomed to being invited to conduct their own internal review and reporting back.

If subject to this type of review by a third party, INGOs may wish to:

- Understand the basis upon which the review is occurring, its scope, aims, and limitations, and the framework in which it does so. An audit on the basis of contractual rights is very different to a criminal investigation;

- Obtain legal advice early and throughout the process, but be cautious about being seen to 'lawyer up' too soon. The presence of lawyers at meetings during an audit may appear escalatory;
- Appoint a Single Point of Contact (SPOC) to co-ordinate relations with the external reviewers and keep track of information requests and questions. This helps not only to ensure that their requests are met, but provides an opportunity for the INGO to gain early warning of the trajectory of the inquiry.

In interactions with the reviewers, ensure that INGO staff:

- Take a constructive and reflective approach. Demonstrate a learning environment, not a defensive one. The organisation as a whole, and the individuals with whom auditors are interacting, should welcome challenge;
- Co-operate rapidly and in full. Do not be perceived to hold back information, delay access to material, or be mealy-mouthed in responses;
- Are wary of deceiving auditors, whether inadvertently or not. Even when the matter being reviewed may result in no case to answer, being caught out in lies or half-truths can have catastrophic consequences;
- Answer questions at this point in time. Describing what the INGO *will* do rather than describing what it *did* do can make it appear that it did nothing. Audits are retrospective. The opportunity to describe an action plan comes later. Failing to be frank about what has happened frustrates reviewers and carries the opportunity cost of exploring *why* the INGO operated as it did.

Remedial action

It is critical to identify and record any lessons from an incident, no matter the outcome – this includes incidents where diversion was not in fact identified. There may be internal controls that need changing, introducing, or even abandoning with the experience of an alleged incident behind us.

With the requirement to consider and capture lessons-learned embedded in the response plan, a helpful structure for a complete reflection on the matters might be to use the components of the ADP. These questions should be asked not just in response to any system failure, but also in the context of ongoing improvement:

- What information has the incident generated to support better risk assessment?
- What opportunities to heighten deterrence have been identified?
- How might an incident be better prevented?
- How might an incident be better detected, perhaps earlier?
- How can the INGO improve its response?
- How can internal and external communications, including training, be improved?

- What can be learned from the matter to support better governance and assurance?
- What feedback can be provided to senior leadership?

Reporting

Diversion issues – whether suspected, proven, or ambiguous – attract a range of potential reporting obligations and the BOR will help INGOs to consider the multiple directions in which they may be required to make reports to external bodies, and the stages at which these obligations may arise. These may be contained in counter-terror legislation, financial regulation, charity or corporate laws, as well as donor funding agreements and contracts with other INGOs.

Agencies that might expect a report can include:

- Criminal justice authorities such as the police;
- Government financial reporting centres or regulators;
- Charity or non-profit regulators;
- Institutional donors;
- Other INGOs in contracting arrangements, such as consortia.

There are several key points to note:

- Consider the threshold at which a notification must be made. For some donors and in some law, only a very low burden of proof is required to issue a notification and this may be before any formal investigation has taken place;
- There may be several notifications required at different points in the response process;
- Each jurisdiction may have its own set of agencies requiring notification;
- There can be serious personal and corporate penalties for failing to notify relevant agencies, or failing to disclose fully.

References

Association of Certified Fraud Examiners (ACFE) 2018. *Report to the Nations 2018: Global study on occupational fraud and abuse.* Austin, TX: ACFE.

Bland, Olivia (@oliviaabland). "Yesterday morning I had a job interview for a position at a company called Web Applications UK. After a brutal 2 hour interview, in which the CEO Craig Dean tore both me and my writing to shreds (and called me an underachiever), I was offered the job. This was my response today." 03:10, 30 January 2019. Tweet.

May, O. 2016. *Fighting fraud and corruption in the humanitarian and global development sector.* Abingdon: Routledge. https://doi.org/10.4324/9781315558301

Ratley, J. 2012. *Fraud indicators for risk management professionals.* Austin, TX: ACFE.

10 Culture, communication, and training

Oliver May

While I was still an officer in the British Serious Organised Crime Agency (SOCA), there was an operation to track down a fugitive who had fled the country. This criminal had managed to dodge the authorities, and now lived a happy life in the sun – lounging by the pool in the day, hitting the gym in the evening, and partying into the night at exotic bars. To stay ahead of law enforcement, he had taken elaborate steps to cover his tracks and practised routine security hygiene like staying off social media.

However clever he may have been, he had vulnerabilities – his friends. He kept his tracks covered, but his associates were not so fastidious. In the end, using a range of techniques, he was apprehended and brought home. His sophisticated attempts to stay on the run were undermined, in part, by the people around him.

So far, we have discussed systems and processes to deter, prevent, detect, and respond to diversion. But diversion, as with all financial crime, has a common denominator: People. It is committed by people, for the benefit of people, and is enabled by other people. We can create all the policies and systems that we like, but if we forget this simple truth then none will be effective. And so, this chapter is about determining how we want our people to behave, and how we influence and equip them to do so.

We know that people are more likely to behave corruptly, for example, when they believe corruption will only cause indirect harm, where unethical behaviour is not punished, and where rationalisations make it more acceptable (Dupuy and Neset, 2018). Diversion is likely to be similar, and cultural development, internal communication, and training are key ways to tackle this. But across all three, perhaps the most common mistake made by INGOs is to default to transmission, rather than reception. Without listening, INGOs cannot effectively influence or equip anybody to manage the risk of diversion. Throughout this chapter, then, we refer to ways that INGOs can ensure that culture and communication is less an agenda, and more a conversation. Meanwhile, a core theme that will emerge is the need to integrate all three activities with wider corporate work.

An anti-diversion culture

Internal culture is a non-negotiable facet of all INGOs, irrespective of size or nature, and a disproportionately powerful enabler or disruptor of diversion. It is no surprise, then, that recognition of its importance has never been greater. Whether it's the CCEW (Hobson, 2018), Australian Securities and Investments Commission (ASIC, 2016), Bond (Williams, 2018), or the Financial Conduct Authority (FCA, 2018), it's hard to find a peak body or regulator or that hasn't stressed the point in relation to integrity risks. But recognising the importance of internal culture, and actually shaping it, are two very different things.

Challenges to developing anti-diversion culture

One does not have to look far to find people who believe that aid sector organisations are less vulnerable to financial crime than those evil, greedy companies – a Humanitarian Exchange article once claimed that the sector faced "much lower levels [of corruption] than the private commercial sector," for example (Larche, 2011). But it is not the case that because INGOs have a moral mission, they will enjoy a culture predisposed to integrity. Organisations with moral missions can be just as vulnerable as those with profit motives (May, 2016a).

INGOs do, however, face unique challenges here. Simple ideas in other sectors like 'do the right thing,' 'speak up,' and 'culture of ethics' are less helpful for INGOs because they operate in ethically-complex spaces. For any given aid worker, for example, the thing that appears 'right' or 'ethical' to them might in fact be something that their organisation would rather they did not do – such as pay a diversionary a fee at a checkpoint.

This tension is often undetected, often due to an over-reliance on artefacts. With a code of conduct and an anti-diversion policy in place – both of which, no doubt, took a lot of time and negotiation to draft – many assume that the cultural work is done. But this is not enough to influence people. Just because we have a values statement, it does not mean anybody in the organisation is actually living out those values.

Further, it is unrealistic to imagine that any organisation can arrive at the point where everybody is pointing in the same direction at all times. Even the idea that we could all agree to the same 'values' is something of a sleight of hand, because in truth we interpret and act upon values differently, and the human ability to rationalise any given action is powerful. In one case of which I am aware, local NGO staff allegedly diverted funds to a diversionary in the belief that, despite the NGO's 'zero tolerance' stance, they were implicitly expected by management to do so.

Meanwhile, though commentators and consultants may stress the importance of 'tone at the top,' INGOs are not always unitary bodies. Many operate with necessarily devolved models of management, and within local contexts with their own cultures and social structures. There might be many 'tops,' and it is unlikely that they will all reflect the expectations of the board at all times.

Should we master the challenges of the sector's ethical complexity, cultural assumptions, and diversity of corporate structures, then we still face further barriers to influencing our people – human factors. These affect not only the way that staff and volunteers respond to our anti-diversion culture initiatives, but also how we design and implement them.

In the light of all this, one may be forgiven for wondering whether there is anything we can do at all to shape internal culture. Of course, there is – but we must be practical, methodical, and committed.

Practical steps to developing an anti-diversion culture

To build on the definition of Hussain (2014), culture is the framework that guides the way people in an organisation think, feel, and act as they go about their work. Importantly, this does not just represent how they think, feel, and act in relation to diversion – it is also about how they think, feel, and act in relation to the systems that deter, prevent, detect, and respond to diversion.

There are four key steps we can explore to influence the way our people think, feel, and act about diversion:

- Define and articulate what an anti-diversion culture is;
- Take steps to shape the culture;
- Determine key positive and negative indicators of that culture, with which to guide development;
- Monitor and review progress towards the desired culture.

Define and articulate

May (2016b) sets out four core characteristics of an anti-fraud and corruption internal culture, with which the characteristics of an anti-diversion culture align. An anti-diversion culture is one in which:

- All commit to, and participate in, reducing the risk of diversion;

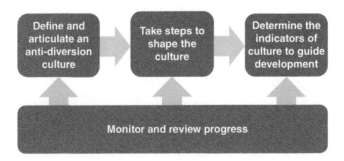

Figure 10.1 Towards an anti-diversion culture.

- The components of the ADP are present, utilised, and effective;
- Anti-diversion activity is considered a fundamental part of programming;
- The honest majority of staff and volunteers are activated and empowered to tackle diversion.

In sum, it is a culture that reduces the likelihood and consequences of diversion. The aspiration to such a culture should be placed on an authoritative footing for the INGO, perhaps as part of a diversion policy, strategy, or programme plan. Similarly, although it is not the whole story, a code of conduct is an important first step. Its content should align with these characteristics, and clearly set out the behaviours required in relation to both diversion and the systems necessary to deter, prevent, detect, and respond to it.

Take steps to shape the culture

As should be clear, the development of internal culture is not a project with a start and end point. Culture is not static, and organisations do not arrive at the right culture overnight. It is ongoing. Managers should avoid implying that anything else is the case, perhaps through insincere grant applications promising that their INGO has such a culture. Believing that such a culture can exist without an ongoing schedule of work can lead to disillusionment and a decline in momentum.

Instead, develop a clear plan for the ongoing development of anti-diversion culture through practical activities and a programmatic cycle: Determine objectives, plan, execute, monitor, and review. The plan should be a 'live document' or collection of documents, helping to track the development of the culture through the phases of the cycle.

Further, work to develop an anti-diversion culture should not happen in isolation from wider cultural development activity. The plan should integrate with other such work, especially around integrity and risk issues. Finally, maintain vigilance for disruptive human factors not only in the implementation of the plan, but in the design of it as well.

Determine key indicators of positive and negative culture

'Measuring' culture is famously challenging, and to be pragmatic we must rely on indicators rather than measurements – events, data-points, and assessments that help to portray a picture based on likelihood. Indicators of peoples' understanding, implementation, and operation of the ADP could be a helpful proxy – giving glimpses into the likely extent and performance of an anti-diversion culture.

Monitor and review

Monitoring is important not just for the optimisation of the development process itself, but also for the maintenance of momentum. Given the breadth of the potential indicators described above, it is clear that both a wide array of

Table 10.1 Example 'think, feel, act' anti-diversion cultural indicators

Element	Positive indicator	Negative indicator
Risk awareness and ownership	The myths in Chapter 2 of this book are routinely challenged.	The myths in Chapter 2 of this book are commonplace.
	Discussions about diversion are marked by a constructive attitude to reducing the risk.	Conversation is marked by terms and tone indicative of complaint, exasperation, defeatism, and a 'do what we need to do' attitude.
	Managers and staff demonstrate a sense of collaborate risk ownership, looking for ways to work together with both back donors and implementing partners to manage it beyond the boundaries of their organisation.	Back donors and/or implementing partners are seen as solely responsible for the management of diversion.
	Managers and staff demonstrate awareness of the specific risks they face in their areas of work.	There is an absence of risk awareness – managers and staff could not describe the risks they face in their area of responsibility with sufficient knowledge.
Governance, leadership and management	Managers can evidence their actions to manage specific diversion risks and detect incidents.	Managers suspect that diversion goes on, but make little effort to detect or understand it ('let sleeping dogs lie').
	Managers show evidence of dynamism, energetically testing new approaches and controls to improve the management of diversion risk.	Diversion is tolerated as a 'necessary evil,' and no genuine belief is evident that it can be reduced.
	Anti-diversion work is proportionately resourced.	Anti-diversion work is disproportionately under-resourced.
Legislation and regulation	Consensus that at least some legislation and regulation play a positive role.	Legislation and regulation are seen negatively in all circumstances.
Prevention	A baseline of compliance with internal policies, procedures, and systems for the management of diversion risk.	Routine non-compliance with internal controls, and the spirit of internal controls.
Detection	Suspected incident reporting levels are credibly aligned with the likely risk.	Detection levels are not credible in the light of the risks.
Response	Incident responses are mostly conducted within the principles of the ADP and in compliance with the response plan.	Suspected incidents are not reported beyond a country programme.

information will be required to monitor and assess progress, and that this assessment will have a strong qualitative dimension.

Material that may inform this ongoing assessment, and the continuous surveillance of indicators can be found all over the organisation, including, for example, in:

- Programme and MEL reports;
- Internal audit and exception-based review reports;
- Feedback from beneficiaries;
- Compliance reviews and control assessments;
- Risk reporting;
- Internal and external communications;
- Incident casefile information;
- Staff surveys – whether electronic or manual, broad or targeted. If used, they are best carried out regularly to enable progress tracking.

Internal communications

I am aware of a particular organisation that was established through a series of mergers. This led to many different staff from diverse backgrounds and internal cultures working together, which in turn apparently led to accusations of bullying. The organisation, keen to define its own culture, launched a huge anti-bullying campaign – there were anti-bullying mugs, lanyards, and posters everywhere. But an unintentional consequence was that some visitors to its buildings would enter, take a look around, and remark: "Wow, you guys must be horrible!"

The clear, specific lesson here for internal communications is that while there may be a message you intend to convey, there may be other messages you unintentionally broadcast too. But there is a general lesson as well – that internal communication is a discipline, requiring careful planning and execution.

The purpose of anti-diversion communication

Communication about diversion is a tool, not an end in itself. As with any tool, we require a clear understanding of the purpose, and a plan to govern the execution of that purpose. The aims of internal communications as part of an ADP might be to:

- Raise staff awareness of their responsibilities, and the systems that support them in executing those responsibilities;
- Prompt each worker's vigilance, and retention of diversion as one of the risks at the top of their mental agenda, commensurate with the risks in their role, locale, and aid modality;

- Influence each worker to think, feel, and act in a way that promotes their responsibilities and supports the INGO's anti-diversion systems;
- Support the development of an anti-diversion culture and the creation of a transparent and open conversation about diversion.

The ADP communications plan can drive the delivery of each of these four aims.

The ADP communications plan

A communications plan can help to ensure that anti-diversion communications are not an afterthought, and helps an INGO to explore and pursue all the opportunities, means, and modes available. Whether the INGO adopts a dedicated anti-diversion communications plan or incorporates these issues into its broader communications strategy, internal communications best practices should be followed.

Developing a communications plan

Getting anti-diversion communications right means starting with analysis. Given our four aims – raising awareness, elevating vigilance, influencing how people think, feel, and act, and supporting culture and an open conversation – what challenges might the INGO have in generating effect? What are the problems with communicating about diversion in the INGO? What are the barriers to communication? What has and has not worked before, and why? What are the opportunities and potential enablers that can be harnessed? The key is to think with breadth and creativity. It is also not an activity that will take place in isolation – it must be integrated with culture and training.

Optimising communications

Diversion is just one of many risks that busy staff need to manage, and good anti-diversion practice is frequently heckled by other priorities, interpretations of values, and messaging. So for maximum effect, anti-diversion messaging will need to be reinforced through multiple media (Leonardi et al., 2012). This requires frequent and varied communication throughout business and programme cycles.

Similarly, only some messaging needs to be informative (perhaps ultimately pointing stakeholders to any position statements, codes of conduct, or policies). Messaging must aim to secure action, rather than merely transmit information. That means that every message must be crafted to facilitate either a change of perspective or an action.

Meanwhile, receptivity of messaging can be heightened by securing endorsement from those who set the 'tone at the top.' In our devolved models, this may not only be senior executives but regional directors, country directors, and local programme managers. The messaging must be clear and echoed by all business units, especially those in high-risk country programmes. A practical way to secure this might be to develop 'conversation guides' for managers, setting out the key messaging that the INGO expects its leaders to communicate about diversion at every opportunity.

Ways to communicate

Once messages have been crafted, a range of channels are available through which to convey them:

- Participation in events such as the ACFE's Fraud Week, or the UN's Anti-Corruption Day;
- Internal newsletter items, pay statements, posters, intranet articles and banners, videos, and multimedia;
- Roadshows, talks, seminars, and agenda items at 'town halls';
- E-mails from senior executives or the board;
- Training and capacity building activities;
- Leveraging influential figures;
- Circulating articles, publications, and podcasts.

Transmit and receive

We have already discussed how many in the sector are reluctant to discuss diversion, which can deny an INGO its visibility of the problem. A fundamental part of anti-diversion communication, then, is not only to broadcast messages but to help create a more open conversation.

Practical ways to encourage dialogue about the risk, and how best to prevent, detect and respond to incidents, might include:

- Q&A sessions with senior managers;
- Publication of 'whistleblower' feedback mechanisms;
- Publicising examples of positive dialogue or good anti-diversion collaborative working;
- Sharing examples of good practices in other organisations;
- Framing diversion as a core values issue.

The keys to good anti-diversion communication

The unique circumstances of the aid sector, INGOs, and diversion itself create special challenges to the four aims of anti-diversion communications. INGOs can overcome many of these by bearing in mind the following keys to good anti-diversion communication: Taking a risk-based approach, clarity, relevance, contingency, integration with wider internal communications, and alignment with external messaging.

A risk-based approach

The content of communications and priority of recipients should be informed by the organisational, business unit, and project risk assessments. A risk-based approach can not only heighten positive effect, but also ensures that communications are proportionate. Weekly reminders to all staff from the SLT, for example, would not be proportionate for an INGO that does not work in any countries with an immanent diversionary threat.

Clarity

INGO operations frequently involve a very high number of stakeholders, managers are often empathetic, and decisions are often consultative and consensus-driven. On flashpoint issues like diversion, this can lead to convoluted position statements. There is no space for these kinds of statements on such high-impact issues. The INGO's expectations of its staff and partners must be unambiguous.

Relevance

Communications must be relevant to those who receive them in order to have impact. This means selecting channels, style, and content that aligns with the INGO's culture and customs. Similarly, communication must be tailored to the specific circumstances of the recipients – their roles, level, corporate function, and the aid modalities they work on.

Contingency

Much can go wrong with internal communication if we get the mode or content wrong. In particular, legal and donor relations risks, and the risks of confusion, offence or concern in local cultural contexts, can all arise from poorly-chosen language. In addition to the guidance of public relations and internal communications professionals, other guidance might be sourced from local expertise, legal advice, and donor management officers.

Integration with wider internal communications

A range of benefits can be captured from engaging the INGO's internal communications team and aligning the plan with its wider internal communications strategy. Firstly, of course, this can reduce duplication, confused messaging, and communications fatigue – and identify opportunities for increased effect through harmonisation with related matter like safeguarding. But it also allows the ADP to access the knowledge and expertise of the internal communications function and existing communications infrastructure.

Staff must trust internal communications for them to attain their full effect, and this can be undermined when internal and external messaging is at odds. Similarly, an INGO that says one thing in public and another thing in private to its staff is waiting for a transparency scandal. Whatever approach the ADP takes to managing the risk of diversion, what it says in public and in private must align. That includes what its executives say in their blogs and on podiums.

Training

Empowering staff to minimise diversion is not only of value, but on integrity risks more broadly, risk-based training has become a regulatory expectation (Ministry of Justice, 2011) and a matter of donor guidance (DFAT, 2019). Meanwhile, research suggests that there may be a reduction in fraud losses of more than a third for organisations with anti-fraud training (ACFE, 2018).

It is especially important for international organisations working in diverse, complex, and volatile contexts through dynamic programmes. Training gives staff the knowledge and skills to make informed and reasonable decisions in the ambiguous situations common in these circumstances. In this way, it is a powerful way to extend the reach of the ADP.

Of course, elevating an INGO's human capability to manage diversion goes beyond its own staff, and even beyond diversion. We will discuss building the capacity of partners in Chapter 13, and it is also important to note that an adequate level of skills, experience, and knowledge is required in disciplines like finance, logistics, HR, and security. But in this section, we focus on taking a holistic, risk-based approach to building staff capability.

The holistic, risk-based approach to training

The holistic approach sets out to equip every member of staff with the knowledge required to deter, prevent, detect, and respond to diversion in their role, how to do it, and influences them to do so. The approach becomes risk-based when the resourcing, mode, and content of the programme is informed by the diversion risks faced by each participant. In a risk-based approach:

- Training Needs Analysis (TNA), whether at organisational, business unit, or project level, is informed by the corresponding diversion risk assessment;
- Recipients of training are identified, prioritised, and the content they receive tailored to the diversion risks they may encounter in their role, location, function, or aid modality;
- The extent and frequency of the training for each recipient is informed by the likelihood and consequence of the risks. Induction upon entry to the

> organisation, or upon assuming certain roles, is the minimum – not the aim;
> • The scale of investment in training is informed by the risk levels.

For example, the training received by staff in high-risk roles, functions, and jurisdictions will be different from that given to those with rare exposure to diversion. This makes this approach practical, proportionate, and action-oriented.

This is quite distinct from a compliance-based approach, in which the unspoken primary purpose might be to evidence that the INGO has told its staff the rules. Where this is the aim, training can become a 'tick-box' affair that affects mode, content, and ultimately success.

Key considerations

Start with a TNA

Whether at an organisational, business unit, or project level, a range of TNA models are available. But in essence, the key is to assess the current state of staff anti-diversion competency and identify gaps relative to the risks, recognise those that training can fill, and create training solutions.

Take a structured approach

The TNA should springboard a methodical, continuous, and monitored training programme. This should be responsive to the INGO's potentially-rapidly changing environment and regularly evaluated. Significant changes – for example, new projects or aid modalities, or evolving diversionary threats – should trigger re-evaluation. Each intervention should be defined by clear learning objectives, by which learning outcomes can be measured.

Passive development

Some capability uplift can be attained from simply making information available to staff about how to deter, prevent, detect, and respond to diversion. This overlaps to some extent with the ADP communications plan, and can include:

• The accessibility of the code of conduct, anti-diversion policy, and related procedures;
• The inclusion of diversion issues in any project or programme guidance or manuals;
• Dedicated anti-diversion handbooks, manuals, or guidance notes;
• A guidance portal on the corporate intranet sharing useful articles, tools, guidance, and resources;

- 'Helpdesk' access to local or organisational anti-diversion focal points for advice and guidance.

Developing capability in this way, however, has limitations and it is likely that these will need to be complemented by more proactive interventions.

Transmitting information versus behavioural change

We have all sat in boring, didactic workshops on a Monday morning that we have completely forgotten about by Tuesday afternoon. Instead, effective anti-diversion training must recognise the difference between information transmission and securing behavioural change. Certainly, there is a place for relaying information about, for example, legal and donor requirements. But to truly manage the risk of diversion, participants must understand how they are to enact these responsibilities and connect with why this is important.

Training design must make space to change behaviour and perspectives. Detailed information, for example, can be provided in handouts and manuals rather that use up workshop time. Workshops, instead, can focus on participation, discussion, exercises, and multimedia techniques, for example.

Be culturally and contextually appropriate

For challenging issues like diversion, the limitations of the clichéd INGO workshop mean it must become a thing of the past. There have been significant developments in the way that we learn in the workplace; learning through non-traditional methods, collaboration, and with self-direction are preferential approaches now. Meanwhile, expected and effective learning styles vary between countries, cultures, and contexts. One size does not necessarily fit all.

Mode and content of anti-diversion training

True as the old trope is that staff are an organisation's greatest asset and liability, it is surprising how much training is still carried out on a shoestring. Poor-quality educational interventions, delivered by non-professional facilitators, lead to sub-therapeutic outcomes. Perhaps where risks are comparatively low in likelihood or consequence, the effect (or absence of effect) of poor-quality training might be masked or immaterial. But for a high impact issue like diversion, there is little space for this.

Mode

The INGO will need to determine which modes best deliver the content for maximum effect in its own circumstances. A wide array of channels through which learning can be achieved are available, but each has its own strengths, limitations, and dependencies. Online platforms, for example, are comparatively inexpensive, facilitate a consistent global approach, and can reliably evidence completion. However, they may have a lower retention rate than more interactive means and can tend to suit information transmission rather than behavioural change. Meanwhile, face-to-face interventions can enjoy stronger retention through higher participation and engagement, give participants the ability to direct their own learning to an extent, and tap into a raft of psychological and sociological benefits around drawing people together. They can be, however, expensive and time-consuming.

Available modes can include:

- Online platforms ('e-learning') and software packages, including smartphone apps;
- Face-to-face workshops, including exercises based along discussion and interaction;
- Seminars and learning events;
- Remote learning (e.g. through online communication tools);
- Blended learning;
- Externally-provided anti-diversion training.

Consolidating retention and heightening growth requires taking learning beyond the classroom. Such measures can include:

- Task books;
- Forums, working groups, and learning hubs;
- Exercises requiring check-ins after the workshop;
- Coaching and mentoring schemes.

Activities within learning that can help to elevate retention include:

- The use of anonymised, sanitised incident reports;
- Gamification;
- Case studies, real or fictitious;
- 'Choose-your-own-adventure' narrative approaches;
- Multimedia, such as video, electronic voting platforms, and other tools that capture the benefits of visual learning and participation.

Content

Generic inputs conducted for show have little proven value, and forensic auditors actively look out for them in the event of integrity breakdowns (see, for example, INEQE, 2019). A risk-based approach means that training interventions and their content will vary between INGOs, but it is likely that at least a basic input for staff, and a further input for managers, is required to reflect differing responsibility levels. Those working in high-risk roles, or high-risk circumstances, may require additional content and further development.

For large INGOs working extensively in a wide, diverse array of challenging circumstances (such as multiple emergencies, in a range of fragile states and conflict zones, through differing modalities), a senior management package may even be necessary.

As a starting-point, helpful content for a basic staff package might include:

- The INGO's expectations of them around diversion;
- An introduction to the INGO's anti-diversion policies and practices, and what this means for participants' role;
- What their personal responsibilities to deter, prevent, detect, and respond to diversion are;
- Guidance on carrying out these responsibilities in their day-to-day work;
- The risks of diversion that they may face in their work, and the consequences of diversion;
- The red flags of an incident, and what to do if they spot them;
- The relevant obligations of both the participants and the INGO;
- Where to find further information and support.

Additional content for a manager-level package might include:

- Conducting business unit and project diversion risk assessment;
- Situational awareness and monitoring diversion risk indicators;
- The long tail of causality – how diversion risks become incidents, and how this can be prevented;
- Tools and guidance for identifying, assessing, and monitoring risks;
- Guidance on what elevates risks and what lowers them;
- How to manage incidents of potentially materialised risk.

References

Association of Certified Fraud Examiners (ACFE) 2018. *Report to the Nations 2018: Global study on occupational fraud and abuse.* Austin, TX: ACFE.

Australian Securities and Investments Commission (ASIC) 2016. *What you walk past is what you accept.* Sydney: ASIC.

Department of Foreign Affairs and Trade (DFAT) 2019. *Fraud control toolkit for funding recipients.* Canberra: DFAT.

Dupuy, K. and Neset, S. 2018. *The cognitive psychology of corruption: Micro-level explanations for unethical behaviour.* U4 Issue 2018: 2. Bergen: Chr Michelsen Institute.

Financial Conduct Authority (FCA) 2018. *Transforming culture in financial services.* London: FCA.

Hobson, J. 2018. *There's no room for doubt around safeguarding: Protecting people is too important.* London: Charity Commission for England and Wales.

Hussain, M. 2014. *Corporate fraud: The human factor.* London: Bloomsbury Publishing.

INEQE 2019. *Oxfam GB independent safeguarding review: Executive summary and recommendations*. Belfast: INEQE.

Larche, J. 2011. Corruption in the NGO world: What it is and how to tackle it. *Humanitarian Exchange*. Issue *52*. London: Overseas Development Institute.

Leonardi, P., Neeley, T., and Gerber, E. 2012. How managers use multiple media. *Organization Science 23(1)*: 98–117. DOI: 10.1287/orsc.1110.0638.

May, O. 2016a. *This is how humanitarian need enables corruption*. FCPA Blog. https://fcpablog. com/2016/04/28/oliver-may-this-is-how-humanitarian-need-can-enable-corrupti/.

May, O. 2016b. *Fighting fraud and corruption in the humanitarian and global development sector*. Abingdon: Routledge. https://doi.org/10.4324/9781315558301.

Ministry of Justice 2011. *The Bribery Act 2010: Guidance about procedures which relevant commercial organisations can put into place to prevent persons associated with them from bribing*. London: HM Government.

Williams, A. 2018. *A respectful organisational culture is crucial to safeguarding*. London: Bond.

11 Leadership, governance, and management

Oliver May

In financial crime scandals such as Wells Fargo, Volkswagen, and FIFA, major incidents are frequently seen in the public space as a failure of leadership (Ochs, 2016; Glazer, 2016; Humm, 2015). Whether the breakdown has been a matter of stewardship, culture, or ethics, the public gaze sweeps swiftly to those who sat in key positions. The same is true of integrity failures in the non-profit sector – the representation of the Wounded Warrior Project (Hennessy, 2016) and Kid's Company (Bright, 2015) issues are high-profile examples.

This reflects a simple truth that the long tail of a diversion incident can start well before the fateful transaction. The culture, systems, and practices of an INGO can enable such incidents. In the most serious and complicated cases, that tail is often made up of a collection of issues threading up through the tiers of management and all the way to the board.

For our purposes, leadership, governance, and management are three different things. Governance represents the running of an INGO at the highest level – how it determines, sets, and monitors its objects, purpose, and the strategy to deliver them. These are matters for its governing body, and how that body has chosen to orchestrate the organisation to deliver its decisions. Management represents oversight of the effectiveness and efficiency of the systems and functions that deliver in line with the direction set by that governing body. Both play a key role in managing the risk of diversion.

But leadership is a different matter, transcending organisational, functional, and process levels. Anti-diversion leadership is not confined to the board, or the Senior Leadership Team (SLT), or even to managers. Any member of staff or volunteer in an INGO can be an anti-diversion leader. And in this confusing and often opaque space, at a turbulent time for aid, doing so is more important than ever. This chapter, then, sets out how the INGO's governance and management tiers relate to the ADP, and explores what anti-diversion leadership might look like.

Governance and management of the ADP

The ADP must be given the mandate to affect the way that business units, such as country programmes, run their operations. Devolved models of responsibility in the aid sector give business units significant autonomy, allowing them to respond rapidly to volatile and diverse circumstances. This enables local business units to manage risks, certainly, but it must be balanced with the protection of the enterprise-level, for whom risks are created at business unit level. OFAC has described 'decentralised' compliance functions, and 'inconsistent application' of sanctions compliance programmes, as root causes of actual breaches of US sanctions (OFAC, 2019). The mandate, then, is critical and it starts with the board and SLT.

Role of the board and SLT

The governing bodies of INGOs vary according to their models and legal obligations, but for clarity we will distinguish between the board and the SLT. The board is the ultimate authority, almost certainly with legal responsibilities and might be analogous to a board of trustees in the UK. The SLT, led by a Chief Executive Officer (CEO), executes the operations of the INGO on behalf of the board, to whom it is accountable.

In addition to managing their own personal development in relation to diversion and other integrity risks, both the board and SLT should:

- Authorise and regularly review the ADP;
- Actively support and foster the ADP, in word and action;
- Communicate their appetite for diversion risk clearly through a risk appetite statement;
- Maintain their visibility of the INGO's diversion risk profile, and make informed decisions to respond to that changing profile.

Authorisation and review of the ADP

The ADP should be fully endorsed by the board and the SLT and their messaging, both formal and informal, internal and external, should reflect this. To endorse it, both groups must understand it, and that will mean creating space to do so through:

- Ensuring the ADP's regular appearance in board papers;
- Creating time at meetings to engage directly with the anti-diversion lead;
- Receiving appropriate management information on the operation, progress, and impact of the ADP.

The board and SLT should ensure that the ADP as a whole is regularly and independently audited, and that all findings are acted upon by management to ensure the ADP's effective, holistic, and proportionate management of risks. The frequency of both review and audit should be linked to the pace and scale of both change in diversionary threats and in the INGO's operations, and could also be triggered by material changes to the INGO. Examples of such triggers might include:

- Significant changes to objects, strategy, or direction;
- Opening or closing a programme in a new country, especially a high-risk country;
- Embarking on a new programme modality;
- Absorbing, or merging with, another organisation;
- Major programmes of organisational change.

Active support for the ADP in word and action

The need for the board and SLT to be supportive of the ADP is clear, and their support must be visible – expressed not only in their interactions with relevant functions but through internal communications like podcasts, global e-mails, or placemats during training events.

Similarly, a well-resourced ADP is a mark of the commitment of the board and SLT. The ADP should enjoy the appropriate capabilities and capacities, and the INGO's models of governance and management should be such that appropriate responsibilities and accountabilities are in place to create compliance and support for it at all levels. Crucially, the board and SLT – as with all tiers of management – should be ready to intervene if more junior lines are not adequately interacting with the ADP, and have lines of reporting to identify when this is taking place.

Use of a risk appetite statement

A risk appetite statement clarifies the risks that an INGO is prepared to bear. It is an important means by which to help managers to make operational decisions within parameters that give the board comfort.

Care is required in the language of the statement. If the term 'no tolerance' is to be used, an object should be attached – to what is the INGO not tolerant? 'Diversion' or 'fraud' for example are not useful objects – all organisations must have some level of tolerance for these risks. A more helpful object to which the INGO might have no tolerance might be, for example, 'perpetrators' or 'inaction.'

Maintain visibility of the INGO's diversion risk profile

With sufficient regularity given the countries and contexts in which the INGO is working, the board and SLT should require:

- Regular reporting of diversion risks and the action being taken by management to respond to them;
- Management Information (MI) that enables them to stay abreast of the performance and effectiveness of the ADP;

- Reporting of the key findings of any audits or reviews of the ADP, and of any diversion incidents, and that such incidents have been reported externally in line with its legal obligations;
- Reporting of the performance of the INGO in respect of its obligations management.

Anti-diversion lead and working group

While all in an INGO's value chain have anti-diversion responsibilities, two functions are particularly important in respect of the ADP: The anti-diversion lead driving the ADP and the anti-diversion working group facilitating it.

Anti-diversion lead

The anti-diversion lead is an important function that:

- Drives the ADP;
- Provides thematic leadership on diversion, and a locus of momentum for ongoing management and continuous improvement;
- Builds the capacity of the INGO and its partners to manage diversion;
- Advises, supports, and influences other business units.

The lead must:

- Be agile, able to assist the INGO to assess risk as its operations change and develop;
- Enjoy a clear mandate;
- Be able to work closely with related disciplines, like ERM or safeguarding.

These are demanding requirements, and the lead must have the appropriate resources to develop an effective and proportionate ADP. OFAC (2019), in particular, has made it clear that this is an expectation. In the event of an incident, an INGO might reasonably foresee regulatory or donor inquiry into the extent to which this was the case.

While one individual should be the anti-diversion lead, whether this is a dedicated role or part of a portfolio of tasks, and whether it is supported by a team or department, depends on the size, breadth, complexity, and scale of diversion risk managed by the INGO. It might, for example, be a particular programme manager, or a counter-fraud, risk or compliance manager.

The function in which the lead best sits will depend on the structure and operations of each INGO, but should be a place in which:

- Sufficient capacity exists for appropriate focus on diversion;
- There is a mandate to develop, co-ordinate, improve, and monitor the ADP;

- It has direct access to all the business units with which it must engage, at all levels;
- It is able to leverage, influence, and hold to account other business units and functions from that location.

In a truly risk-based approach, there may be functions that have traditionally held this brief, but may need to cede it. The lead's role to operationalise the ADP may mean, for example, that legal or internal audit departments should be freed to carry out their independent roles in respect of the ADP, rather than administrate it.

Anti-diversion working group

As a group of risks controlled by, arising in, and having consequences for a range of different functional areas, it is important to take a collaborative approach. A senior working group for the ADP can help to:

- Guide and support the anti-diversion lead;
- Ensure commitment in different functional areas for the ADP;
- Help the ADP to take account of the perspectives and requirements of different functions.

It is likely that the working group would include representatives from programme, finance, any central logistics functions, audit, risk, HR, and legal. It might also incorporate SMEs from the INGO's different aid modalities, and where contexts are very different, regions or country programmes.

Responsibility architecture

There must be a comprehensive arrangement of responsibility for deterrence, preventing, detecting, and responding to diversion in all parts of the INGO and at all levels. Specificity here is critical. All components of the holistic approach rely on individuals having, and knowing they have, responsibility for managing the risks in their own area of autonomy.

INGOs should be cautious of diluting this, and be particularly on the lookout for situations where:

- Outside of the board, responsibility or accountability for diversion is vested in a group, rather than individuals;
- Responsibility or accountability for managing diversion is 'assumed' to apply to individuals, but that responsibility is not documented or expressed;
- An individual or function has the responsibility but not the capacity, scope, or reach to meet it – while an individual or function with the capacity, scope, or reach does not have the responsibility;

- Responsibilities are discharged to outside organisations. While certain anti-diversionary functions may be outsourced or occur in partnership, each INGO must ensure that individuals within their management line retain responsibility for the arrangement.

Instead the ownership of diversion as a risk will likely follow the same 'golden thread' in the INGO's risk and control architecture as other issues like fraud, safeguarding, or even non-integrity based risks. But in essence, an identified person must be responsible for the work that deters, prevents, detects, and responds to diversion in every business unit, function, and process in the INGO. Each person must know that this is their responsibility, and they must be equipped to meet it and incentivised to do so. This framework can be enabled by:

- Clear directions relating to diversion in contracts and role descriptions;
- Comprehensive capacity-building like training;
- Diversion or ADP-related objectives in performance plans, such as a requirement to support the implementation of the ADP:
- Sufficient scope within day-to-day work to deliver the responsibilities;
- The articulation of diversion related responsibilities in policy.

Management review

In addition to the review of the ADP, there should be regular reviews of each component of it, and exception-based review in relation to significant changes to the environment of the component. Further, each business unit should review its implementation of the ADP, and the effectiveness of the ADP, for its own context and operations. Where gaps or tensions are found, this must be fed back to the owner of the ADP.

Exception-based review of both ADP components, and the application of the ADP in business units, might be triggered by:

- New systems or platforms;
- Operating in new jurisdictions, places, or with new methods or modalities;
- Changes to the legislative, regulatory, or diversionary threat environment.

For example, an INGO might review anti-diversion data analytics on an annual basis but should instigate an exception-based review if it introduces new software platforms offering additional analytical opportunities, such as financial management, supply chain, or payment platforms. A country programme, meanwhile, might review the ADP following the emergence of a new diversionary organisation with an aggressive approach to operating fees and taxation.

Independent review

As with any organisational function or process, the ADP should be subject to independent audit within a risk-based audit programme, and, potentially, self-assessment between such audits. Particular themes that auditors may wish to consider might include:

- That the components of the ADP are appropriately risk-based;
- The presence, extent of implementation, and enforcement of these components;
- That the ADP's capability and capacity is proportionate to the risks faced by the INGO;
- The reach of the ADP within the organisation.

Monitoring, performance measurement, and management information

Each ADP requires a bank of measures that provide an overview on the performance of its components, both in terms of their implementation, and their effectiveness. These measures should be reported to the anti-diversion lead, SLT, and board.

What does anti-diversion leadership look like?

There is a clear trend towards 'management commitment' as an expected component of financial crime programmes. Both OFAC (2019) and the UK Ministry of Justice (2011), for example, have incorporated such a provision into their expectations of regulated entities or inferred their intention to do so. That phrase has been around for a long time – as has its sibling, 'tone at the top,' which was hotly followed by 'mood in the middle' and 'buzz at the bottom' (see Feldman, 2015). But what does it all really mean? What is anti-diversion leadership, how does one practise it, and what would we expect if we went looking for examples?

Certainly, we can point to factors in the sector that can discourage, harry, or obstruct such leadership. Organisational models with devolved responsibility can make a consistent management message difficult, the compelling moral mission of INGOs can mean that programme issues enjoy more sympathy than business support ones, and the relentless funding and programme cycle can suck leaders into short-termism. Examples of poor leadership that emerge from these circumstances might include failing to seek visibility of the risks and how they are managed, failing to manage our own human factors, and failing to appreciate the value of risk management. We do not, of course, have to operate like this, and there are some key ways in which leaders at all levels can practise anti-diversion leadership.

Seek visibility of the risk and assurance of its effective control

One key reason that many forms of diversion are able to hide is that links in the funding chain may be disincentivised from accurately describing them.

Telling the truth can mean risk-averse and heavy-handed responses, perhaps involving an end to funding and even personal consequences. "If I say it's not safe or that sometimes we have to pay at checkpoints, will I lose my job?" an Afghan INGO worker told Jackson and Giustozzi (2012), poignantly. "I have promised the people support, will they be abandoned?"

Meanwhile, and perhaps consequently, the damaging prevalence of 'don't ask, don't tell' described by Pantuliano et al. in 2011 has remained a disappointingly consistent feature of the humanitarian landscape for nearly a decade (Jackson, 2014; O'Leary, 2018). Sometimes leaders see this as a trust, empowerment, and delegation issue, relying on their line reports to escalate when necessary. But the current sector ecosystem discourages that escalation. Silence in low-risk environments may be expected, in high-risk environments it is suspicious.

The marks of good leadership in this context, then, involve piercing the veil and extending the reach of sound, safe management. Leaders must role-model transparency and communication. They must not only maintain energy and focus in setting up and optimising systems to identify these risks, but have the courage and sensitivity to ask difficult and probing questions. In doing so, they must avoid inadvertently stoking a 'blame culture' and instead foster an environment of curiosity and collaboration. This, of course, might primarily be in one's own area of responsibility, but it also requires us to consider how we share information and help other functions and programmes to manage the risks. Risk-sharing is not just an inter-agency ideal, but an intra-agency one too.

With a clearer picture of the risks, leaders must also promote effective control. This is not the same thing as alleviating the risk – in fact, as we

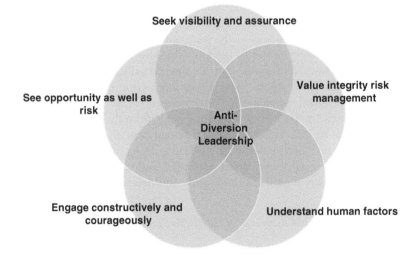

Figure 11.1 Characteristics of anti-diversion leadership.

described in Chapter 1, unbridled risk transfer is no assurance of control at all. Effectively controlling the risk requires leaders to apply balance and rationality in the face of uncomfortable truths.

Value the integrity risk management agenda

While some diversion risks are external, many belong to a family of stewardship and protection risks that arise from basic human frailty. These are best thought of as 'integrity' risks, and they might also include bribery and corruption, internal fraud, conflicts of interest, and sexual exploitation and abuse. They have so much in common with diversion that anti-diversion leadership means valuing that whole space.

The breadth of risk, and the scale of operational complexity that modern INGOs must manage, is enormous, and many leaders have expressed concern at the seemingly exponential growth of issues they must address. This attitude however is misguided – all these risks must indeed be managed, but there are harmonies. Leadership means recognition, not lament, of the breadth of risks and complexity. Effective management of integrity risks is not optional, it is a ticket-to-play in today's aid sector.

The journey to effective management begins with leaders truly valuing integrity management in word and action. That means striving to balance operational ambition and resources, so that there is sufficient capacity for deterrence, prevention, detection, and response activities.

Coupled with capacity, of course, is capability – and valuing integrity means investing in the necessary systems and functions, and seeking and listening to the advice of risk experts. These might include in-house counter-fraud, safeguarding, risk, compliance, business support, and legal teams. Leadership is about balance, and sometimes those voices can struggle to compete with the prominent, morally-compelling voices of programme functions. Leadership means allowing for this. This, in turn, can mean resisting laudable but over-reaching aims, especially when under pressure from important stakeholders like donors, governments, and trustees.

None of this, of course, means wasting money and time on complicated and expensive risk management systems. It means appreciating, and demonstrating appreciation for, sober, practical, and thoughtful consideration of integrity risk. It means respecting the frailty and complexity of both people and operations.

Anti-diversion leaders recognise that by doing so, they can not only reduce the likelihood and consequence of diversion incidents, but they also enable their INGO to seize the humanitarian and development opportunities that effective risk management facilitates. They can also gain other benefits associated with organisations that manage risks like these well – perhaps improved staff morale, productivity, safety, and retention.

Understand human factors – including one's own

In 2011, Oxfam GB carried out an investigation into sexual abuse allegations concerning, amongst others, its country director in Haiti. The 2018 statutory inquiry by the CCEW into how Oxfam's senior managers handled this investigation made for sobering reading (CCEW, 2019), but one striking factor in the Commission's report was the extent to which reputation was a key factor in several of the decisions later criticised in the press.

From one perspective, it is understandable why reputation played such a role. The link between reputation and funding is strong, while the confidence of beneficiaries, local partners, and governments is vital to delivery. The problem, of course, is that a focus on short-termist reputation management can lead to decisions that are ultimately more damaging, and the Commission's report itself noted that "dealing properly with incidents … reporting them, and ensuring lessons are learned and acted on [protects] the reputation of a charity in the long term."

It is unfair and naïve to suggest, as some commentators have, that Oxfam's senior managers at the time were somehow ethically different to others. In fact, allowing the preservation of reputation to impede the right outcomes of integrity incidents is so common that we could speculate it might even be the norm. It is easy to see why when we apply the lens of human factors.

Cognitive errors, biases, and heuristics affect our ideas and decisions. Learned helplessness might leave aid workers believing that corruption and diversion are 'just how things are done here,' for example. Group norms and reinforced beliefs can preserve myths and misconceptions about diversion. And just as companies may be encouraged to pay bribes through fear of being unable to compete in a given market (Søreide, 2009), aid workers might worry that failing to embrace the provision of material benefit to terrorists rules them out of providing aid at all (though while potentially true on some occasions, it is certainly not the case in all). And, of course, the bias towards short-termist thinking in threatening scenarios (Gray, 1999) might explain questionable reputational management decisions.

These psychological factors shape stakeholder perspectives, and means that it is not enough to see preventing integrity incidents as a matter of being 'more ethical.' A better approach is for leaders to be smarter about how they manage inevitable human frailty, including their own.

To protect the ADP from the cognitive errors, biases, and heuristics of ourselves and others, the starting point is for leaders to know about them. Anti-diversion leaders must engage with the heavy weight of research in this area, so that they can allow for these variables. They must also combine self-awareness, emotional intelligence, and rationality to challenge their own perspectives and those of others. Is a diversion-free programme really impossible in that particular country context, for example? Is there really no other way of helping those beneficiaries without providing some kind of benefit to an armed group? Are there issues we are putting on the back burner that could come back to bite us?

And of course, they must promote the practice of managing human factors in their programmes and functions. The more that practitioners are aware of these challenges to rationality, the better we can allow for them.

Engage constructively and courageously in the public space

Research suggests one in three people worldwide lack confidence in NGOs, especially in Australia, the US, and Europe (Younis and Rzepa, 2019). Antagonists and ideologues, for whom diversion may be merely a lever, have been amplified by a string of high-profile controversies. The aid sector, arguably, is in the grip of a trust crisis. In the reputation economy, that is an unhealthy position.

Anti-diversion leadership means participating in this dialogue. Unlike antagonists, who focus on the problem, leadership must focus on progress, improvement, and – perhaps ultimately – solutions. To do so, engagement must avoid:

- Rehashing old tropes that lack credibility, like equating the fate of any given INGO with the fate of beneficiaries;
- Polarising the discussion. The effects of diversion are severe, and regulation and donor requirements do serve a purpose as a lever for integrity in the sector;
- Defensiveness.

Instead, despite the challenges of the 'post-truth' era, engagement must be evidence-based and the messaging clear. That messaging must go in all directions – the public, regulators, donors, lawmakers, the media, and the sector itself. It must be consistent, and raise awareness on:

- The effects of legislation, regulatory enforcement trends, and donor requirements;
- The reality of trying to carry out necessary programming in high-risk places;
- The impact of the 'overhead myth' and the need for investment in protecting people and resources;
- The vital importance of the work affected by these issues.

See opportunity as well as risk

While managing diversion risk is about pursuing aid opportunities as safely as possible, it is still a common misconception in the sector that managing risk is about managing *hazards* (CFG, 2016). This is a crucial difference. Sometimes INGOs are urged to run 'more like businesses,' which is an odd aspiration given their fundamentally different nature – and from one perspective would merely mean exchanging one set of risks for another. But perhaps what these voices are really asking for is more decisive, effective, and efficient leadership –

and the private sector's entrepreneurial bend for opportunity is a key characteristic.

Managing diversion demands courage. But if leaders commit to transparency, use the information generated by it to manage the risks as effectively as possible, through systems upon which they can rely, then they can have the confidence to operate in high-risk circumstances. That means reaching beneficiaries.

Even where the reputation economy threatens to punish INGOs for whom incidents occur, or where overreaching new legislation threatens aid, there are opportunities. These circumstances create scope for dialogue and for INGOs to advocate on behalf of the humanitarian and development sector (May, 2019). That can be very powerful – consider Bond's successful campaign for change to the UK's Counter-Terrorism and Border Security Bill (Bond, 2018).

At programme and project levels, the complexity of the circumstances in which diversion risk can be found means that leaders need to be creative, optimistic, and agile to minimise it. This can only be enabled by the right training, experience, and access to local knowledge.

References

Bond 2018. *Counter Terrorism Bill: Lords pass amendment to protect aid workers*. London: Bond.

Bright, M. 2015. Kids Company: A charity so toxic everyone who supported it is tainted. *The Guardian*.

Charity Commission for England and Wales 2019. *Statement of the results of an inquiry: Oxfam*. London: Charity Commission for England and Wales.

Charity Finance Group (CFG) 2016. *Rethinking risk: Beyond the tick box*. London: CFG.

Feldman, E.R. 2015. *It's not just tone at the top: How companies can build a corporate ethical culture and prevent fraud*. Ethics and Compliance Institute.

Glazer, R. 2016. The biggest lesson from Volkswagen: Culture dictates behaviour. *Entrepreneur*.

Gray, J.R. 1999. A bias toward short-term thinking in threat-related negative emotional states. *Personality and Social Psychology Bulletin* 25(1): 65–67. https://doi.org/10.1177/0146167299025001006.

Hennessy, R. 2016. Failure of stewardship was at the heart of Wounded Warrior Project firings. *Entrepreneur*.

Humm, S. 2015. Was FIFA's corrupt organisational culture developed by its leaders? *HR Review*.

Jackson, A. 2014. *Humanitarian negotiations with armed non-state actors: Key lessons from Afghanistan, Sudan and Somalia*. HPG Policy Brief 55. London: Overseas Development Institute.

Jackson, A. and Giustozzi, A. 2012. *Talking to the other side: Humanitarian engagement with the Taliban in Afghanistan*. London: Overseas Development Institute.

May, O. 2019. Is your non-profit suffering from regulatory fatigue? Pro Bono Australia. https://probonoaustralia.com.au/news/2019/03/non-profit-suffering-regulatory-fatigue/

Ministry of Justice 2011. *The Bribery Act 2010: Guidance about procedures which relevant commercial organisations can put into place to prevent persons associated with them from bribing*. London: HM Government.

O'Leary, E. 2018. *Principles under pressure: The impact of counterterrorism measures and preventing/countering violent extremism on principled humanitarian action*. Geneva: Norwegian Refugee Council.

Ochs, S. 2016. *The leadership blind spots at Wells Fargo*. Harvard Business Review. https://hbr.org/2016/10/the-leadership-blind-spots-at-wells-fargo.

OFAC 2019. *A framework for OFAC compliance commitments*. Washington, DC: United States Department of the Treasury.

Pantuliano, S., Mackintosh, K., Elhawary, S., and Metcalfe, V. 2011. *Counter-terrorism and humanitarian action: Tensions, impact and ways forward*. HPG Policy Brief 43. London: Overseas Development Institute.

Søreide, T. 2009. Too risk averse to stay honest? Business corruption, uncertainty and attitudes toward risk. *International Review of Law and Economics 29*: 388–395.

Stoddard, A., Czwarno, M., and Hamsik, L. 2019. *NGOs & risk: Managing uncertainty in local-international partnerships*. Humanitarian Outcomes/InterAction. https://www.humanitarianoutcomes.org/publications/ngos-risk2-partnerships.

Younis, M. and Rzepa, A. 2019. One in three worldwide lack confidence in NGOs. Gallup. https://news.gallup.com/opinion/gallup/258230/one-three-worldwide-lack-confidence-ngos.aspx.

12 De-risking

The intersection of a bank's AML/CTF programme and the INGO

Paul Curwell

The challenge of de-risking intersects legislation, guidance, and enforcement action opinions issued by global regulators, bank reputation risk, and financial crime compliance programmes (Human Security Collective, 2018; Durner and Shetret, 2015). Much of the de-risking literature focuses on the social impact, rather than the root causes. This chapter, however, explores some of these root causes, what is de-risking, and how it can be undertaken.

Contrary to popular belief, de-risking is not something that affects only INGOs. Much has been written on the de-risking of Money Services Businesses (MSBs) and correspondent banking relationships, but patent attorneys, gaming, and foreign embassies have also been affected.

At the heart of de-risking is the Customer Risk Assessment. We explore this, reviewing the concepts of 'high risk customer' and 'high risk jurisdiction,' before considering the main factors influencing a bank's customer retention decisions. We then turn to a discussion of the practical steps which INGOs can take to minimise de-risking. These include a more collaborative, 'relationship management' approach in which INGOs work with their bankers to help inform their customer risk rating, and where possible to remove the cost and complexity associated with the bank's due diligence processes.

As with any regulation, understanding the conditions against which you are to be risk-assessed is critical if you are to influence the outcome. This chapter aims to provide this foundation.

De-risking, demystified

For FATF, 'de-risking' is "the phenomenon of financial institutions terminating or restricting business relationships with clients or categories of clients to avoid, rather than manage, risk" (Caribbean Financial Action Task Force, 2019). In this chapter, this 'risk' primarily relates to financial crime risks such as money-laundering, terrorist financing, or economic and trade sanctions. The role of FATF, as described in Chapter 3, is such that all FATF member countries must require their banks and Designated Non-Financial Businesses and Professions, which includes accountants, notaries, and lawyers, to identify and address their money laundering and terrorist financing risks (FATF, 2012).

While INGOs are generally excluded from the resulting legislative re-quirements, they are most greatly affected when accessing the global financial system. Whilst banks rarely discuss de-risking decisions due to staff concerns about committing the criminal offence of 'tipping off,' compliance costs and risk appetite are also common root causes (FATF, 2015). Taking a macro view, de-risking is defeatist in terms of both financial inclusion and financial system integrity, as customers who should be subject to more intense scrutiny are removed from the bank which detected the problem, potentially to an-other bank with a less mature compliance capability, or out of the formal banking system altogether and into underground banking markets.

When considering a bank's financial crime maturity, it should also be noted that smaller banks may not have the resources or expertise required to manage compliance risks associated with an INGO operating in a high-risk jurisdic-tion. Banks are not permitted to accept financial crime risk at the portfolio level in lieu of the customer, and it is here where the de-risking tension lies.

Customer due diligence: A bank's perceptions of INGO AML/CTF risk

Customer Due Diligence (CDD) is a key AML/CTF control in the banking system and encompasses:

- Identifying and verifying a customer's identity;
- Establishing a baseline of expected transactions for a given customer's profile for the purpose of detecting anomalies;
- Determining the financial crime risks posed (FATF, 2012).

CDD starts upon commencement of the relationship (account opening) and continues throughout the customer lifecycle ('ongoing customer due dili-gence'). Understanding the CDD Customer Risk Assessment (CRA) process is critical for INGOs, as banks use this in the same way as the preliminary risk rating for KYP (see Chapter 8) to determine the requisite due diligence scope for each customer (AUSTRAC, 2019). Where the CRA is performed im-properly, such as in situations where a compliance officer does not understand an INGO's risk context, inappropriate customer risk ratings may be assigned which in turn generate a heavy compliance burden.

The Customer Risk Assessment

The CRA is one of a suite of risk assessments that must be performed by a bank to comply with its AML/CTF regulations. A customer's first CRA is performed on account opening, with the rating being determined by factors such as their:

- Legal entity type;
- Industry;

- Operating jurisdiction(s);
- Beneficial owners;
- Applicable financial products or services.

Further risk factors may include the customer's transaction activity and associations with third parties. In jurisdictions such as the USA, the banking regulator (Federal Financial Institutions Examination Council, FFIEC) defines various checks that must be performed during a CRA (FFIEC, 2014). Aside from having a general understanding of an INGO customer's legal structure and operations, US regulators require banks to also understand the risks posed by donors as well as the INGO's funding and disbursement criteria, amongst others.

Whenever an INGO receives a request for information from its bank relating to this kind of information, it can assume that its customer risk rating may be under review. To obtain the most positive outcome possible, INGO managers should be prepared to talk about these points and, where necessary, provide evidence to verify any claims, including in relation to controls viewed by their bank as being critical to the INGO's management of financial crime risks.

As bank compliance officers perform the CRA, they will look for specific red flags indicating 'high risk' status (Financial Conduct Authority, 2016). In addition to triggers recommended by regulators, banks may also identify their own risk factors. Typically, there are only two outcomes from a CRA: A customer is either rated as low/medium ('normal risk') or 'high risk,' with customers rated as 'high risk' likely to be subject to Enhanced Due Diligence (EDD) as outlined in guidance from the pre-eminent Joint Money Laundering Steering Group (JMLSG, 2017).

Enhanced Due Diligence

A customer can be rated as a 'High Risk Customer' (HRC) at any stage in their lifecycle with their bank. As with the CRA, the FFIEC also defines various EDD criteria for INGOs banking in the USA (FFIEC, 2014). Irrespective of specific jurisdictional requirements, three structural characteristics of the aid sector can attract further scrutiny during the EDD process, being:

- Legal entity type;
- Nature of business activity;
- Jurisdiction risk.

Legal entity types

Directors and Trustees should understand the role that legal entity type can play in any HRC rating or de-risking decision. Some types of legal entity are more frequently associated with unlawful activity, perhaps due to reduced transparency, and therefore attract increased scrutiny. Whilst there is no definitive list, higher risk legal entities are typically those where beneficial ownership is obscured, or where a lack of regulatory oversight results in minimal transparency in relation to ownership, financial arrangements, or business activity. Publicly listed companies on a reputable stock exchange are considered to have the highest level of transparency, whereas the trusts and private foundations often found in the INGO sector can be seen as less transparent (ACAMS, 2016).

Nature of business activity

For bank compliance officers, a customer's business activity is an important part of interpreting the dynamics that will affect its risk rating. The four INGO programme delivery models identified by the CCEW (2016) can help to support an INGO's conversation with its bank about its business activity. Table 12.1 presents the four models and their respective advantages and disadvantages from the perspective of financial crime risk, and gives an indication of the way a bank compliance officer is likely to perceive each delivery model:

Table 12.1 Perceived financial crime risk of the four CCEW programme delivery models

Programme delivery model	Advantages	Disadvantages	Bank's indicative perception of risk
INGO undertakes all work using direct delivery.	INGO has ability to develop and implement robust anti-diversion systems and internal control frameworks.	INGO is solely accountable if frameworks are inadequate.	LOW – MEDIUM
INGO undertakes and supervises the work itself, but uses local representatives or individual partners to assist where the INGO has no local presence.	INGO has ability to develop and implement robust anti-diversion systems and internal control frameworks.	Extent of programme oversight by INGO influences level of compliance by local representatives/partners.	LOW – HIGH
INGO works in collaboration with, and alongside, other organisations (INGOs and non-INGOs).	INGO can team with like-minded partners to create a lower risk environment.	Reputations are easily tarnished by partners with poor controls – requires assurance over teaming partners.	LOW – MEDIUM
Giving grants or using local NGOs and other delivery partners to carry out charitable projects.	Allows INGO to disburse offshore or in inaccessible regions.	INGO has limited control over use of funds upon receipt, visibility of who actually receives the funds, or their actual use.	HIGH (greater where high-risk jurisdictions are involved)

Whilst the perceptions of risk outlined in this table are indicative, they can help to structure conversations with bankers as part of the CDD process. Meanwhile, one major factor influencing the customer risk rating for an INGO will be the combination of its programme delivery model and jurisdictional risk.

Jurisdictional risk

AML/CTF programmes incorporate the risk rating of countries based on a variety of political, social, economic, and legal factors identified by each bank for this purpose (Cortez, 2015). Jurisdictional risk ratings are maintained by each bank and will include, but not be limited to, countries subject to economic or trade sanctions. Banks typically prohibit their customers from transacting with jurisdictions they consider to be 'high risk' without an exemption from an accountable senior executive, ensuring customer risk remains within the bounds of what the bank considers manageable given its resources and risk appetite.

Jurisdictional risk presents a challenge for INGOs, as many countries in which they operate are likely rated 'high risk' by their bank, and because many banks do not have compliance resources with the requisite depth of understanding in these jurisdictions to properly assess and manage the risk. Bank stakeholder management is particularly important for INGOs operating higher risk business activities in 'high-risk' jurisdictions.

The cost of an HRC to a bank

Aside from exposing a bank to regulatory risk, HRCs demand a disproportionate level of compliance resources during both initial onboarding and throughout the customer lifecycle (Artingstall et al., 2016). Acceptance for a customer operating in a 'high-risk' jurisdiction typically requires a written exemption from a senior executive (JMLSG, 2017).

Those exemptions are often predicated on additional in-country due diligence being performed to inform risk acceptance. This work is increasingly outsourced to local specialists, with market rates typically ranging from US$5,000 (£3,807) to US$25,000 (£19,000) per case, and I have seen cases in which costs exceeded US$50,000 (£38,000).

Additionally, ongoing monitoring must also be performed throughout the customer lifecycle, which could amount to a large percentage of a compliance officer's workload. It is increasingly common to find customers being asked to reimburse the bank for its due diligence costs where costs cannot be recovered through other fees and charges.

The de-risking process

The mere fact of classification as an HRC is not generally enough to trigger the de-risking process for an onboarded customer. Instead, de-risking is usually commenced in the wake of an event such as a financial crime red flag, suspicious transaction, or adverse media reporting involving a customer. At a minimum, a bank's media monitoring programme is likely to focus on what FATF refers to as 'designated categories of offences,' essentially any predicate offence to money laundering or terrorist financing (FATF, 2012). Automated media alerts are typically established by the bank which include predicate offence keywords, as listed below:

- Organised criminal activity (including, but not limited to, kidnapping and extortion);
- Terrorism and terrorist financing;
- Human trafficking, people smuggling, and slavery offences;
- Sexual exploitation (including child sexual exploitation), either as a 'seller' or 'consumer' of such services;
- Trafficking in illicit commodities including drugs, arms, and stolen goods;
- Corruption, bribery, fraud, forgery, insider trading, robbery and theft;
- Counterfeiting (currency and products), smuggling, and piracy;
- Environmental crime;
- Murder and assault.

Once a customer has come to the bank's attention, it may be referred to a specialist team for investigation. Notably, this team's understanding of any referred customer, and the time allocated to them to perform any such task, is limited. Any material provided in advance by the customer, such as briefing packs, to help understand the risk context and assess materiality of an adverse event, is useful.

These reviews typically examine a customer's historical transaction activity and account profile for biographical risk indicators, suspicious activity, or adverse associations. Associations here could include depositors (i.e. donors), beneficiaries, and partners. Names of associates will be searched in various databases and matches flagged. For example, using a delivery partner which is a front company for a known diversionary will likely lead to de-risking. Mandatory bank reporting may initiate a criminal investigation.

Typically, a customer review report is compiled and sent to a bank committee with authority to make a retention or termination decision, with the latter usually having immediate effect. It can be difficult to reverse a termination decision, not least as this may indicate an 'ineffective AML/CTF programme' to banking regulators. For this reason, it is imperative that INGOs actively manage their banking relationships to proactively minimise any likelihood of de-risking. If an INGO is seeking to reverse a de-risking decision, legal advice should be sought as to available options.

Proactively managing banking relationships to minimise de-risking

So far, this chapter has outlined the concept of de-risking, explained the AML/CTF CDD process as it applies to INGOs, and explored the de-risking process within a bank. A key theme that emerged is the need for engagement, and four ways in which INGOs can foster this include selecting the right bank in the first place, looking out for early warning indicators of de-risking, adopting a proactive stakeholder management approach, and being responsive to information requests.

Selecting the right bank for your INGO

When we as consumers think about opening a bank account, the decision on where to place our money is often derived from trust – our family may have used a specific bank before, or a bank's brand may resonate with us. However, for INGOs, selecting the right bank should be a more informed decision. For INGOs, picking the right bank might be guided by two considerations:

- That the bank has the compliance capacity to support its operations;
- That the bank has interest in doing so.

At their most basic level, banks are businesses, and some customers are more profitable than others. Some banks are genuinely interested in helping effect social change, and demonstrate this not just in word, but in action. Picking the right bank starts with the relationship manager, the banker assigned to an INGO as a customer and responsible for selling their products, services, and maintaining the customer's account. When selecting a bank, INGOs may wish to consider one with a dedicated non-profit team – such banks likely have a better understanding of INGO programme delivery models, risks, and governance frameworks.

The second consideration is driven by the nature of the INGO's operations. INGOs which fall into a lower risk category probably don't need to consider their bank's compliance capability. However, an INGO engaging in activity which may result in their classification as an HRC would be best selecting a banking partner that has a demonstrated commitment to the sector, paired with the requisite risk and compliance capability. This might include a presence in the countries in which the INGO operates or a familiarity with emerging markets. This will help to minimise any confusion or misunderstanding between the INGO and the bank which could trigger de-risking.

Early warning indicators of impending de-risking activity

INGOs, particularly those conducting activity perceived to be high-risk or which operate in high-risk jurisdictions, should be particularly attuned to the nature and tone of any communications from their bank. Typically, de-risking is not something that happens overnight, with no notice. There are often indicators, such as:

- Being asked to re-verify account holder identities, beneficial owners, or directors;

- Being the subject of adverse media or an active law enforcement investigation (this can extend to actual or perceived organised criminal actions of the INGO's staff, such as involvement in child sexual exploitation);
- Being asked to explain the purpose and counterparty of a payment to/ from a foreign jurisdiction which could be considered high risk;
- Evidence that the bank is struggling to understand the nature of an INGO's operations or programme delivery model, or finding it difficult to manage its compliance obligations in relation to the INGO's customer risk.

INGO managers should look out for these. For example, has there been a material change in the INGO's operations or geographic footprint? Has its account received a large, unexplained donation from a new donor located in a high-risk jurisdiction? Any communications from the bank subsequent to a change in the INGOs operations or some other activity should be taken seriously, as de-risking can happen because events or context are misinterpreted.

To manage these risks, all bank communications should go through one senior person or a core team who understand both the INGO and have an understanding of the bank's AML/CTF regulatory obligations so events can be placed into context and accurate information provided to the bank at the right time. A comparable model may be donor relationship management.

Adopt a stakeholder management approach

Whilst customers can get annoyed by their bank's questions about their account activity, even to the point of suggesting it is none of the bank's business, this is exactly the expectation placed on financial institutions by global AML/CTF regulators. In respect of financial crime, banks are held accountable, in a sense, for their customers' actions. Therefore, like any relationship, INGOs should take proactive steps to nurture and grow the relationship within an environment of trust and transparency. This means INGOs should consider initiating meetings with their banker to brief them periodically on their operations, donors, governance, risk and compliance processes. INGOs may also wish to ask the banker to invite their assigned compliance officer as this will provide an opportunity to proactively engage, clarify any concerns or misinformation, and provide input to any future re-evaluation of the risk posed by the INGO as a customer of the bank.

INGOs should proactively contact their bank's relationship manager in the event of an incident involving 'suspected unlawful activity' or generating adverse media coverage, rather than hoping the bank doesn't realise. Notably, banks receive court orders and 'notices to produce' from law enforcement agencies and regulators in relation to their customers.

Depending on the notice and jurisdiction, these communications may reveal the nature of any alleged offence(s), meaning a bank probably knows more about its customers' activities than they realise. Whilst specific details of an incident need not be disclosed, the high-level nature of the matter might be outlined, followed (more importantly) by the steps being taken by the INGO to prevent any reoccurrence and the implementation timeframe.

For example, initial discussions should demonstrate transparency through words and actions and that the INGO takes the compliance obligations of both itself and the bank seriously. These are opportunities to prove to a bank that the INGO is worthy of its continued trust, otherwise if something adverse happens it is likely the bank will opt for de-risking as the first and easiest option.

Being prepared to respond quickly to any request for information from your bank

Previously, we indicated that de-risking decisions are usually undertaken quickly to minimise the regulatory risk to the bank between the date and time when a customer was identified as being associated with an 'adverse event,' and when a completed customer review report is sent to the committee for a retention or termination decision. Further, many banks have been fined by regulators for failing to exit a customer marked for termination.

Consequently, INGOs should always be ready in the event of a call from their bank requesting more information for the bank's Know Your Customer (KYC) or AML/CTF purposes. One way to do this is to have a pack prepared in advance that contains all relevant public and non-public information in a single location and which can easily be shared with the bank at a moment's notice. Such a pack should be reviewed and updated periodically, at a minimum annually, to ensure all information is accepted by the bank as being current. INGOs might also wish to include a signed letter from a senior 'accountable authority' (ideally this person would also be listed on the bank's customer profile) attesting that all enclosed information was true and correct at the time of issue.

To make it as easy as possible for your Banks' compliance team, these briefing packs might consist of at least two sections. The first section might include:

- An overview of the INGO and its operations in clear, easy to understand language;
- Details of typical donors and beneficiaries;
- Delivery partner arrangements;
- Geographical presence.

The second section should contain all the information required by the bank to typically perform its CDD and assess your customer risk, including copies or extracts of company or charity registrations and other such material. If the INGO has been subject to previous incidents, regulatory enforcement, or adverse media reporting, it may be worthwhile adding additional sections to outline steps taken to improve governance, risk and control frameworks to minimise recurrence, and high-level up-to-date action plans for any remediation work.

Many organisations would understandably be reluctant to release such information to an external party, at least without a formal non-disclosure agreement. However, given the short window of time available to avoid de-risking, any reluctance to share such information or requests to sign non-disclosure agreements may compound any negative perceptions of the INGO by their bank. To avoid this, INGOs may consider releasing such documentation to their bank in a way that enacts the privacy and banking customer secrecy provisions of the applicable jurisdiction, such as use of appropriate caveats or other conditions stated in the documentation itself.

To help minimise the risk of misinformation being provided to the bank, clear procedures should govern who can have these conversations, what information can be disclosed, and if briefing packs are prepared in advance, where the latest version can be located. Additionally, smaller INGOs should ensure appropriate staff are available in case of a call. INGOs may wish to consider providing awareness training to all staff and volunteers, including who they need to refer calls from their bank to within the organisation. At a minimum, any member of senior management or the board, the risk, compliance or legal teams, or anyone from the finance team nominated as a contact for the bank account, should be conversant in such protocols.

Actions in the event of a blocked transaction

Legislation providing for the blocking (seizure) of payments typically relates to sanctions. Transactions which are blocked become property of the government of the applicable jurisdiction and must be deposited into an account controlled by that government at the bank (US Department of the Treasury, nd).

Blocked payments get more complicated with international transfers involving correspondent banks, as payments are subsequently reviewed by multiple, independent financial crime teams as the transaction passes through each bank's systems (Eckert, Guinane, and Hall, 2017). This situation establishes the scenario where one bank will process an international payment, only for one of its correspondent banks to block it. Where this happens, it is often because the correspondent bank has more detailed information about the associates of sanctioned parties. One limitation with many PEP and sanctions lists, including commercial databases, is that they vary considerably in their coverage (Human Security Collective, 2018).

This variation in coverage extends to reliable details on indirectly sanctioned ('sanctioned by extension') entities and individuals, which requires considerable investigative research and expense to identify close associates of a sanctioned party such as family members, friends, business associates, lawyers, and accountants. As a consequence of these coverage gaps, companies across a range of sectors with a higher sanctions risk profile often establish in-house programmes to identify and map indirect sanctions with a nexus to their operations to minimise this exposure. Where a customer's funds are blocked, the starting point to try and have them unblocked and released is the relevant national regulator for the blocking action.

References

Association of Certified Anti Money-Laundering Specialists (ACAMS) 2016. *Study guide: CAMS certification exam.* Miami, FL: ACAMS.

Artingstall, D., Dove, N., Howell, J., and Levi, M. 2016. *Drivers & impacts of derisking: A study of representative views and data in the UK.* London: Financial Conduct Authority.

AUSTRAC 2019. *Money laundering/terrorism financing risk assessment.* https://www.austrac.gov.au/business/how-comply-guidance-and-resources/amlctf-programs/risk-assessment (accessed 13 December 2019).

Caribbean Financial Action Task Force 2019. De-risking. https://www.cfatf-gafic.org/home/cfatf-news/449-de-risking (accessed 13 December 2019).

Charity Commission for England and Wales (CCEW) 2016. *Compliance toolkit: Protecting charities from harm.* London: CCEW.

Cortez, A. 2015. *High risk countries in AML monitoring.* Miami, FL: ACAMS.

Durner, T. and Shetret, L. 2015. *Understanding bank de-risking and its effects on financial inclusion: An exploratory study.* Oxford: Global Center on Cooperative Security/Oxfam.

Eckert, S.E., Guinane, K., and Hall, A. 2017. *Financial access for U.S. nonprofits.* Washington, DC: Charity & Security Network.

FATF 2012. *International Standards on Combatting Money Laundering and the Financing of Terrorism & Proliferation (The FATF Recommendations).* Paris: FATF.

FATF 2015. *Combatting the abuse of non-profit organisations (Recommendation 8).* Paris: FATF.

Federal Financial Institutions Examination Council 2014. *Bank Secrecy Act/Anti-Money Laundering Examination manual.* Virginia: FFIEC.

Financial Conduct Authority (FCA) 2016. *High-risk customers, including politically exposed persons.* London: FCA.

Human Security Collective 2018. *At the intersection of security and regulation: Understanding the drivers of 'de-risking' and the impact on civil society organisations.* Human Security Collective/European Center for Not-for-profit Law. http://ecnl.org/wp-content/uploads/2018/05/Understanding-the-Drivers-of-De-Risking-and-the-Impact-on-Civil-Society-Organizations_1.pdf (accessed 28 April 2020).

Joint Money Laundering Steering Group (JMLSG) 2017. *Prevention of money laundering/combating terrorist financing. Guidance for the UK Financial Sector, Part 1.* London: JMLSG.

US Department of the Treasury nd OFAC FAQs: Sanctions compliance. https://www.treasury.gov/resource-center/faqs/Sanctions/Pages/faq_compliance.aspx#block (accessed 13 December 2019).

13 Working in partnership

Oliver May

The way that the aid community, and the social impact sector more broadly, sees partnership should be a differentiating characteristic. While organisations that exist for social good should also enjoy the benefits of controls like contracting, for example, these organisations are supposed to exist for a purpose beyond their own benefit, or the benefit of a demarcated group, in a way that is not true of the private and public sectors. That should release them to exponential collaboration in a unique and powerful way. It is sad, then, that 'partnership' is too often a euphemism for outsourcing, and a fig-leaf for simple, subcontracting relationships.

There are a number of core issues at the heart of how we, as a global community, ensure that our charitable intentions evolve successfully into safely-delivered aid interventions, free of diversion. Tackling these can only be achieved with change to the way that we work in partnership both in specific relationships, and as a global community.

Though hardly an exhaustive list, there are five themes to the impediment of anti-diversion progress here. The first is risk transfer. Generally speaking, the greater any given risk, the more effort we should see to control it. But we do not always see that in this dynamic. Instead, we see the risk passing to actors less able to control it, with fewer resources to do so, while the preceding agency retains reputational liability.

The second is disparate, even contradictory, inter- and intra-agency agendas. The third is related, and that is a degree of corporate tribalism; some blame INGOs for a perceived lack of progress, while some INGO workers blame their institutional donors. The problem, of course, is that those who truly suffer through this collective intransigence are beneficiaries.

The fourth is the diversity and the dynamism of the risks and contexts in which they arise – and arguably the failure of actors across all agencies to appreciate that. Diversion is not static, the places in which it occurs are in a constant state of short-, medium-, and long-term change, and no two contexts are identical. Fifthly, diversion in aid – as with wider financial crime – still suffers from underinvestment in capacity and capability.

To move forward, alleviating these issues requires fundamental change to the approach of all actors: Institutional donors, INGOs, regulators, wider government departments, lawmakers, aid sector peak bodies, private supporters, the media, and, of course, the public. This chapter makes some suggestions that aim to address these themes.

Residual risk and 'zero tolerance'

"Humanitarian assistance has a terrorism problem," wrote Jessica Trisko Darden of the American Enterprise Institute in a 2019(a) article. The response from Joel Charny of the Norwegian Refugee Council was almost immediate. "The US approach to counter-terrorism has a humanitarian problem," he wrote. Whether these authors intended to or not, their exchange neatly captured a key difference of perspective at the heart of this issue: Who created this problem?

It is not a particularly helpful dynamic. As with many wicked problems, and as we saw in Chapter 1, a huge array of factors are at play. But one stands out in particular. This book has touched on the tension between the political and enforcement-derived language of 'zero tolerance,' and the discipline of risk management. In reality, to reach the people who most need aid will mean working in challenging environments in which the risk of diversion can be reduced, but not eliminated. The only way to eliminate the risk is not to work there, and this is unlikely to be either morally acceptable, or palatable within IHL.

Perhaps a helpful approach might be to speak less in terms of 'zero tolerance,' and more in terms of managed residual risk. There is much that INGOs can do to lower that residual risk, and it is true that not all INGOs are doing as much as they should. But true progress will only be made when all stakeholders in the aid sector adopt a more nuanced approach, and more nuanced language.

To be clear, this book is not advocating that the aid sector should tolerate diversion. Far from it. It is advocating a more considered approach to reducing it, and more accurate language to describe how we do that.

Institutional donors

There are certainly some general actions that institutional donors could take – there is a need to continue to work towards a common language on risk and diversion, and to harmonise requirements on partners between donors (such as due diligence) as far as possible. But there are also some specific ones. Institutional donors should adopt the risk-based approach, and foster it amongst their partners. They should take the lead on addressing the phenomenon of humanitarian risk transfer, achieve a more equitable balance of prescription and agency in contracting, and assist to articulate – to a sceptical public – the need to accept residual risk.

Adopt a risk-based approach to managing diversion with partners

Institutional donors should require partners to demonstrate evidence of an ADP. A donor should clearly articulate what a holistic, proportionate, and effective approach looks like (and the programme outlined in this book offers a starting point), but – and this is key – the control activities should not be limited to the project that donor might fund. The prospective partner should demonstrate how it controls its own diversion risks.

The scale of the risk in any given funding arrangement might inform the extent of the donor's inquiry into a prospective partner's ADP. But it is likely that a donor should seek evidence of strategy, monitoring, policy, procedure, the components of the programme, and audit. Such evidence might be obtained through not only documentary review, but interviews and testing.

Secondly, at the project level, donors should expect meaningful diversion risk assessment in any project they intend to fund in an elevated risk context. That may mean declining funding applications from partners that are unable to evidence an appropriate level of diversion risk management, particularly rejecting proposals in high-risk contexts where there is no evidence of a meaningful risk assessment.

Thirdly, the assessment of an ADP must be part of a consistent, integrated approach to evaluating a partner's capacity and capability. The awarding of funding beyond a partner's capacity and capability to manage it is still very common. Guarding against this also requires re-assessment should a partner be provided funding in excess of the original capacity and capability assessment. And it must include reflective, evidence-based evaluation of the donor's own capacity and capability to manage diversion in the context of the project. This must go beyond policy, procedure, and commitment, and instead take in systems, resources, skills, and local knowledge.

At the other end of the funding cycle, how donors respond to suspicions of diversion may require their urgent review. A partner reporting a suspicion offers either an opportunity to encourage transparency and improve anti-diversion resilience, or to make a partner wish they had not (and it is notable that a significant proportion of humanitarians feel unable to be honest about diversion, according to Burniske and Modirzadeh, 2017).

It may also be time to retire the term 'zero-tolerance.' As language imported to risk management from the law enforcement and political space, it generates confusion and is often differently-defined between agencies. While it is often felt to broadcast a particular values-based stance, that effect is undermined by the baggage it carries at an operational level. If its use is to persist, it must come with an object – that is, 'zero-tolerance for perpetrators,' for example. Without clarification of its operational meaning, the term in relation to broad phenomena like diversion or fraud is no longer helpful.

Foster the risk-based approach among partners

In addition to setting expectations that incentivise holistic, proportionate, and effective ADPs, there is some truth to the common INGO refrain that institutional donors do not provide sufficient scope in their grants for 'administrative' or 'overhead' costs.

Allowances for these costs are often determined by consistent, value-based rules. But any such standing rule is unlikely to be nuanced enough in the diverse array of contexts in which projects are implemented, and the restricted nature of such funding disrupts economies of scale and harmonies of risk management.

Some may see it as a tough ask to expect institutional donors, particularly governments, to effectively fund the development of INGOs at the same time as the projects these organisations are engaged to deliver. In effect, this might be perceived as making INGOs a form of beneficiary. Jessica Trisko Darden disagrees in particular 2019(b). For Trisko Darden, "throwing money at NGOs" will not improve their behaviour. This view, however, is puzzling – prudent investment in capacity and capability is necessary for its improvement – and inadequately recognises the value chain of institutional donors, which are often reliant on partner delivery. These would not be lost funds, but value chain investments.

Donors, of course, will need to be able to show that such investment has met their own aims – and that becomes harder if donors are forced to rearticulate their missions to favour the political and economic interests of their countries, rather than humanitarian interests.

Take the lead on addressing risk transfer

Chapter 1 noted the potential impact of the use of risk transfer in international aid operations. It observed that risk transfer often follows the funding chain with improper consideration, and each agency in the funding flow, from back-donor to local implementing partner, passes on risk and liability to the next link in the chain. As a result, agencies often fail to:

- Adequately assess the capability of a partner to manage diversion risks;
- Sufficiently support partners in the management of diversion risks;
- Enter into arrangements for joint liability of diversion risks;
- Respond proportionately or reasonably upon the potential detection of diversion.

While this is one of the thorniest issues in diversion, it must change. As the first links in the chain, institutional donors are in a strong position to instigate that change. Donors need to explore ways to move beyond simple risk transfer and associated contracting – perhaps exploring ways to 'share' risk. After all, donors and partners already share consequences like reputational damage, how can they share other consequences, and the likelihoods? In doing so, how can they more effectively control the risk together?

Balance prescription and agency

Agencies increasingly issue prescriptive due diligence requirements of INGOs working with local actors. While requiring extensive checks carries a friction benefit – that is, making it a little harder for a bad actor to secure funding – we have shown how this level of granularity is inherently flawed, in a number of ways:

- Checking an entity against a list relies, to a large extent, on the information provided by the entity, giving them effective control over what is checked;
- Checking lists does not control for the risk of association – that is, a member of diversionary group will not necessarily be named on a sanctions list themselves;
- The approach can carry the sense that it is really controlling for the risk of being challenged by the public or the media in the event of a diversion incident, rather than diversion itself. Onerous controls that are really for the risk of outside challenge may not be proportionate.

The focus for institutional donors should be how to encourage partners to manage risks, and how to avoid perpetuating a compliance-based approach through granular contracts. Donors must explore new ways of managing risk amongst their partners that avoid detailed requirements, especially around due diligence. The Australian DFAT model, in which the highest fence is entry to a pool of approximately 60 partners, rather than in relation to specific funding agreements, is an interesting approach.

Refocussing donor expectations of partners towards their ADPs may also help to reduce the diversity of obligations those partners face. Harvard Law School (2014) found significant variance in diversion policies between donors. And yet, while specifics differ between organisations, there has been a significant converge of consensus on what a meaningful approach to managing risks like these looks like – across fraud, bribery, corruption, and even wider integrity risks like sexual exploitation and abuse. Requiring partners to evidence the effectiveness of ADPs, rather than process controls, could help to harmonise expectations between donors and therefore reduce duplication for stretched INGOs.

A further point here is to reflect on the circumstances of INGO and local partners and how better to design more enabling programmes and projects. Project inception periods, for example, can create space to re-contextualise the plan and carry out risk assessment. And local partners, too, are a key part of donor value chains – how many such donors make space in their grants (or establish specific programmes) to help build local partner capacity in risk management?

Assist to develop public understanding

To participate in aid, whether as a donor, implementer, or some other role, an organisation's credibility must depend on its readiness to articulate to the public that in some extreme circumstances, where the places in which aid happens are difficult, dangerous, and chaotic, diversion must be accepted as a hazard. Without accepting that residual risk exists and sometimes materialises, aid cannot be delivered. Institutional donors must, as must INGOs and other actors, begin to challenge media-led myths about this.

INGOs

INGOs, themselves, meanwhile need to re-examine the role that they play in their own vulnerability, and that of the wider sector. While the introduction of an ADP is certainly a starting point, and indeed a bare minimum, there are more fundamental changes needed.

Hold an honest internal conversation

Aid must be made available to those who need it. However, not all actors in the space have the capacity and capability to deliver it to an acceptable level of safety, at all times, in all theatres. Each INGO must identify and accept the limits of its reach. Some will be able to operate in very high risk, high complexity contexts. Others will not. INGOs that do not identify the risks in a project, and attain confidence that they have the capacity and capability to manage them, should not undertake that project.

Shift perceptions

Even holding that conversation may require a shift in perception for some. It is time for INGO managers to recognise and internalise that they are part of a sophisticated, professionalised, and regulated sector. Regulation, while sometimes clumsy, blunt, or outright wrong, is a broadly positive force and necessary for an INGO sector that receives £22bn ($27.3bn) a year (Development Initiatives, 2018) in humanitarian aid alone, affecting hundreds of millions of people.

Similarly, a reconsideration of the value of business support needs to take place. Contrary to many sector voices, the overall value of aid delivered is not the right benchmark for the cost of such activities (where such activities are effective and proportionate, of course). High risk environments demand a rise in control activities. Pragmatic and effective activities to manage risks are not at the expense of programming, they are part of programming.

This is important and could help to reduce aggregate risk in the system. But another shift is important for the reduction of risk within an INGO's own footprint. This is to abandon the assumption that diversion is purely a donor or legal issue, and instead see it as an integrity issue that INGOs must manage for themselves. Seeing the matter as a compliance issue fosters an unhelpful, blame-the-donor culture, and makes it more difficult to detect the boundary between what it is reasonable to expect INGOs to do, and what is unreasonable, persecutorial, and a symptom of shrinking civil society space.

Invest in capacity and capability

Having adjusted perceptions, INGOs need to align their investment in the 'business support' costs necessary for anti-diversion capacity and capability, with the scale of the risks in their programming. While individual organisations differ, the need is often true across all aspects of anti-diversion: Financial management, systems, logistics, risk management, counter-fraud, legal knowledge, local knowledge and experience, and governance.

While waivers, licences, and exemptions might alleviate some legal pressures, they do not alleviate the moral requirement to do no harm. This must still involve the careful application of a well-resourced ADP to minimise diversion.

Examine reliance on restricted funding

Donors have been criticised in recent years for 'risk aversion' in their reluctance to operate in certain ways, in certain places. But all organisations, donors included, must be allowed to set their own risk appetite. INGOs must respect this, and while of course they must advocate on behalf of communities requiring assistance, they must accept that not all donors are prepared to operate in the ways advocated. If donor funding cannot be secured for operations within an INGO's mission, then it must raise the funds from another source, including private contributions. After all (as noted by Stoddard et al., 2019), INGOs with unrestricted funding enjoy more flexibility.

In the short and medium term, it seems unlikely that governments will balance their competing internal agendas, or that we will see resolution of the tensions between IHL and CTF. And yet, at the same time, our world is arguably experiencing the most severe humanitarian crises for a generation. While donor cash is readily available and tempting, if it comes with requirements that negatively affect holistic, proportionate, and effective diversion management it may no longer be feasible for an INGO to accept it.

Do unto partners as you would have done unto you

May (2016) sets out an approach to managing the risk of financial crime in local implementing partners, the principles of which should be followed for the management of diversion. But a key part of that approach is building local partner capacity and capability. This is something which INGOs often demand of their own donors in the context of improved administration margins in grants, but Stoddard et al. (2019) found that most INGO–local relationships in their study were 'directive', sub-granting relationships. INGOs should explore ways in which this can change.

Collaborate with other INGOs and local actors

While much activity is already in train, INGOs should continue to practise collective advocacy on counter-terrorism – but improve the sharing of information and practices, and heighten dialogue with local actors. The transfer of capability and funding is one avenue for the localisation that the sustainability of global development needs. This point also holds for INGOs and their relationship with donors and potential donors. Contracting needs to be a negotiation, in which INGOs are cautious about the risks and liabilities they take on, and in which donors are receptive to proposed contractual variations.

Aid sector peak bodies and researchers

There has been substantial success in advocacy for the humanitarian and development sector on diversion in recent years. From Bond's leadership in the UK, to the work of the Global NPO Coalition on FATF, it has never been a more important time to advocate for the sector. We should be cautious, however, of wrapping up beneficiary advocacy with that of our organisations, of course.

Further, there is a need for more research on how INGOs (in particular) manage these risks. While there has been some outstanding and insightful work in recent years, much more data are needed. Humanitarianism in particular, can be a closed tribe. More illumination is needed in more contexts. A relatively small number of incidents make it into the public space. Peak bodies must support further research, and encourage the transparency that is needed to foster understanding.

Meanwhile, a vein of defensiveness runs through the sector's literature. This is entirely understandable; the legal and political environment is frustrating to humanitarians watching beneficiaries, quite literally, die. But the sector must have the right expectations: Large-scale, blanket humanitarian exemptions to CTF law are unlikely, donors must be able to manage their own risk appetite, and INGOs on average do have room for improvement in their anti-diversion capacity and capability.

Regulators, government, and lawmakers

Outside of government donor agencies, wider stakeholders can also play an important role in reducing the effects of diversion and heightening the scope for vulnerable people to be served by the aid community.

Firstly, consultation on existing and proposed reform needs to be broader and deeper. Intensifying legislation and corresponding enforcement are the go-to of governments worldwide. But the aid sector is different – here, operations are motivated by a moral need. Aid organisations do not respond like other industries. While businesses weigh up the risks to themselves, humanitarians weigh up the risks to others. Legislation and enforcement are not always the answer, and where they are being considered, they must be contemplated carefully.

Governments must, then, engage fully and openly with the aid sector when formulating policy and legislation likely to affect it. It cannot be allowed to become acceptable in the twenty-first century, for example, that humanitarians could be banned from access to any given geographical space (Bond, 2018), that peacebuilding activities could become unlawful, or that aid workers might not be allowed to hold dialogue with armed actors in order to facilitate aid but without any transaction of material benefit (Debarre, 2018). Where appropriate, humanitarian exemptions should be created.

Secondly, while regulators are an important lever on INGOs, they should be careful to calibrate risk-based targeting. A large INGO, for example, does not necessarily have the capacity and capability to manage diversion. It must have a proportionate ADP. Focussing too tightly on small and medium charities, for example, might seem like a wise use of limited resources but it belies that the charities of focus should be those without proportionate controls. Those might very well be large agencies.

Meanwhile, in respect of individual matters of alleged diversion, the principle of 'public interest' must be applied with a sober analysis of each case. This should be not only by prosecutors and the courts, but by private individuals and organisations seeking to utilise the law for their own purposes. To accuse an INGO of providing material benefit to a sanctioned entity because it provided cookies and water during peacebuilding activity is preposterous. That is not to say, however, that cases where machinery or equipment have been provided would not be significant – each case must be considered on its own merits. But governments must be cautious about the claims made by bounty activists.

Finally, where licence regimes exist, the speed with which these can be accessed by aid organisations must align with the urgency of their work. That may require not only standing operating agreements between government departments, but between governments. More coherence, and more rapid results, may be one of the only ways in which some of the challenges of value chain diversion can be palliated.

The public and the media

Aid organisations, and perhaps particularly INGOs, are in an uneasy partnership with the public, which funds them through private donations or government taxes. Public assumptions and perceptions about aid work overseas, often driven by Victorian ideas about charity, do not easily sit alongside the reality of modern aid work.

In respect of diversion, that tension is compounded by ignorance and stereotypes about terrorists. Meanwhile, civil society is under stress, squeezed by regulatory currents, aggressive political and regulatory zeal, and the 'culture war' that threatens to engulf and polarise all aspects of Western political economy. It is not surprising that Harvard Law School (2014) reported that NGO staff perceived an increased level of scrutiny by external authorities and the media.

To accept how their funds will be used, and to ensure that currents of public thought are reflected in how INGOs do their work, the public must be educated and enlightened in the realities of anti-diversion work and the kinds of programming at risk of it. The public must:

- Understand that the most desperate people are often to be found in the highest risk contexts, where diversion is a key risk and operating safely is extremely difficult;
- Recognise that not all diversion can be prevented, and a certain degree of acceptance must be reached in order to help people;
- Appreciate that the majority of funds in the average aid project are likely to make their way to the correct destination;
- Internalise that reducing the risk of diversion is a complex, challenging, and iterative process for all organisations;
- Encourage INGOs to exist in a virtuous circle of constant anti-diversion improvement;
- Remember that penalising INGOs for individual incidents can be counter-productive.

Certainly, as Chapter 11 described, this can be the aim of advocacy in anti-diversion leadership by sector actors. But this goes beyond the sector: The media must play a role in delivering these points. The media has a vital role in exposing failures of accountability, transparency, and integrity in the aid sector. But in our post-truth, culture-conflict reality, that privilege must be accompanied by promoting the importance of aid, the difficulties of operating in places where diversion is a key risk, and the nuance of these issues. They are not simple, and simplistic or ideological reporting is not journalism. Diversion management is an operational discipline – not a political football.

In particular, the media must be particular cautious when formulating stories that will:

- Challenge 'support side,' 'administrative,' or 'overhead' costs;
- Propose a cure-all solution for diversion, such as data, or technology, or which will oversimply diversion issues;
- Involve bounty activists, or those with ideological motivations;
- Support outdated narratives about charity.

Ending the open secret

I once led an investigation into alleged terrorist financing amongst aid agencies working in Africa. Meanwhile, another professional was leading an informal project to understand diversion risks, driven by a set of confidential conversations between humanitarians. Notably, senior managers in the agencies concerned gave my investigation the 'party line' – that diversion was a matter of 'zero tolerance' and was not accepted. But my colleague told me what senior humanitarians were saying off-the-record – that it was believed to go on but that they avoided lifting too many stones in case they found something they would have to pick up.

Terrorism, as a device, relies on the creation of fear in order to leverage public policy. Fear is contagious, and it has infected the humanitarian and global development sector's management of diversion risks. This is entirely understandable, but it is time for more openness, and less secrecy.

The sector does not need to mumble its way into another crisis. It is time for transparency, courageous conversation, and investment in capacity and capability. All actors in the sector, and beyond it, must participate. We must be clear that diversion is often a high risk, and sometimes cannot be avoided. Failing to accept and grapple with the risk, however, leads to an even worse consequence – that vulnerable people who desperately need urgent humanitarian and development assistance are left alone. If we would not wish that for our children, we must not accept it for theirs.

References

Bond 2018. *Counter Terrorism Bill: Lords pass amendment to protect aid workers.* London: Bond.

Burniske, J. and Modirzadeh, N. 2017. *Pilot empirical survey study on the impact of counter-terrorism measures on humanitarian action.* Cambridge, MA: Harvard Law School.

Charny, K. 2019. Counter-terrorism and humanitarian action: The perils of zero tolerance. War on the Rocks. https://warontherocks.com/2019/03/counter-terrorism-and-humanitarian-action-the-perils-of-zero-tolerance/.

Debarre, A. 2018. *Safeguarding medical care and humanitarian action in the UN Counterterrorism Framework.* New York, NY: International Peace Institute.

Development Initiatives 2018. *Global Humanitarian Assistance Report 2018.* Bristol: Development Initiatives.

Harvard Law School 2014. *Counterterrorism and Humanitarian Engagement Project: An analysis of contemporary anti-diversion policies and practices of humanitarian organizations.* Cambridge, MA: Harvard Law School.

May, O. 2016. *Fighting fraud and corruption in the humanitarian and global development sector.* Abingdon: Routledge. https://doi.org/10.4324/9781315558301.

Stoddard, A., Czwarno, M., and Hamsik, L. 2019. *NGOs & risk: Managing uncertainty in local-international partnerships.* London: Humanitarian Outcomes/InterAction.

Trisko Darden, J. 2019a. Humanitarian assistance has a terrorism problem. Can it be resolved? War on the Rocks. https://warontherocks.com/2019/01/humanitarian-assistance-has-a-terrorism-problem-can-it-be-resolved/.

Trisko Darden, J. 2019b. It's time to take foreign aid theft seriously. American Enterprise Institute. https://www.aei.org/foreign-and-defense-policy/terrorism/its-time-to-take-foreign-aid-theft-seriously/.

Appendix

Example ADP Health Check

A risk-based approach

1 Does the INGO formally adopt a holistic and risk-based approach to managing diversion through an ADP?
2 Is the INGO able to demonstrate that its resourcing of anti-diversion activities is proportionate to the scale of its risk?

Risk assessment

Risk management

3 Is diversion managed within the context of an integrated framework for the management of risks at organisational, functional, and project levels?
4 Do diversion risks appear in the INGO risk register?
5 Has the risk appetite been defined in respect of diversion?

Risk assessments

6 Has a documented organisational diversion risk assessment been carried out within the last two business cycles?
7 Have documented risk assessments been carried out for business functions, business units, or country programmes operating in contexts with diversionary threats?
8 Has a documented risk assessment been carried out for every project in a context with a diversionary threat?
9 Are risk assessments updated sufficiently regularly, given the changing profile and situation of the INGO, its contexts, and its programmes?

Risk registers

10 Do business units maintain risk registers, in which relevant diversion risks appear?

11 Do the managers, staff, partners, vendors, and suppliers of the INGO practise situational awareness?
12 Do managers assess and respond to diversion dynamically, using risk assessment as a basis for daily, monthly, and annual decision-making?

Deterrence

13 Does a schedule of work exist to deter internal parties from participating in diversion, particularly through:

   i   Initiatives to reduce the pressures on individuals that may drive them towards participation in diversion;
   ii Reducing the perception of opportunity to participate in diversion, and elevating the perception of detection;
   iii Tackling rationalisation strategies?

14 Is there work to support and encourage INGO staff to deter external parties from participating in diversion, particularly through:

   i   Dialogue with diversionaries;
   ii Collective action with other INGOs;
   iii Building and maintaining a reputation of refusal;
   iv Leveraging of local relationships;
   v Use of passive physical security measures?

Prevention

Due diligence

Risk-based due diligence framework

15 Has the INGO identified a range of contextually-viable forms of research that it can use to understand the risks presented by a particular second or third party?
16 Has the INGO carried out a risk analysis that results in the proportionate use of forms of research on categories particular second or third parties, based on their risk?
17 Does the INGO have a consistently-applied set of due diligence checks for the categories of:

   i   Partner;
   ii Vendors, suppliers, contractors, and consultants;
   iii Staff?

18 Are informed and recorded decisions made about engagement with those second and third parties made on the basis of the results of that due diligence?

Obligations management

19 Is there a process to develop and maintain a Business Obligations Register, enabling the INGO to maintain visibility of its legislative, regulatory, and policy obligations?
20 Is the Business Obligations Register a single repository used to support harmonisation of approach?

Policy framework

21 Is diversion considered within a code of conduct?
22 Is there a clear anti-diversion policy?

Framework of internal controls

23 Is there a framework of preventative and detective controls that modify specific, identified diversion risks at organisational, functional and business unit, and process levels?

Detection

Proactive

Management review

24 Do proactive reviews of business processes take place to identify potential red flags of diversion, with business processes for review determined on a risk prioritised basis? Are these reviews:

  i   Carried out by persons with a risk-based understanding of diversion red flags?
  ii Carried out with a regularity informed by assessed level of diversion risk?

25 Does independent transaction testing, informed on a risk basis, take place?

Data analytics

26 Are available sources of structured and unstructured electronic data lawfully and ethically exploited to identify:

  i   Potential diversion incidents;
  ii Changing diversion risk profiles of INGO operations?

Reactive

Overt reporting system

27 Do all staff, volunteers, and third parties have a clearly-articulated obligation to report suspected diversion to a line manager or other manager of the organisation?
28 Is there a clearly defined process for making reports through the management line?
29 Are managers appropriately trained to handle such reports?
30 Is guidance provided to staff, volunteers, and third parties in making such a disclosure?

Confidential reporting system

31 Do all staff, volunteers, third parties, and the public have access to appropriate, usable means to make a confidential (including anonymous) report of a suspicion of diversion?
32 Are beneficiary reporting mechanisms integrated with the wider organisational reporting system in respect of diversion?
33 Is guidance provided to staff, volunteers, and third parties in making such a disclosure?

Information sharing agreements

34 Do formal and informal agreements exist between the INGO and its third parties to share information relating to diversion suspicions? This might include:

   i   Contracts with suppliers, vendors, and implementing partners;
   ii   Consortia and collective operations;
   iii   Donors;
   iv   Other INGOs working in the same spaces;
   v   Sector working groups and collective initiatives?

Response

Incident management

35 Is there an incident response plan covering diversion, which:

   i   Sets out roles and responsibilities, including a single response manager and a stakeholder panel for each matter;
   ii   Incorporates triaging to align capability, capacity, and priority of incident response with the risk and complexity of the incident;

    iii Establishes clear, phased workflow for all suspicions arising from point of generation to closure;

    iv Creates scope for initial and full investigations;

    v Ensures that corporate memory will be created and maintained, through recording, retention, review and revelation?

Investigation

36 Is there a capability for the INGO to carry out internal investigations to:

    i Fact-find into whether diversion may have occurred;

    ii Determine any loss;

    iii Identify any control gaps or failures;

    iv Explore the possibility of negligence?

37 Is there an investigation procedure, doctrine. or manual covering internal investigations into diversion to ensure lawfulness, consistency, and completeness of investigations?

38 Is there a system to ensure that investigations are carried out with the right capability, capacity, and independence?

Remedial action

39 Does the INGO ensure that remedial action is always explored and all aspects of the ADP are considered?

Reporting

40 Does the INGO have a system to ensure that all external reports required are made transparently and in good time?

Culture, communication and training

Cultural development

41 Has the INGO defined and articulate what an 'anti-diversion culture' means in its operations?

42 Has the INGO determined what the positive and negative indicators of its anti-diversion culture will be?

43 Is there a schedule of work, aligned to or integrated with wider cultural development work, to develop an anti-diversion culture?

44 Is the anti-diversion culture monitored and regularly reviewed?

Communications plan

45 Are anti-diversion communications considered within the ADP's own communications plan, or a wider organisational strategy?

46 Do anti-diversion communications derive from the aims and priorities of the ADP and its development?
47 Are there planned and regular anti-diversion communications across a range of media?
48 Do anti-diversion communications:

  i Raise staff awareness of risks and their responsibilities;
  ii Elevate staff vigilance about diversion;
  iii Influence staff to think, feel, and act about diversion, and the systems that tackle it, as the ADP requires;
  iv Support the development of the ADP?

Training

49 Is anti-diversion training based on the specific risks that any given member of staff or volunteer will encounter in their work, and targeted to their specific role, level, and context within the INGO?
50 Is the extent, mode, and content of anti-diversion proportionate to the risks faced by participants and the INGO?
51 Are there at least separate training packages for operational staff, and for managers?
52 Do the training packages empower participants to deter, prevent, detect, and respond to diversion, and support the ADP?

Leadership and governance

Governance

53 Does the board and Senior Leadership Team (SLT):

  i Authorise the ADP, monitor, and review it;
  ii Actively support the ADP in word and action;
  iii Maintain their visibility of the INGO's diversion risk profile?

54 Does an anti-diversion working group:

  i Support the development and success of the ADP;
  ii Ensure commitment to the ADP across all relevant functions;
  iii Assist the ADP to take account of perspectives and requirements of all relevant functions?

55 Does a single, identified anti-diversion lead:

  i Have the mandate to assist the organisation manage the risk of diversion;
  ii Drive the development and implementation of the ADP;
  iii Build the capacity of the INGO and its partners to manage diversion;
  iv Advise, support. and influence relevant business units?

56 Is there a coherent structure of responsibility across the entire INGO, so that individuals are responsible for identifying and managing the risk of diversion in all operations and transactions?

57 Are all components of the ADP owned and regularly reviewed?

58 Is the ADP independently audited?

59 Does a suite of measures of the performance of the ADP exist, and are these monitored and use to continually improve the ADP?

60 Is the ADP expressed in a single plan or strategy document?

Articulation of leadership expectations

61 Does the INGO define and articulate its expectations of anti-diversion leadership to all relevant staff and volunteers?

Humanitarian advocacy

62 Does the INGO engage courageously but constructive with key global stakeholders to ensure that its humanitarian and development footprint are considered by lawmakers, regulators, donors, and the public?

Index

Note: citations within tables are indicated in **bold**, and citations within figures, are indicated in *italics*.

For Product Safety Concerns and Information please contact our EU
representative GPSR@taylorandfrancis.com Taylor & Francis Verlag GmbH,
Kaufingerstraße 24, 80331 München, Germany

Printed and bound by CPI Group (UK) Ltd, Croydon, CR0 4YY
08/05/2025
01864481-0001